To Rev. J. A. Nelson

With the respects of

The Author

Indianapolis Ind

April 24, 1876

Eng'd by W. Wellstood

REV. F. C. HOLLIDAY

INDIANA METHODISM:

BEING AN ACCOUNT OF THE

INTRODUCTION, PROGRESS, AND PRESENT POSITION
OF METHODISM IN THE STATE;

AND ALSO A

HISTORY OF THE LITERARY INSTITUTIONS

UNDER THE CARE OF THE CHURCH,

WITH

SKETCHES OF THE PRINCIPAL METHODIST
EDUCATORS IN THE STATE,

DOWN TO 1872.

BY

REV. F. C. HOLLIDAY, D. D.

CINCINNATI:
HITCHCOCK AND WALDEN.
1873.

PREFACE.

IN writing the following account of Methodism in Indiana, I have desired not only to rescue from oblivion valuable information that would soon be lost, but also to pay a feeble, but justly merited, tribute to the heroic pioneers and founders of Methodism in our state. The record of their toils is found chiefly in the numerous and flourishing Churches that have sprung up all over the state, in the multitudes of living witnesses to the truth and power of the Gospel that they preached, in the schools of learning which they founded, in the vigor of the benovolent institutions which they fostered, and in the educational effect produced by their earnest and evangelical preaching on the public mind and conscience.

The pulpit is always a popular educator, and its teachings are the basis of doctrinal belief, to a great extent, in every Christian community. This is especially true in a community where books are scarce, and in a state of society where the opportunities for reading are limited. Such was necessarily the case with the early settlers in Indiana.

Methodism, with its itinerant system, and its extempore method of preaching, found ready access to the people. Its doctrinal basis, so consonant with reason and revelation, was readily accepted by the masses. Total depravity—not total in degree, but in its univer sality as to the powers of the soul—universal redemption, the duty of immediate repentance, justification by faith, regeneration, and perfect love, were the grand themes upon which they dwelt. They preached experience doctrinally, and they preached doctrines experimentally. They were too busy to write the results of their labors. Their work was grander than their estimate of it; they planned and builded wiser than they knew. The function of the pulpit as a popular educator is grand. Its mission, always glorious, is preeminently so in a new country.

The founders of Methodism in Indiana were, many of them, great preachers. Had the sermons of Allen Wiley, James Armstrong, Calvin W. Ruter, George Locke, James Havens, and Richard Hargrave, been reported as they preached them, when, in the days of their vigor, the multitudes that were gathered from far and near attended their camp-meetings and quarterly-meetings, they would have been regarded as grand specimens of pulpit eloquence. They would have compared favorably with the productions of the pulpit in any age or country. The pulpit with them was a sort of telegraph-office, and the people were so many wires in the hand of the preacher. They put themselves in full sympathy with their hearers; their words vibrated from nerve to nerve. There is a power in human sympathy that is almost irresistible. They were men of deep, earnest convictions, and loving hearts. And who can resist the fascination of a loving nature? They were the prophets and pioneers of a better day.

Their ministry was not only characterized by deep, earnest convictions, and true human sympathy; it had clearness, knowledge, force—convincing the judgment, arousing the conscience, establishing faith, nourishing earnestness, sustaining zeal, and satisfying the felt wants of the soul. They felt an agonizing determination to speak the words of truth to their fellow-men at all hazards. They were impelled by yearnings of super-human import. And while the modern pulpit has gained some in breadth and culture, some in refinement and surface acquirements, it is well if it has lost nothing of the earnestness and honesty of the early days.

The mission of the pulpit is the same to-day that it has ever been. It is the grand instrument, the Divinely appointed instrument, of the world's evangelization. And if the pulpit in our day has rare opportunities for usefulness, it is also beset with remarkable difficulties. The platform is no mean rival to the pulpit. Popular lectures on current themes engross a large share of public attention in towns and cities, and command much of the attention of the better educated classes. And thus the platform becomes a rival to the pulpit. If the pulpit would retain the pre-eminence that it should, the sermon must have as much freshness and culture, as much breadth of thought and ease of manner, as the lecture, and it must have superadded the unction of the Holy Ghost.

The modern pulpit has another rival in the press, and especially in the style of modern literature. The paper, the magazine, and many of our books, are written in the most fascinating style. This is a reading age, and for the pulpit to retain its hold upon the popular mind, the sermon must be as interesting as the paper, the magazine, or the book. No book can perform the peculiar office of the pulpit. The pulpit is missionary in its character; its office is to dig in the garden of the soul, to excavate a road for moral manhood, to indicate a pathway to moral attainments. No book can so well arouse flagging and exhausted powers, no book can so well grapple with wandering convictions, no book can so well quicken generous and active impulses, and no book can rebuke vice with the same withering, scathing force, as the voice of the living preacher. And while we honor the Fathers, and claim that theirs was an efficient ministry, and adapted to the times, we can not admit that the pulpit, upon the whole, has lost any of its power. Some of the early founders of Methodism in Indiana yet remain with us, most of them suffering from the infirmities of age, while a few, as Dr. A. Wood, of the Northwestern Conference, and Dr. E. G. Wood, of the Southeastern Conference, retain much of the sprightliness and vigor of their earlier years, with the ripeness and maturity of age. The spirit of Methodism is retained in its vigor, while its modes of operation have been modified to suit the changed condition of society.

Thus the large circuit system has been superseded by smaller charges, and week-day preaching has nearly disappeared. Church interests and ministerial cares have greatly increased as Church institutions have multiplied, and while long journeys and physical exposure have greatly diminished, intellectual exertion and moral responsibility have greatly increased.

No notice has been taken of a number of ministers, who, for various causes, have seen fit to leave the ministry, some for positions in other Churches, and some for secular pursuits. Such cases have been few, and subsequent history will do them justice. It is enough at present to say that none of them have profited by their changes, and that the men who have remained faithful to their ministerial vows have been the men of the largest influence and the greatest success.

Many interesting details in the history of Methodism in the state have been necessarily passed by, and much local history has been omitted for want of room. A full history of Indiana Methodism would fill three volumes of the size of this. What has been aimed at in this volume, is to make such a record of the introduction, progress, and present position of Methodism in Indiana, as will convey to the mind of the reader a just estimate of what Indiana Methodism is, what it has achieved, and the circumstances under which it has wrought out its results, without attempting a minute and consecutive history. It is hoped that the plan of the work will be acceptable to the majority of readers.

I am indebted to the kindness of brethren in different

parts of the state for valuable information. I have had free access to the Journal of Dr. A. Wood, and he has also furnished many valuable items from his own memory. The difficulty, and in many cases the failure, to obtain needed information, can not be appreciated, except by persons who have labored in the same field.

Elliott's "Life of Bishop Roberts," Cartwright's "Autobiography," Smith's "Indiana Miscellany," "The Life and Times of Wiley," the *Indiana School Journal*, "The Census of the United States," and Dillon's "History of Indiana," have been consulted in the preparation of this work. Where local history has been written by parties on the ground, the names of the writers appear in connection with their articles.

This work has been written under the pressure of ministerial duties, and does not claim to be invulnerable to criticism. With devout thanks to God that the writer has been enabled to complete his self-imposed task, and with a sincere prayer that the work may, to some extent, be useful, it is submitted to the public.

F. C. HOLLIDAY.

INDIANAPOLIS, *June* 5, 1872.

CONTENTS.

———•———

CHAPTER I.

CHAPTER II.

(9)

CHAPTER III.

CHAPTER IV.

CHAPTER V.

CHAPTER VI.

GENERAL NARRATIVE.

CHAPTER VII.

FROM 1841 TO 1856.

CHAPTER VIII.

CHAPTER IX.

CHAPTER X.

CHAPTER XI.

CHAPTER XII.

CHAPTER XIII.

CHAPTER XIV.

THE FATHERS.

CHAPTER XV.

METHODIST EDUCATORS.

CHAPTER XVI.

METHODIST EDUCATIONAL INSTITUTIONS.

CHAPTER XVII.

INDIANA BISHOPS.

CHAPTER XVIII.

FROM 1870 TO 1872.

INDIANA METHODISM.

CHAPTER I.

Early Civil History—First Romish Church built in the Territory—First Governor and Civil Officers—First Session of the "General Court of the Territory of Indiana"—First Grand Jury—Members of the House of Representatives—Governor's Message—Convention to form a Constitution for the State of Indiana—First General Assembly of the State—Indiana admitted into the Union—First Senators elected—Early Public Men—Hugh Cull—Dennis Pennington—Ezra Ferris—James Scott—Influence of the Early Itinerants.

THE first white settlements in the territory of Indiana were made by French traders. The villages of the Miamies, which stood at the head of the Maumee River, the Wea villages, situated about Oniatenon on the Wabash River, and the Piankeshaw villages, which stood near the present site of Vincennes, were regarded by the early French fur-traders as suitable places for the establishment of trading-posts. As early as 1719, temporary trading-posts were erected at the sites of Fort Wayne, Oniatenon, and Vincennes. The Romish Church, with a zeal and perseverance which must command our highest admiration, are found on the frontiers of civilization. The missionary of the Church was close on the track of the fur-trader and the trapper. The first Church in the territory was established by a Romish.

missionary by the name of Meurin, at the Piankeshaw village, in 1749, where the city of Vincennes now is. In 1750 a small fort was built at the same place, and another slight fortification was erected, about the same time, at the mouth of the Wabash River. Vincennes received considerable accessions to its white population in 1754, 1755, and 1756, by the arrival of emigrants from Detroit, Kaskaskia, Canada, and New Orleans. On the division of the territory of the United States north of the Ohio River, by the act of Congress of May 7, 1800, the material parts of the ordinance of July 13, 1787, remained in force in the territory of Indiana, and the inhabitants of the new territory were invested with all the privileges and advantages granted and secured to the people by that ordinance. The seat of Government was fixed at Vincennes.

On the 13th of May, 1800, William Henry Harrison was appointed Governor, and on the next day, John Gibson, a native of Pennsylvania, and a distinguished pioneer, to whom Logan, the Indian chief, delivered his celebrated speech, was appointed Secretary of the Territory. Soon afterward John Griffin, Henry Vanderburg, and William Clark were appointed Territorial Judges. The civilized population of the territory was estimated in 1800 at 4,875. Governor Harrison and the Territorial Judges held their first meeting at Vincennes, January 12, 1801, for the purpose of adopting and publishing "such laws as the exigencies of the times" required, and "for the performance of other acts conformable to the ordinances and laws of Congress, for the government of the Territory." The Territorial Judges commenced the first session of the General Court of the Territory of Indiana at Vincennes, March 3, 1801. The first grand jury impaneled in the territory consisted of nineteen persons, as follows: Luke Decker, Antoine Marchal, Joseph Baird, Patrick Simpson, Antoine Petit, Andre Montplaiseur, John Ockiltree, Jonathan Marney, Jacob Tevebaugh, Alexander Valley, Francis Turpin, Fr. Compaynoitre, Charles Languedoc, Louis Severe, Fr. Languedoc, George Catt, John Bt. Barois, Abraham Decker, and Philip Catt. It will be readily inferred from these names that a large per cent of these early settlers were Frenchmen. The members of the first Legislature of the Indiana Territory convened in Vincennes, pursuant to the proclamation of the Governor, on the 29th of July, 1805. The members of the House of Representatives were Jessie B. Thomas, of Dearborn County, Davis Floyd, of Clark County, Benjamin Park and John Johnson, of Knox County, Shadrach Bond and William Beggs, of St. Clair County, and George Fisher, of Randolph County. In his message, delivered on the 30th of July, 1805, the Governor congratulated the members of the General Assembly "upon entering on a grade of government which gave to the people the important right of legislating for themselves." The Convention to frame a constitution for the State of Indiana held its session in Corydon. The Convention was composed of clear-minded, practical men, whose patriotism was above suspicion, and whose morals were fair. The first General Assembly, elected under the authority of the State Constitution, commenced its session at Corydon, then the capital of Indiana, on the 4th of November, 1816. The Territorial Government was thus superseded by a State Government, and the State formally admitted into the Union by a joint resolution of Congress, approved on the 11th of December, 1816. On the 8th of November, 1816, the General Assembly, by a joint vote of both Houses, elected James Noble and Walter Taylor to represent the State of Indiana in the Senate of the United States.

Although the history of Fort Wayne and Vincennes date back to the time of Louis XIV, when missionaries and traders led small colonies far from the homes and comforts of civilized life, and ambitious statesmen sent military forces across the ocean and along our northern lakes; and although the Swiss have cultivated the sunny slopes of the Ohio, in the vicinity of Vevay, from the beginning of the century, it was not until after the close of the war with Great Britain and the suppression of Indian hostilities that population began to flow into the territory of Indiana. Although the representatives of nearly all nations are found among us, yet a large majority of our people are of the sturdy English stock, which, under the extraordinary influences consequent upon the stirring events of the seventeenth century, spread along the Atlantic coast, from Maine to the region of the tropics. Our population is truly composite. Like some grand piece of mosaic, in which all the colors are united, to the obscuring of none and the enhancing of the luster of each, the typical Indiana man is dependent on every element for completeness, yet as a whole is dissimilar to any part. He is neither German nor Scotch, nor Irish nor English, but a compound of the whole. The conqueror of our forests and the plowman of our prairies is possessed of a spirit of personal independence that may be sharpened into insolence or educated into manly self-respect. Quite a number of the early public men of Indiana were men of high moral character, and not a few of them were men of decided piety; and they left their impress upon general society. Hugh Cull, one of the delegates from the County of Wayne to the Constitutional Convention, to frame the first Constitution for the

State, was a local preacher in the Methodist Church, lived to the extraordinary age of one hundred and one years, retaining his faculties, his untarnished Christian character, and the esteem of all who knew him, to the last. He lived to see the county which he represented in the first Constitutional Convention of the State, become the empire county of the State, and a garden-spot both in physical and moral culture, and the population of the State increase from a few thousand to a million and a quarter of inhabitants. Dennis Pennington, from Harrison County, was also an active and influential member of the Methodist Church. He served a number of years in the State Legislature under the Constitution which he had helped to frame, and died at a good old age, having served his generation faithfully and well. Ezra Ferris, a member of the Constitutional Convention from Dearborn County, was a Baptist preacher of a liberal spirit and great Christian influence. He resided in Lawrenceburg till the close of his life, which occurred near the age of eighty years. James Scott, from Clark County, who was subsequently, for a number of years, one of the Supreme Judges of the State, was an exemplary and earnest Christian, a member of the Presbyterian Church, but in hearty sympathy with all Christians. He also lived to a good old age.

Such were some of the men that framed the first Constitution for the State of Indiana. A high responsibility is devolved upon, and rare opportunities are enjoyed by, the men who lay the foundations of society, whether civilly, socially, or ecclesiastically. Society, like the individual, has its educational period, during which it takes on those characteristics by which it is afterward distinguished and known. History teaches us that social and intellectual peculiarities are almost as transmissable as physical traits. John Knox yet lives in the Psalm-singing and rugged Calvinistic theology of Scotland. Every country furnishes illustrations of this truth; and that community is highly favored whose early leaders possessed the requisite intellectual, social, and moral qualities. A decidedly religious impression was made upon the minds of a large proportion of the early settlers in Indiana by the preaching of, the Methodist itinerants, and the value of their services is recognized by men of all parties. Our itinerant system carried the means of grace to the remotest settlements, gathered the people into societies in the country, as well as in the towns and villages, and went far toward molding the minds and morals of the people. Preaching every day in the week, they lived among the people, sharing their privations and enjoying their scanty but cheerful hospitality. Under their labors "the wilderness and the solitary places have been made glad, and the desert has blossomed as the rose." It is fitting that the means, the processes, and the agencies by which Methodism has wrought out her work in Indiana, should be a matter of permanent record.

CHAPTER II.

First Protestant Sermon preached in the Territory—First Methodist Society formed—Mr. Cartwright's Encounter with the Shakers—First Pastoral Charge in the Territory—First Methodist Meeting-house—Whitewater Circuit—Indiana District organized—Indiana District in 1809—First Protestant Preaching at Vincennes—William Winans—Indiana District in 1810—Prominent Members of the Conference—William M'Kendree—Charles Holliday—John Collins—Leander Blackman—John Sale—James Quinn—Solomon Langdon—William Burke—James B. Finley—John Strange—James Axley—Division of the Western Conference—Missouri Conference organized—Introduction of Methodism into Decatur County—First Prayer-meeting in the County—First Class formed—Anecdote of Mr. Garrison—Preaching established in Greensburg—Thomas Rice—Salaries of the Early Preachers—Illustration—First School taught in the Territory—Geo. K. Hester's account of the School—Sketch of the introduction of Methodist Preaching into Clark County by Rev. Geo. K. Hester—First Traveling Preachers sent to the Grant—Benjamin Lakin and Ralph Lotspiech — First Society formed—Silver-creek Circuit organized—Camp-meeting held near Robertson's—Revivals—The New-lights—Memorable Revival in 1819—Illinois Conference held at Charlestown in 1825—Both Bishops M'Kendree and Roberts attend and preach.

AMONG the first Methodist sermons ever preached in the territory of Indiana were those preached by the venerable Peter Cartwright in 1804. Some Methodist families had removed from Kentucky, and settled in Clark's Grant, now Clark County, north of the Ohio River, nearly opposite Louisville. Among them were the Robinsons and Prathers, who settled near the present town of Charlestown, the county-seat of Clark County. This was in 1803. In 1804 Benjamin Lakin and Peter Cartwright traveled Salt-river and Shelby Circuits in Kentucky, and Mr. Cartwright, in his "Autobiography," says that he and Mr. Lakin crossed over the river that year, and preached at Robinson's and Prather's. This was between two and three years before the organization of Silver-creek Circuit by Moses Ashworth.

Mr. Cartwright has also the honor of organizing the first Methodist society in the south-western part of the state, at a place known in the early history of the state as the Busroe settlement, which, for a time, was the stronghold of Shakerism. We will let Mr. Cartwright tell the story of his encounter with the Shakers in his own language:

"I will here state a case which occurred at an early day in the state of Indiana, in a settlement called Busroe. Many of the early emigrants to that settlement were Methodists, Baptists, and Cumberland Presbyterians. The Shaker priests, all apostates from the Baptists and Cumberland Presbyterians, went over among them. Many of them I was personally acquainted with, and had given them letters when they removed from Kentucky to that new country.

"There were then no Methodist circuit-preachers in that region. There was an old brother Collins, a local preacher, who withstood the Shakers, and in private combat was a full match for any of them; but he was not eloquent in public debate; and hence the Shaker priests overcame my old brother, and by scores swept members of different Churches away from their steadfastness into the muddy pool of Shakerism. The few who remained steadfast, sent to Kentucky for me, praying me to come over and help them. I sent an appointment, with an invitation to meet any or all of the Shaker priests in public debate; but, instead of meeting me, they appointed a meeting in opposition, and warned the believers, as they called them, to keep away from my

meeting; but, from our former acquaintance and intimate friendship, many of them came to hear me. I
preached to a vast crowd for about three hours, and
I verily believe God helped me. The very foundations
of every Shaker present were shaken from under him.
They then besought me to go to the Shaker meeting
that night. I went; and when I got there, we had a
great crowd. I proposed to them to have a debate, and
they dared not refuse. The terms were these: A local
preacher I had with me was to open the debate, then
one, or all of their preachers, if they chose, were to
follow, and I was to bring up the rear. My preacher
opened the debate by merely stating the points of difference. Mr. Brazelton followed, and, instead of argument, he turned every thing into abuse and insulting
slander. When he closed, Mr. Gill rose; but instead
of argument, he uttered a few words of personal abuse,
and then called all of the Shakers to meet him a few
minutes in the yard, talk a little, and then disperse.
Our debate was out in the open air, at the end of a
cabin. I arose, and called them to order, and stated
that it was fairly agreed by these Shaker priests that
I should bring up the rear, or close the argument. I
stated that it was cowardly to run; that if I was the
devil himself, and they were right, I could not hurt
them. I got the most of them to take their seats and
hear me. Mr. Gill gathered a little band, and he and
they left. They had told the people, in the day, that
if I continued to oppose them, God would make an example of me, and send fire from heaven and consume
me. When I arose to reply, I felt a sense of the ap-
probation of God, and that he would give me success.
I addressed the multitude about three hours, and when
I closed my argument, I opened the doors of the Church,

and invited all that would renounce Shakerism to come and give me their hand. Forty-seven came forward, and then and there openly renounced the dreadful delusion. The next day I followed those that fled; and the next day I went from cabin to cabin, taking the names of those that returned to the solid foundation of truth, and my number rose to eighty-seven. I then organized them into a regular society, and the next Fall had a preacher sent them; and perhaps this victory may be considered among the first fruits of Methodism in that part of the new country. This was in 1808. They were temporarily supplied with preaching until 1811, when they were regularly included in the Vincennes Circuit, then under the care of Thomas Stillwell as preacher in charge."

The first entire pastoral charge in the territory of Indiana was Silver-creek Circuit, in Clark's Grant, now Clark County, under the ministry of Rev. Moses Ashworth.

The first Methodist meeting-house in the territory was built in what was then, and is still, known as the Robertson neighborhood, near Charlestown. Mr. Ashworth was an enterprising, energetic man. Three meeting-houses were built on this circuit during the first year of its history, and, although they were necessarily cheap log-houses, they evidenced the piety and liberality of the people. They made provision for the public worship of God, as good as they were able to make for the comfort of their own families. Mr. Ashworth returned, at the end of the year, one hundred and eighty-eight members.

Whitewater Circuit, on the eastern border of the state, and lying then principally in the state of Ohio—though that part of the circuit lying in Indiana retained the name—had been organized the year before under the labors of Rev. Thomas Hellams and Rev. Selah Payne. What classes, if any, were organized by them in Indiana, and at what points, is not now known. The circuit, as organized a few years later, included Brookville, Brownsville, Liberty, Connersville, and all of the settled parts of the Whitewater country, from the mouth of Whitewater to as far north as what is now Randolph County.

In 1808, Indiana District was organized as follows:

INDIANA DISTRICT—SAMUEL PARKER, Presiding Elder.

Illinois—Jesse Walker.
Missouri—Abraham Amos.
Merrimack—Joseph Oglesby.
Coldwater—John Crane.
Whitewater—Hector Sanford and Moses Crume.
Silver-creek—Josiah Crawford.

Here was a district extending from the western border of the state of Ohio to Mexico. There is something sublime in the heroism that planned such fields of labor—a single presiding elder's district embracing what is now the three great states of Indiana, Illinois, and Missouri. The mode of travel was on horseback. The streams were unbridged, and could often be crossed only by swimming. The roads were mostly bridle-paths, "blazed," as the backwoodsmen called it, by hatchet-marks on the trees. The country was full of Indians, some of them friendly, but many of them exasperated by the encroachments of the white men. Salaries were scarcely thought of; they lived among the people, sharing their scanty, but cheerful hospitality, encountering perils in the wilderness, from floods and swamps and savage men, often compelled to sleep in the woods. Their meeting-houses were the rude cabins of the pioneers, where one room served as kitchen, bed-room, and chapel. These were lion-hearted men; they "endured as seeing

Him who is invisible;" they saw that these fertile valleys were to be seats of empire, that populous cities would rise on the margin of these mighty rivers, that commerce would burden these navigable streams, knowing that they were laying the foundations of Christian civilization that should bless uncounted millions in after years. Grand as were their conceptions, the facts have out-run them, and the reality is already grander than their most sanguine imaginings. Giving them credit for great fore-sight, they, nevertheless, built wiser than they knew.

In 1809, Indiana District stood as follows:

INDIANA DISTRICT—SAMUEL PARKER, Presiding Elder.

Illinois—Abraham Amos.
Missouri—John Crane.
Merrimack—David Young and Thomas Wright.
Coldwater—Isaac Lindsey.
Cape Girardeau—Jesse Walker.
Vincennes—William Winans.

Vincennes appears for the first time on the list of appointments. Catholic priests had previously officiated there, for Post St. Vincent was an early French trading-post, but it was now an American settlement. General William Henry Harrison, Governor of Indiana Territory, had established his head-quarters there; and William Winans was the first Protestant preacher to visit the place. One of his first services was a night appointment for preaching in the fort. The Government officers, a few English and French settlers, and two or three Indians, make up the audience. A few tallow candles furnish all their light for the occasion. One of these is kindly held by Governor Harrison for the young preacher, while he reads his text and hymn. And in that dingy room young Winans delivers his Gospel message in such a manner as commends both the preacher and his message to the hearts of his hearers. Winans was a young man of fine personal appearance; not handsome, but commanding in his appearance; a little above the medium height, with an open countenance, a clear, strong voice, an easy, rather negligent manner, that showed perfect self-possession and self-reliance, qualities of great value to the frontier missionary, who has no treasury to depend on, and whose audiences are, for the most part, composed of strangers. Winans did not disappoint the expectations of his friends. He rose to eminence, and was for many years a recognized leader of the forces of Methodism in the state of Mississippi, into the bounds of which Conference he fell by the division of territory.

In 1810, Indiana District is continued as follows:

INDIANA DISTRICT—SAMUEL PARKER, Presiding Elder.

Illinois—Daniel Fraley.
Missouri—Thomas Wright.
Merrimack—John M'Farland.
Coldwater—George A. Colbert.
Cape Girardeau—Jesse Walker.

Why it should have been called Indiana District, as thus constituted, is not apparent at the present day. The charges in Indiana were as follows: St. Vincent's, as it was then written in the Minutes, with Thomas Stilwell as the preacher, and included in the Cumberland District, Learner Blackman as presiding elder; Silver-creek, included in Green-river District, with Isaac Lindsey for the preacher, and William Burke as presiding elder; Whitewater, in Miami District, with Moses Crume for the preacher, and Solomon Langdon for presiding elder. The numbers returned for this year were as follows: Silver-creek, 397; Vincennes, 125; Whitewater, 638. In 1811, Lawrenceburg Circuit, on the eastern border of the state, and Patoka, on the south-western part of the state, were added to the organized work in Indiana. Walter Griffith

traveled the former, and Benjamin Edge the latter.
Down to this time, the Church within the bounds of the
Western Conference had accumulated but little property
in the way of churches, parsonages, or school-houses. In
the Winter the log-cabins of the early settlers were the
preaching-places, and in the Summer they worshiped
in the grand old woods. The early settlements were
along the rivers and creeks, as these were the natural
highways of the country; and hence the early circuits
derived their names from some river or creek upon which
they were located, or to which they were contiguous;
and not as is the present custom, from city, town, or
post-office, for the very good reason that there were no
cities, and very few towns and post-offices, after which
they could have named them. The old Western Conference included in its ranks a large proportion of strong
men—men of intellectual vigor, and mighty in the Scriptures. William M'Kendree, the enterprising and efficient
presiding elder and prince of preachers, was elected
bishop in 1808. He was a true champion and a recognized leader in the old Western Conference. Charles
Holliday, than whom few men were ever more familiar
with the Scriptures. He was, a number of years, Book
Agent at Cincinnati. At the close of his Book Agency
he was transferred to the Illinois Conference, where he
continued to labor until the Fall of 1846, when he took
a superannuated relation, and in 1849 was called from
labor to reward. The sweet-spirited, saintly, and successful John Collins, who won thousands as jewels for
his Master. Learner Blackman, John Sale, James
Quinn, and Solomon Langdon were eminently fitted to
lead on the Church from "conquering to conquest."
William Burke was a man of decided ability and impressive manners, and for many years stood in the front rank

of Methodist preachers. In an evil hour he withdrew from the Church, but lived long enough to repent the rash deed. He now rests, with the co-laborers of his early manhood, in the better land. James B. Finley, known as the Old Chief, survived most of his early associates, and, through a long life, declaimed against vice, and proclaimed the Gospel message, with a power and success equaled by few. The thrilling eloquence of John Strange, and the sturdy sense and occasional eccentricity of James Axley, are still themes of conversation among those who still remember them. The last session of the old Western Conference was held in Cincinnati, October, 1811. Bishops Asbury and M'Kendree were both present at this Conference. At the General Conference of 1812, the Western Conference was divided into two conferences, called Ohio and Tennessee. The Ohio Conference embraced the Ohio, Muskingum, Scioto, Miami, and Kentucky Districts. At the General Conference held in the city of Baltimore, in May, 1816, the Missouri Annual Conference was constituted, embracing Indiana, Illinois, and Missouri. There were at that time, in Indiana, Lawrenceburg and White-river Circuits, on the eastern border of the state, included in Miami District, Ohio Conference; and Patoka, Vincennes, Harrison, Blue-river, and Silver-creek Circuits, embraced in Illinois District, Missouri Conference; Missouri Conference being bounded on the east by a line running due north from the city of Madison.

Methodism was introduced into Decatur County as follows: John Robins came to Decatur County, March 28, 1822, and settled on Sand Creek, three and a half miles south of where Greensburg now stands. The town was laid out that same Spring. There were but few persons then in the county. The only family then

in the limits of what is now Greensburg, was Colonel
Hendricks, an honored citizen and a liberal-minded Presbyterian. At this time there was no Church organization
in the county. The first Methodist society, which was
the first religious organization in the county, began
on this wise: The few scattered Methodists, feeling
their need of spiritual aid and the fellowship of the
Church, resolved to see what could be done. John Robins began to hunt for a preacher that could take them
into his circuit, and supply them with preaching. Meanwhile he appointed prayer-meeting at his own house.
At that first prayer-meeting there were present John
Robins, Ruth Robins, John H. Kirkpatrick and wife,
and Nathaniel Robins; and shortly after, John Steward
joined them.

Late in the Summer of 1822, James Murray, who was
then traveling Connersville Circuit, which was included
in the Ohio Conference, sent an appointment to Greensburg, to the cabin of Colonel Hendricks, to preach. He
came; and here he was met by John Robins, who solicited him to make an appointment at his house. Mr.
Murray made a conditional promise. He would come
if he could. In a short time after this, Mr. Robins
received a class-paper, made out in due form by Mr.
Murray, and forwarded to him, not by mail—for such a
luxury was then unknown by the early settlers—but
conveyed by friends from one neighborhood to another.
With that paper was the request that he would open the
doors of the Church, and receive such as were willing
to join in with them to form a class. Mr. Robins proposed, if enough joined to justify it, that he would
report the society to the next session of the Missouri
Conference. When Mr. Robins presented the question
of the organization of a class, seven persons gave their

names, to wit: Abram L. Anderson, Nancy Anderson, Jacob Stewart, Elizabeth Garrison, Nathaniel Robins, John Robins, and Ruth Robins. These formed the first Methodist class and the first religious organization in Decatur County. Mr. Robins reported the organization of the class to Mr. Murray, and the class was reported in due time to the Missouri Conference. In the Fall of 1823, Aaron Wood was appointed to Connersville Circuit, and, as he was surveying his new field of labor, he met with Mr. Robins, and an arrangement was effected for a regular appointment at his house; but Wood had hardly got possession of this new society, when Jesse Haile, of Indianapolis Circuit, Missouri Conference, appeared, with John Robins's house on the plan of his circuit. The east line of the Missouri Conference being a line due north from the city of Madison, Greensburg was found to be in the Missouri Conference, and Mr. Wood had to vacate. From Mr. Wood's first sermon at Mr. Robins's house, it became a regular preaching-place, and, although nearly half a century has passed by, the results are yet visible: "The handful of corn on the top of the mountain shakes like Lebanon." A good Church and a flourishing Sabbath-school still mark that country appointment, while two flourishing Churches exist in the town of Greensburg. Rev. George Horn was the colleague of Mr. Haile, and they received for their support during the year the sum of $27.

In the year 1822, there moved into Mr. Robins's neighborhood a man by the name of Garrison, an old local preacher in the *United Brethren Church;* and, being zealous for his own denomination, the contest would at times wax warm between him and his Methodist neighbors. Elizabeth Garrison, one of the old man's daughters, joined the Methodists, and was one of the original seven of whom the first class was composed; and, not long after, a married daughter of the old gentleman joined, and, a short time after that, his wife also joined. That put an end to the old man's opposition to Methodism; and, in a short time, he himself united with the society. Soon after his union with the Church, the old man applied for license as a local preacher; but Mr. Haile, who was in charge of the circuit, learning that the old gentleman was not entirely sound on "Doctrine and Discipline," arranged to have an interview with him on his next round; and, accordingly, at his next appointment, after dinner, he entered into conversation with him. Finding him unsound on many points, as he judged, he labored with him until late in the afternoon; but failing in his efforts to convince him of his errors, Mr. Garrison was not licensed. The interview ended, Mr. Haile started for his next appointment, which was twelve miles distant, and his way lay through a dense wood, with only a few marks on the trees to guide him. He missed his way, and paid for his devotion to Methodist "Doctrine and Discipline" by spending a night in the dense and chilly forest.

In 1823, Haile and Horn established regular preaching in Greensburg, in the house of Colonel Hendricks, which then stood on the south-east corner of the public square, where the "Moss House" now stands. In the Fall of that year, Haile and Horn were followed by Thomas Rice, under whose labors the work greatly prospered.

Mr. Rice was somewhat eccentric, and, like many of the early preachers, had marked individuality of character. While on the Sangamon Circuit, as his custom was, he directed his heaviest artillery against slavery, whisky, tobacco, and worldly fashions. While holding a meeting at one of his appointments, a brother got very happy, and began to shout, and, in his evolutions, Mr. Rice spied a plug of tobacco in the happy brother's pocket, and he called out immediately, "Do n't shout any more, brother, until you get that tobacco out of your pocket." The rebuke was a damper on the services for that hour. Rice came from the Holston Conference. At the conference in Charleston, in 1825, when Mr. Rice's case was under consideration, John Strange, who was his presiding elder, made some allusion to his eccentricities, which Bishop Roberts feared might damage him before the conference, and he arose to make some remarks in Rice's favor. He said : " True, brother Rice is an eccentric man. While we were passing through Tennessee, in company, when at family worship, brother Rice would pray, 'O Lord! bless this household; bless the parents and the children, and the poor negroes too. Help this master and mistress to be good and kind to their slaves, not to whip, beat, or starve them. Help them, that they may see the great sin of slavery, and that they may let the oppressed go free.'" At the conclusion of the bishop's remarks, William Cravens, who had been listening intently, and who hated human slavery as but few men could, cried: "I 'll vote for him, my honeys! He prays at them; he prays at them." Of course Rice's case passed the conference all right. Rice was followed by Stephen R. Beggs, and he by James Havens. The work was then divided, and Greensburg was placed in Rushville Circuit. Havens was followed by Joseph Tarkington and William Evans. The circuit then embraced thirty-four appointments, which had to be filled every twenty-eight days. Tarkington and Evans received each, for their year's labor, the sum of $63. But the preachers were relatively as well supported then as now, and it required more effort for the people to raise the pittance then paid than it does the salaries of the present day.

Take the following as an illustration: A brother of small means, now residing in Greensburg, pays annually, for the support of the Gospel, the sum of $20. In an early day, he had a small tract of land near the town, with four acres cleared. His quarterage was one dollar a year. The conference year rolled on, and brother —— had no money. A good brother in town proposed to take corn-meal and sell it, and give the preacher the benefit of it. But brother —— had no corn to spare, not more than enough to do him until he could raise a crop. But the preacher was in need; so he resolved to divide. He shelled two bushels of corn, took it to mill, and had it ground, took the meal to Greensburg, turned it over to Silas Stewart for twenty-five cents a bushel, and got credit for half his quarterage. Those were the days of moral heroism and self-denial, both on the part of preachers and people.

Tarkington and Evans were followed by Amos Sparks and John C. Smith.

The first school of any kind held in the territory of Indiana was taught one-and-a-half miles south of Charlestown, the present county-seat of Clark County, in 1803. Rev. George K. Hester, who was a pupil in this school in 1804, says: " Our first books were generally very far from facilitating an education, or affording materials for the mental culture of youth. My first two reading-books were ' Gulliver's Travels,' and a ' Dream Book.' We had to commence the first rudiments of language in ' Dilworth's Spelling-Book.' The rigid discipline exercised, the cruelty practiced on delinquent scholars, as well as the long confinement of children to their books, from soon after sunrise to sunset, with only vacation at noon, was detrimental to their advancement in learning."

Rev. George K. Hester, who is undoubtedly the best living authority on the subject, says: "The first introduction of Methodist preaching into the Grant—as Clark County was then called—from the most reliable sources, was by Rev. Samuel Parker, and Edward Talbott, in the Spring of 1801. They attended a two-days' meeting, in a village called Springville, which had just been laid out, and was situated about one-and-a-half miles west of the present town of Charlestown. Parker and Talbott were then both of them local preachers. Benjamin Lakin and Ralph Lotspeich were the first traveling preachers that were sent into the Grant. They came in 1803. Lakin first visited Gazaway's neighborhood, five miles east of Charlestown, and preached in the woods, as early in the Spring as the weather would permit. He then proposed to take them and Father Robertson's, which was five miles north of Charlestown, into his regular work. To these, at first, he devoted but one day in each round, preaching alternately at each place. These appointments were included in Salt-river Circuit, Kentucky. It is believed that the first society formed in the state was organized at Father Robertson's. It has been supposed that the first society was formed at Gazaway's, but Hezekiah Robertson distinctly recollects that the first society was organized at his father's. And old sister Gazaway has often been heard to say to persons, when excusing themselves for their neglect in attending class-meetings, on account of the distance, that she had uniformly gone to Nathan Robertson's to class-meeting every two weeks, a distance of four miles, which makes it evident that the first class was organized there. This must have been in the Spring of 1803. Then came M'Guire and Sullivan. In 1805, Peter Cartwright preached in the Grant, and, in the Fall of 1805, Asa Shinn and Moses Ashworth preached there. In 1806, Joseph Oglesby and Frederick Hood also preached in the Grant. And in 1807, the work on this side of the river was organized into Silver-creek Circuit, with Moses Ashworth for their preacher. Moses Ashworth closed his year with a camp-meeting, which was held in the neighborhood of Father Robertson's. Rev. William Burke was the presiding elder. This was a novel affair in our new country, and called together a vast multitude of human beings." No special revivals of religion are noted until 1810, when many were converted and brought into the Church, and preaching was established in the town of Charlestown. These infant societies were not free from trouble. Most of the population came from Kentucky. Arianism, as taught by Marshall and Stone, and as held by the New-lights, as they were called, was advocated strenuously. Their chief attacks, so far as Methodism was concerned, were against the Divinity of Christ and the Discipline of the Church. They opposed all articles of faith and rules for Church government. The New-light meetings attracted a good deal of attention, because of the prevalence of a peculiar exercise, which attended many of their meetings, known as "the jerks."

In 1819, a memorable revival of religion prevailed in this part of the country. It began at a camp-meeting held on what was known as Jacob's camp-ground. The good work continued long after the close of the camp-meeting, and extended to every neighborhood within the bounds of the old Silver-creek Circuit.

Bishop M'Kendree and Bishop Roberts both attended

the session of the Illinois Conference at Charlestown, Indiana, in 1825. Bishop M'Kendree arrived at the seat of the Conference a few days before the opening of the session, and visited a few of the adjoining neighborhoods, and preached to the people. He preached twice during the session of the Conference, much to the edification and delight of both preachers and people. Bishop Roberts also preached twice during the session of the Conference. He preached on Saturday, at 11 A. M., and on Sabbath afternoon. Dr. Martin Ruter preached on Sabbath morning. Bishop Roberts's sermon on Sabbath afternoon was one of remarkable power, founded on the text, "Yea, doubtless, and I count all things but loss for the excellency of the knowledge of Christ Jesus my Lord."

CHAPTER III.

Allen Wiley and C. W. Ruter admitted on Trial in the Ohio Conference—Friendship of Wiley and Bigelow—Incidents—First Camp-meeting held in Indiana—Incidents of the Meeting—First Camp-meeting held near Madison—Allen Wiley preaches—Results of the Meeting—Camp-meeting near Cochran—Impressive Closing Services—Remarks on Camp-meetings—Charges in Indiana in 1818—John Schrader's account of his early Labors—Appointed to Silvercreek Circuit—Administers the Sacrament for the first time in New Albany—Appointed to Spring-river Circuit, Arkansas Territory—Preaching under Difficulties—Appointed to Corydon Circuit, Indiana—Organization of the Missouri Conference—Appointed to Missouri Circuit—First Camp-meeting at Boone's Lick—Heroism of the Early Preachers—Early Jesuit Missionaries—Romanism and Protestantism contrasted—Number of Methodists in Indiana in 1810—Number in 1820—Charges in Indiana—Memoir of Samuel Parker—James Havens admitted on Trial—William Cravens received in the Missouri Conference—His hatred of Slavery—An Incident—Remarks on the Labors of Havens and Cravens—Appointments in Indiana in 1821—Cravens appointed to Indianapolis—Connersville Circuit organized—Extract from the Journal of the Quarterly Conference for Connersville Circuit in 1822—Appointments in Indiana in 1823—Dr. A. Wood's account of his Journey to his new Circuit—Account of his Year's Work—Division of the Missouri Conference—Appointments in Indiana in 1824—Appointments on Madison Circuit.

AT the session of the Ohio Conference, in Zanesville, September, 1817, Rev. Allen Wiley and Rev. C. W. Ruter were received on trial in the traveling connection. Ruter was appointed as junior preacher on Steubenville Circuit, under James B. Finley as presiding elder, and Wiley was apointed as junior preacher on Lawrenceburg Circuit, with Samuel West in charge. Wiley and Ruter will hereafter figure largely in the history of Indiana Methodism. Wiley had traveled a part of the preceding year on Lawrenceburg Circuit, under the direction of the presiding elder, with Russel Bigelow in charge. He had yielded to the importunity of Bigelow to travel three months; but instead of terminating with three months, it became the business of a long life. Bigelow and Wiley were united in the bonds of friendship as closely as David and Jonathan. There were several incidents connected with Wiley's first year on Lawrenceburg Circuit with Mr. Bigelow, that are worth relating. Although their circuit extended from the vicinity of Brookville down to Madison, on the Ohio River, they materially enlarged its bounds during the year, and added a number of new appointments. In several of the societies there were glorious revivals of religion during the year. Wiley's own house was made a preaching-place, and although, a few months previous, there was not a dwelling within two miles of his, yet such was the emigration, and such the work of God among the new-comers, that during the year a society of forty members was raised up. One night, when there was an appointment for Bigelow to preach at Wiley's house, a crowd collected, and during the first prayer the power of God was manifested among the people, and many began to cry for mercy. So great was their distress that preaching was dispensed with, and penitents were at once invited to the mourners'-bench; and great was the work of the Lord among the people. During this year there was a glorious revival of religion at Allensville, a small village in the northern part of Switzerland County. One day Wiley was preaching in Allensville from the words, "The eyes of the Lord are over the righteous." In the exposition of the text, he remarked that when the Scriptures ascribed eyes and hands and other bodily parts to the Deity, they were not to be understood literally, but as expressive of attributes and operations of the Deity. There was present a lady who had been a confirmed Deist for a number of years. She had supposed that Christians believed all such expressions were to be understood as physically descriptive of God, and she always regarded with contempt such a petty and local God as these expressions seemed to intimate the God of the Bible to be. She was led to think more seriously about the Bible and its doctrines than she had formerly done. Not long after hearing this sermon, she was riding alone through the woods, when a limb fell from a tree and came near striking her, and in her fright she exclaimed, "Lord Jesus!" This alarmed her the more, to think that she should invoke a name for which she felt no respect. This incident fastened conviction upon her mind. Not long afterward she went to hear Mr. Bigelow preach. She became powerfully convicted, and was soon afterward happily converted to God; and her conversion was followed by a powerful revival of religion all over the neighborhood. There had settled in the vicinity of Buchanan Station, a post about midway between Madison and Versailles, a man by the name of John Richey, who had been a local preacher in Kentucky, but who had got out of the Church, and was a miserable backslider. One day he came to hear Wiley preach, and he was so deeply impressed that he remained after the sermon, to converse with the preacher about his condition. He stated that he had not heard a traveling preacher for some years, and that he had not read a chapter in the Bible for three years, that it tortured him beyond endurance to read the Bible. Two weeks after, when Bigelow came around, he united with the Church, and in a short time was reclaimed, and was made a class-leader, then an exhorter, and afterward a local preacher. And he became one of the most useful and popular local preachers in all the land.

A new society was formed during this year, about nine miles south-west from Brookville, and another on the dividing ridge between South Hogan and Laughery, near where Mount Tabor meeting-house now stands. During this year there were two glorious camp-meetings held within the bounds of Lawrenceburg Circuit. One had been held the year previous, about five miles above Harrison, on Whitewater, near what is known as the Lower Narrows. This meeting was under the superintendence of Hezekiah Shaw. This was the first camp-meeting ever held in Indiana. Mr. Shaw was very anxious to secure good order during the meeting, but was not the most judicious in the use of the means he employed. He posted at the different cross-roads, and other public places throughout the neighborhood, written notices, threatening the public with three dollars' fine, to be assessed by a magistrate in the neighborhood, for Sunday breaches of order. There was, however, no disturbance; but a witty fellow, by the name of Breckenridge, paraphrased Shaw's posters in a kind of doggerel poetry, every stanza ending with "three dollars' fine." This furnished a great deal of sport among the idlers around the encampment. During this meeting an intelligent gentleman, by the name of Merwin, whose education had been in another Church, was struck under deep conviction, while listening to a sermon from William Houston, who was that year traveling the Cincinnati Circuit. He went home that evening greatly excited on the subject of religion. His soul's salvation had become the absorbing subject of his meditations. He retired to bed with a heavy heart, mourning his sins and imploring the Divine mercy. While in this state of mind, all at once light broke into his mind and love flowed through his heart, and he felt as though he was in a new world. With him all things had become new, he shouted aloud, and spent most of the night in praising the Savior.

In 1817 there were two camp-meetings held on the Lawrenceburg Circuit, which that year enjoyed the labors of Russel Bigelow, aided by Allen Wiley. The first of these was on the bank of Crooked Creek, within the limits of the present city of Madison. Down to Saturday morning the meeting dragged heavily. The appointment for eleven o'clock, on Saturday, had been reserved for Thomas Hellum, one of the preachers from Whitewater Circuit, who was expected at the meeting. Just before the hour of meeting, as Mr. Hellum had not arrived, Bigelow said to Wiley: "You will have to preach." Up to this time Wiley had preached more from a conviction of duty than from any love of preaching. But on that morning he remarked that he felt, for the first time, a desire to preach. And when told that he must preach at that hour, the intelligence was welcome. He requested Bigelow to tell him where the following passage could be found: "The wicked is driven away in his wickedness; but the righteous hath hope in his death." Bigelow named the chapter and verse, and Wiley immediately commenced the service of the hour. As he advanced, God filled his mind with ideas, and his heart with zeal, and he preached with great success. At the close of the sermon twelve or fifteen came forward for prayers; and the work of conversion commenced, and continued to the close of the meeting. Bigelow preached the closing sermon on Monday, which was one of decided ability, and was attended with displays of Divine power. The results of the meeting were truly glorious. Many substantial citizens, who lived for years as ornaments of piety, and earnest workers for the Lord, were added to the Church. The revival did not close with the camp-meeting, but continued with unabated interest for some time. The local preachers in the vicinity kept up the meetings in the absence of the traveling preachers, and the work went gloriously forward, and many were converted at their houses, as well as at the place of meeting.

The other camp-meeting was held near the bank of South Hogan, nearly opposite the village of Cochran, and at the foot of the hill, on the left of the road leading from Aurora to Wilmington, on the land of Mr. Milburn. At this meeting Bigelow closed his official labors on Lawrenceburg Circuit. There were, perhaps, as many conversions at this camp-meeting as there had been during the progress of the Madison camp-meeting; but its influence was not as extensive, nor its permanent fruits as great. The meeting closed on Monday, in a very solemn and impressive manner. Bigelow formed the congregation into a company, like soldiers, in double file, and marched around the encampment, singing appropriate farewell hymns. After which the preachers took their stand at some convenient point, and bade them all farewell by shaking hands with each of them, and getting pledges from as many as they could to meet them in heaven. It was truly a heart-melting time. Christians had been associated together in the worship of God for several days on what was to them a consecrated spot. It had been made holy ground by reason of the displays of Divine power and mercy. There they had prayed and rejoiced together, and many of them had found peace in believing; and now they were about to separate, never all of them to meet again on earth. Bigelow was bidding adieu to his flock, and he exhorted them, in touching strains of eloquence, to meet him in heaven. The results of such meetings will never be fully known until God shall collect his ransomed ones. The Lord shall count, when he righteth up the people, that "this man was born there;" for many shall date their spiritual birth-place upon that camp-ground. And we hold it as a good omen that camp-meetings are again reviving. Notwithstanding the number of commodious churches, both in town and country, camp-meetings will produce a popular effect that no other meetings will. They break up the current of wordly thought, and, by their continual daily services, make a profounder impression than the brief services in our churches can possibly do. Let us perpetuate our camp-meetings, and not desert the venerable groves,

> "God's ancient sanctuaries, and adore
> Only among the crowd, and under roofs
> That our frail hands have raised."

In 1818, the charges in Indiana were as follows: Whitewater, Lawrenceburg, and Madison, in the Lebanon District, Ohio Conference; and Silver-creek, Indian-creek, Blue-river, Harrison, Vincennes, Patoka, and Pigeon, in what, for that year, was called Illinois District, Missouri Conference.

As an illustration of the exposure, privations, and labors endured by the traveling ministry of that day, I insert the following, furnished me by the veteran and truly venerable John Schrader. He says:

"I was removed to the Silver-creek Circuit, on the Ohio, embracing the country from the mouth of Blue River up to Madison. Rev. J. Cord had been appointed to this circuit by the bishop, but, his house being consumed by fire, he was compelled to quit traveling for a season and return to his friends. I came to Cord's

appointment at Gazaway's, and found him preaching
from, 'The Lord is my Shepherd; I shall not want.' It
was a good sermon, preached by a good man. After
service, I told him that I had come to take his place.
He appeared glad to be released, and hastened home.
I now entered on my work with much fear and trembling. Revivals had commenced at different points on
the circuit under Cord's preaching, and on me rested
the responsibility of carrying on this great work, which
extended all over the circuit, and, during the year,
nearly six hundred were taken into the Church on
trial. I took into the circuit, as new preaching-places,
New Lexington, Jeffersonville, and New Albany. Some
seven or eight members of the Church had formed
themselves into a class in New Albany, and called on
me to preach for them, which I did in a tavern, occupied
by a Mrs. Ruff. In this tavern I administered the
Sacrament of the Lord's Supper, for the first time, I
suppose, that it was ever administered in New Albany.

"At the close of this year, by the direction of my presiding elder, I went to Cincinnati to meet Bishop M'Kendree, and conduct him to the seat of the Missouri Conference, which was to be held at Bethel meeting-house,
near the present town of Washington, the county-seat
of Daviess County, Indiana. I was taken sick the first
day of the Conference, but was well taken care of at the
house of William Hawkins. My appointment for the
ensuing year was Spring-river Circuit, Arkansas Territory. It was some time before I sufficiently recovered
from my sickness to enable me to ride; but while yet
feeble, I started for my field of labor, which required a
journey of five hundred miles. My circuit embraced a
large extent of territory; it was mountainous and rocky,
the settlements were very scattering, and it was far

between the appointments. The inhabitants were mostly hunters, and lived on the game they caught. They generally brought their guns and dogs with them to meeting. The dogs very often differed with each other, and a quarrel ensued, and this ended in a general dog-fight. This always produced a stir in the congregation, and consumed some time before peace could be restored and ratified. The preacher would be interrupted in his sermon, or perhaps forget his text, and have to finish with an exhortation. At other times the hunters would return home during divine service, with venison, bear-meat, and dogs. But we were not easily disturbed in those days. We had plenty of venison, bear-meat, and wild turkeys to eat; but our bread was corn, and coarse at that. In many places we had no way of grinding our grain except on what was called Armstrong's mill. This was generally a long cedar pole, with one end made fast to the ground, and supported in the middle by two forks, with a pestle fastened to the small end; under it we placed a mortar, and thus we prepared our breadstuff; and this we frequently baked without sifting, and perhaps this is the reason why we did not have the dyspepsia. In some parts of the circuit, however, we fared well for the times, found warm friends, and at two or three appointments had good revivals of religion. At the close of the year I traveled as far west as the Arkansas River, and attended a camp-meeting on its banks. We had a good meeting, at the close of which I started for Conference, which sat at M'Kendree Chapel, near Cape Girardeau, Missouri. My next appointment was Corydon Circuit, Indiana. I was much pleased with this appointment, and felt myself at home among old friends."

In 1816 the Missouri Conference was organized and held its first session at Turkey-hill Settlement, in Illinois.

The following is Father Schrader's account of the organization of the Conference, and his first appointment therefrom: "Bishop M'Kendree and myself started from Louisville, Kentucky, for Vincennes, from whence Walker, Scripps, and others were to travel with us through the wilderness, to the Missouri Conference. After camping in the wilderness three nights, we arrived at the seat of the Conference. When the Conference was organized, we found that we had seven members present, and some few were admitted on trial. These are all now dead (1853), except J. Scripps and myself. The Conference extended over four different states. Most of the members of Conference were young men. We had received very little quarterage from our circuits and consequently were in tolerably straitened circumstances. Bishop M'Kendree gave the Conference one hundred dollars; and this, added to our share of the funds, made us a pretty fair dividend. From this Conference we scattered over this immense territory. My appointment was to Missouri Circuit, embracing the settlements between the Mississippi and Missouri Rivers. I commenced preaching in St. Charles, in a tavern; some of the bacchanalians would leave their worship and listen to me awhile, and sometimes they would swear that I was preaching the best sermon that they had ever heard. We had a good revival on the Missouri, above St. Charles. In the Fall of this year, 1817, the presiding elder and myself traveled up the Missouri River as far as Boone's Lick, and held a camp-meeting, the first ever held in that part of the world. Having to lodge in the woods six nights, going and returning, I was taken very sick, and had like to have died in the wilderness."

Such energy, devotion, and toil, such cheerful self-denial and unostentatious moral heroism, as was displayed by the early Methodist preachers in the West, has never been equaled in the history of our country, except, perhaps, in the case of the early Jesuit missionaries of the Romish Church. They were the first in the field; they came with the early French trappers, traders, and troops. The Jesuit missionaries were the first historians and geographers of the Great West; they not only visited the trading-posts and small colonies established by the French, but they followed the Indian to his hunting-ground, threaded the forests, swam rivers, and endured all kinds of hardships in prosecuting their spiritual work, and in furthering the objects of the French Government. The best and only authentic account of the country, bounded on the north by the lakes, on the east by the Wabash, on the south by the Ohio, and on the west by the Mississippi, one century ago, is to be found in the missionary reports of these Jesuit Fathers. One of these reports was written by Father Gabriel Maust, missionary of the Company of Jesus, and directed to Father Germon, of the same Company, and dated at Kaskaskia, then an Indian village, November 9, 1712. An edition of these reports was published in Paris in 1761; but while the influence of the Jesuit Fathers was doomed to decline, the influence of Methodism was destined rapidly to increase. The causes which tended to produce these opposite results in the two systems are apparent to the unprejudiced mind upon a moment's reflection. There is, and has ever been, a strong sympathy between Romanism and monarchy, or with despotism in some form. It has never been the friend of free thought and personal liberty. Its central idea is an aggregation of power; and, hence, its affinities and tendencies are all to a state of absolutism. But while the central idea of Romanism was power, the central idea of Methodism was salvation from sin. Methodism, in common with most forms of Protestantism, has its sympathies, tendencies, and affinities all on the side of republicanism, on the side of liberal institutions and free goverment, and all it asks of the State is to be let alone in its holy mission of saving sinners, and of building up the spiritual kingdom of Christ in the earth. The pioneer founders of Methodism in the West found the seal of their apostleship in the multitudes that were converted to God through their instrumentalities.

In 1810, the population in Indiana was 24,520, and Methodism numbered 755. In 1820, the population had increased to 147,178, and Methodism to 4,410. The charges in Indiana were Whitewater, Lawrenceburg, and Madison, on the eastern border of the state, all included in Miami District, Ohio Conference; and in Indiana District, Missouri Conference, Charlestown, Blue-river, Bloomington, Vincennes, Patoka, Ohio, Mt. Sterling, and Corydon Circuits. The preachers were stationed as follows:

Whitewater—James Jones.
Lawrenceburg—J. P. Durbin and James Collard.
Madison—Allen Wiley and William Quinn.

These charges were included in the Miami District, with Walter Griffith as presiding elder; Indiana District, Missouri Conference, with Samuel Hamilton for presiding elder.

Charlestown—Calvin W. Ruter and William Cravens.
Blue-river—John Scripps and Samuel Glaize.
Bloomington—David Chamberlin.
Vincennes—Job M. Baker.
Patoka—Elias Stone.
Ohio—John Wallace.
Mount Sterling—George K. Hester.
Corydon—John Schrader.

The growth of Methodism was keeping even pace with that of the population. Every settlement and

block-house was visited by these bold itinerants, who
did not scorn to preach in the bar-rooms of the taverns,
in the towns, in forts, in block-houses, and in the groves,
as well as in the cabins of the early settlers. Their
message was to every creature, and, relying on the
promise, "Lo, I am with you always," solitudes were
cheerful, and "all rest was labor to a worthy end :"

> "A toil that grows with what it yields,
> And scatters to its own increase,
> And hears, while reaping outward fields,
> The harvest-song of inward peace."

The arduous labors and privations of the early itinerant preachers, although endured with a martyr heroism, and with a spirit of consecration to their work that
counted it all joy to suffer for Christ, nevertheless
brought them to early graves. Samuel Parker, who
was the first presiding elder on Indiana District, having
been appointed to that district in 1809, when it included the settled portions of Indiana, Illinois, and Missouri, closed his earthly labors, December 20, 1819. He
was a native of New Jersey. His parents were pious,
and occupied a respectable social position. He was converted to God in his youth. He was licensed to preach
in 1800, at the age of twenty-six. In 1805, he became
a member of the traveling connection, and at the end of
four years he was admitted to elders' orders, and appointed presiding elder on Indiana District, at that time
one of the most difficult and laborious positions in the
old Western Conference. It is impossible at this day
fully to appreciate or comprehend the amount of moral
heroism and physical endurance demanded by such a
position at that time. He was a young minister to be
placed in so responsible a position; but he fully met the
expectations of the bishops. He remained four years

on the district, when it was found necessary to divide the district, so rapidly had the work grown on his hands, and "so mightily grew the Word of God and prevailed." In 1813, he traveled Deer-creek Circuit, in the Ohio Conference, and his labors were greatly blessed. In 1814, he was appointed presiding elder of Miami District, and, in 1815, presiding elder of Kentucky District, where he continued four years. A position of great importance in the estimation of the bishops had to be filled in the Mississippi Conference; and, although it was one that called for great sacrifices, and was beset with difficulties, and, withal, was in a very sickly climate, when the matter was proposed to him—for the bishops saw in him just the man that was needed—he said: "Here am I, send me; I count not my life dear, so that I may finish my course with joy, and the ministry which I have received of the Lord Jesus." He went; but failing health and an early death disappointed the expectations of the Church. God removes the workmen, but the work goes on. He is not dependent upon any class of instrumentalities. The early death of a useful minister is a mysterious providence; but as the standard bearers fall, the "Captain of our salvation" has some one ready to seize the standard, and bear aloft the banner of the Cross, and lead the hosts of Immanuel on to greater victories. Although many of our pioneer preachers died young, yet, if we measure their lives by events, and not years, they lived long. Their ministry was rich in results; their efforts were heroic, and their achievements morally grand; "they rest from their labors, and their works do follow them." Parker's death was peaceful and triumphant. The Gospel he had so faithfully preached to others sustained him in the hour of death. His funeral sermon was preached by Rev.

William Winans, a young man of great promise, whom Parker had induced to enter the ministry, who was once stationed at Vincennes, Indiana, but whose long and successful ministerial career was chiefly in connection with the Mississippi Conference.

At the session of the Ohio Conference, held in Chillicothe, August 8, 1820, James Havens was admitted on trial. His name appears at the end of a list of thirteen, which list is headed by the venerable Alfred Brunson, who is still in the front of the battle, and doing valiant service in his Master's cause in Wisconsin. Havens will hereafter figure largely in the struggles and triumphs of Methodism in Indiana. Few men have entered the itinerant ministry under greater discouragements than James Havens, and few have achieved more signal success, all things considered. His education was so limited that he could barely read. He had a large family of young children; he was poor, and the Church could only promise a meager support. Havens was endowed with remarkable force of character. Though of medium size, he possessed remarkable physical strength, and his courage often deterred the lawless, and served as a protection to those who wished to worship God in quietness. His strength of will was only equaled by his energy in executing. Having consecrated all his powers to the service of God, his labors were greatly blessed. He not only succeeded in gathering multitudes into the Church, but he succeeded equally in the work of personal culture. He made himself familiar with science and general literature. As a theologian, he was an able defender of the doctrines of Christianity, and of all that was peculiar in the doctrines of his own Church, and was better read in both medicine and law than many who follow those professions exclusively.

REV. JAMES HAVENS.

The same year, William Cravens entered the itinerancy, in connection with the Missouri Conference, and was appointed to Charlestown Circuit, as junior preacher, with Calvin W. Ruter. Cravens spent his ministry in Indiana. He, too, was a man of remarkable physical strength, and undaunted courage. A Virginian by birth, he was an uncompromising enemy of human slavery. He had sought a home in the North-western Territory that he might be free from the blight and curse of the peculiar institution. Mr. Cravens had been a local preacher for several years in Virginia, previous to his emigration to Indiana, and had acquired great notoriety from the faithful and fearless manner in which he denounced vice in all its forms. He had a special abhorrence to sins of drunkenness and negro slavery. Against these he was accustomed to declaim with a directness and force that made the guilty quail before him, even on slave territory, and in the aristocratic parts of old Virginia. While residing in Virginia, Mr. Cravens had an infidel neighbor by the name of " T.," who was a slaveholder. Cravens had labored in vain to convert him, either to anti-slavery principles or to the truths of Christianity. At length Mr. T. was taken seriously ill, and it soon became apparent that he would likely die. The near approach to death shook his faith in his infidel principles, and he became deeply concerned for his soul's salvation; and, as his convictions increased, he desired some one to instruct him in the way of salvation. At length he sent a servant, with a request that Mr. Cravens would call and see him. Judging correctly as to the cause of the invitation, he hastened immediately to the home of the sick man, whom he found dangerously ill, and deeply distressed on account of his sins.

"O!" said the sick man, "I am glad to see you. I

want you to pray for me, and tell me what I must do to be saved."

"Ah, Mr. T., I thought it would come to this. What have you done with your negroes?"

"I have provided for them in my will," said Mr. T. "I have divided them among my children, as I wish them to remain in the family."

"I can not pray for you," said Cravens. "God will never have mercy on you until you are willing to do justly. You will never get religion until you set your negroes free."

So saying, Cravens returned home. But in a short time another messenger came for him.

"Massa wants to see you immediately," was the substance of the request.

The sick man felt that his condition was a perilous one. Death was rapidly approaching, and the preacher in whose honesty and faithfulness he had full confidence, had refused to pray for him. He needed mercy, and yet he had failed to exercise it. The will was called for and altered, and the minister again sent for. On his arrival he said:

"Well, Mr. T., how is it now?"

"Mr. Cravens, I want you to pray for me, and tell me how I can be saved."

"What have you done with your slaves?" said Cravens.

"I have altered my will," said Mr. T., "and have provided for their emancipation."

"I will pray for you now," said Cravens. "And, more than that, God will have mercy on you too."

In answer to their united prayers, God did bless him with an assurance of pardon and a bright hope of heaven.

Christian civilization is deeply indebted to the chivalrous and indefatigable labors of such moral heroes as James Havens and William Cravens. They were born leaders; and, having that sort of magnetism that attached others to them, they were a tower of strength in any cause. They were just the men to lay the foundations of Christian society in a new country; they were men of comprehensive views; they occupied no doubtful positions, and gave no uncertain utterances on questions of doctrine or morals. Their style was perspicuous, if not polished, and their dauntless courage, and cheerful self-sacrifice exerted an inspiring effect upon their co-laborers, especially upon their junior brethren. Cravens continued his denunciations of slavery after his arrival in Indiana; for he found some here who had hired out their slaves, and had removed with their families to a free state, that they might raise their children free from the corrupting influences of slavery, but who were, nevertheless, drawing the wages of their slaves, and living by their unrequited toil. Others had sold their slaves, and, with their prices, had purchased homes in a free state. These he was accustomed to denounce as blood-stained hypocrites, and worse than those who retained their slaves and treated them kindly. He rarely preached a sermon without making those who made, sold, or drank intoxicating drinks, feel uneasy. On one of his circuits a brother was accused of "unnecessarily drinking ardent spirits." He was cited to trial, and found guilty. The committee was anxious to save him to the Church, if possible, and wished to know if he would not quit his habit of dram-drinking. After some reflection, he said he would try to quit. It was evident, however, that he did not feel that any particular guilt attached to his conduct, and that the action of the Church was rather an interference with his personal rights; but rather than leave the Church, he would promise to try to quit; and on that promise the committee retained him. But said Cravens, " Brother, you *must* quit." That was more than the brother would promise, and Cravens carried the case up to the next session of the quarterly conference; and the brother was required either to give up his drams or give up the Church. He concluded to give up the former; and doubtless owed his salvation from a drunkard's grave to the uncompromising integrity of his pastor.

In 1821, the Ohio Conference met in Lebanon, and the Missouri Conference at Cape Girardeau. From the Ohio Conference there were sent to circuits in Indiana:

Whitewater—Allen Wiley and James T. Wells.
Lawrenceburg—Henry Baker.
Madison—James Jones and James Murray.

And from the Missouri Conference:

INDIANA DISTRICT—SAMUEL HAMILTON, Presiding Elder.

Charlestown—James Armstrong.
Flat-rock—George K. Hester.
Blue-river—John Wallace and Joseph Kincaid.
Bloomington—John Cord.
Honey-creek—David Chamberlin.
Vincennes—John Stewart.
Patoka—James L. Thompson.
Mount Sterling—Ebenezer Webster.
Corydon—Job M. Baker.
Indianapolis—William Cravens.

There were but few settlements in Central Indiana when William Cravens came to organize Indianapolis circuit, in the Fall of 1821. A few families had settled at Indianapolis as early as 1819; but it was the policy of the Church to keep even pace with the tide of population, and Cravens was just the man for this pioneer work. He made an impression in favor of Methodism, and against slavery and intemperance, that has never faded out.

Indianapolis had been selected by the Commissioners as the seat of Government for the state in 1820, and emigration was beginning to set in to the new capital of the state.

Connersville Circuit was organized in 1822, under the presiding eldership of Alexander Cummins, who was in charge of Miami District, and who employed John Havens to travel Connersville Circuit. I have before me a transcript copy of the Journals of the quarterly conferences of Connersville Circuit, from its organization, in 1822, down to 1843. The following extract, for 1822, shows the meager support received by the early pioneer preachers, and the efforts put forth by the people to furnish even that meager support:

THE STEWARDS OF CONNERSVILLE CIRCUIT, *Dr.*

To Cash received from Lewis's Class ....$	50
To " " " Curtiss's "	50
To " " " Connersville Class......................	2 50
To " " " Abbott's "	1 00
To " " " Hardy's "	87½
To Bridle-leathers...	62½
To Cash from Fuller's..	1 25
To Shoe-leather and Corn...	1 75
To Cash from Lowers's...	1 25
To 12 yards Linen from Bridges's.................................	3 00
To 9 " " " J. Lowers's.............................	2 56¼
To 1 pair Shoe-soles..	50
To Cash from Roberts's..	4 65
To " " Hardy's..	75
To 2¼ yards Linsey..	1 12½
To Cash from E. Abbott's...	1 32
To " " Curtiss's..	50
To 7 yards Linen, "	1 75
To 1 small pair Shoes...	1 00
To 7¾ yards Linen from Alley's...................................	1 93¾
To 2½ " Linsey " "	1 25
To 8¾ " " " Lewis's...................................	3 27
To 1 pair Socks " "	43¾
To Cash from Gregg's...	2 12½
Total..$36	12½

Cr.

By Cash to A. Cummins, Esq........................	$ 50		
By " " J. Havens, expenses......................	1 50		
By " " A. Cummins, allowance.................	3 75		
By " " J. Havens, "	30 37½		

                                                     $36 12½

NATHAN LEWIS, *Recording Steward.*

CONNERSVILLE, *April* 27, 1822.

In September, 1823, the Ohio Conference met in Urbana, and the following appointments were made in Indiana:

Whitewater—John Everheart and Levi White.
Lawrenceburg—W. H. Raper and John Janes.
Madison—John F. Wright and Thomas Hewson.
Connersville—A. Wood.

Dr. Wood gives the following account of his journey to his new circuit, on the eastern border of Indiana: "On the 12th of September, 1823, I left my father's for the circuit to which I had been appointed. I met brother Bigelow in Springfield, and we rode on to Father Moses', who lived twelve miles from Dayton. Saturday, we started early, and rode to Dayton for breakfast, went on to Eaton, and after tea rode on to Centerville, where we arrived about midnight, sixty miles from where we started in the morning. Here I remained during Sunday, and preached in the court-house. On Monday, the 15th, I arrived in Connersville, which was a new circuit."

During the year, Mr. Wood traveled, according to his diary, now before me, two thousand, two hundred and fifty miles, preached two hundred and eight-eight times, and received for his year's salary fifty dollars. The preaching-places established on the circuit that year were as follows: Connersville, Hawkins's, Hinston's, Hardy's, Connell's, Crist's, Alley's, Lewis's, Miller's, Imley's, Short's, Gregg's Meeting-house, Young's, Taylor's, Grove's, Patterson's, Jacob Lowden's, Morris's, Newcastle, Sand-ford's, Joseph Lower's, and Briggs's. Here was a circuit of twenty-one appointments, extending from Pipe Creek, in Franklin County, to Newcastle, the present county-seat of Henry County. At the close of this year Mr. Wood was admitted into full connection in the Ohio Conference, which met for that year in Zanesville, and was ordained deacon by Bishop Roberts. At the General Conference, in 1824, the Missouri Annual Conference was divided, and Illinois Conference constituted, including the States of Illinois and Indiana. The appointments for that year, in Indiana, were as follows:

MADISON DISTRICT—JOHN STRANGE, Presiding Elder.

Madison Circuit—Allen Wiley and A. Wood.
Lawrenceburg—James Jones and Thomas Hitt.
Whitewater—Peter Stevens and Nehemiah B. Griffith.
Connersville—James Havens.
Rushville—Thomas Rice.
Indianapolis—John Miller.
Flat-rock—Thomas Hewson and James Garner.
Eel-river—John Fish.

INDIANA DISTRICT—JAMES ARMSTRONG, Presiding Elder.

Charlestown—James L. Thompson and Jacob Varner.
Corydon—George K. Hester and Dennis Willey.
Salem—Samuel Low and Richard Hargrave.
Paoli—Edward Smith.
Booneville—Orsenith Fisher.
Patoka—W. H. Smith and George Randle.
Vincennes—Edwin Ray.
Honey-creek—Samuel Hull.
Bloomington—Daniel Anderson and John Cord.
Vermilion—Hackaliah Vredenburg and Robert Delap.

As a sample of the better class of circuits in the older settled portions of Indiana, in that day, we give the appointments on Madison Circuit, which were filled by Allen Wiley and A. Wood: Rising Sun, Buell's Mill, Green's, Davis's, Spoon's, Campbell's, Vevay, Mount Sterling, Slawson's, Alfray's, Bellamy's, Brook's, Crooked-creek Meeting-house, Simper's, Hyatt's, Overturf's, Brown's, Herkul's, Versailles, Wiley's, Allensville, Downey's, Dexter's, including all of Switzerland and Ohio Counties, and the larger portions of Jefferson and Ripley Counties.

CHAPTER IV.

First Session of the Illinois Conference—Charges in Indiana in 1825—
Appointments made at the Illinois Conference for Indiana—Preach-
ing-places in Vincennes District in 1825—Remarks on Circuits and
Stations—Sketch of Rev. William Beauchamp—His Eloquence—
Incident—Second Session of the Illinois Conference in 1826—Num-
ber of Members returned for Indiana—Appointments made in In-
diana—Preaching-places in Indianapolis Circuit in 1825—Honey-
creek Church in 1825—Paoli Circuit in 1826—Appointments for
Indiana at the third Illinois Conference—Radical Controversy at
Madison—Indiana Members reported at the Illinois Conference in
Madison in 1828—Extent of Madison District—Revival in Law-
renceburg District—J. V. Watson—Indianapolis Station—Fall-
creek—Camp-meeting at Pendleton—Incident connected with the
Meeting—Illinois Conference at Edwardsville, Illinois, in 1829—
Incidents concerning John Strange—Illinois Conference at Vin-
cennes in 1830—Number of Members reported—Incident of Allen
Wiley—Meeting Held in Fort Wayne.

ILLINOIS CONFERENCE convened in session, for
the first time, in Charlestown, Clark County, Indiana,
August 25, 1825. There were present two bishops—
M'Kendree and Roberts—and forty-four traveling preachers, gathered from the various charges in Indiana and
Illinois. The charges in Indiana stood numerically as
follows:

MADISON DISTRICT.

Madison Circuit..700
Madison Station...139
Lawrenceburg Circuit...707
Whitewater 942
Connersville...412
Rushville..268
Indianapolis...304
Flat-rock..642
Eel-river..365
                                                           ———
Making for Madison District, members.......... 4,481

INDIANA DISTRICT.

Charlestown 975
Corydon...648
Salem..455
Paoli...422
Booneville...439
Patoka 335
Vincennes..532
Honey-creek..385
Bloomington..601
Vermilion...200

Total on Indiana District............................ 4,992

While there was but one presiding elder's district in Illinois, with a membership of only 3,505. Why the Conference was named Illinois is not apparent, any more than why, previous to this time, the charges included in Missouri, Illinois, and Indiana, were named Missouri Conference, when a large majority of the charges were in Indiana, and but a small fraction of them in Missouri. The appointments made at the first session of the Illinois Conference, held at Charlestown, Indiana, August 25, 1825, for the work in Indiana, were as follows:

MADISON DISTRICT—JOHN STRANGE,, Presiding Elder.

Madison Station—Samuel Bassett.
Madison Circuit—George K. Hester.
Lawrenceburg—James L. Thompson.
Whitewater—James Havens.
Connersville—N. B. Griffith.
Rushville—Stephen R. Beggs.
Flat-rock—James Jones and Thomas S. Hitt.
Indianapolis—Thomas Hewson.

CHARLESTOWN DISTRICT—JAMES ARMSTRONG, Presiding Elder.

Charlestown Circuit—A. Wiley and G. Randle.
Corydon—Samuel Low and George Locke.
Paoli—John Miller.
Bloomfield—Eli P. Farmer.
Crawfordsville—H. Vredenburg.
Bloomington—Edwin Ray.
Salem Station—William Shanks.
Salem Circuit—John Cord.

WABASH DISTRICT—CHARLES HOLLIDAY, Presiding Elder.

Vermilion—James Hadley.
Honey-creek—Richard Hargrave.
Vincennes—A. Wood.
Patoka—James Garner and J. Tarkington.
Booneville—William H. Smith.

We have given Connersville and Madison as specimens of the size of the circuits of that day in the eastern part of the state. Take Vincennes as a specimen of the size of the circuits in the south-western part of the state. In 1825, Vincennes included the following preaching-places: In the county of Knox: Vincennes, Cane's, Thomas's, Snyder's, Terebaugh's, Nicholson's, Hawkins's; in the county of Davis: Bethel Meeting-house, Stuckey's, Thomas Havell's, Widow Stone's, T. Stafford's, Ballon's; in the county of Martin: Hammond's, Clark's, Mount Pleasant, Love's Maner's, in Green County; and back again, in Davis County, to Bratton's, Williams's, Osmon's, and Florer's.

It will be seen from the appointments for this year that there were two stations in Indiana—Madison and Salem. While the circuit system is admirably adapted to a new country, and a sparse population, enabling a number of congregations to unite in one pastoral charge, and thereby secure, at regular intervals, the preaching of the Word of God and the administration of the sacraments of the Church, yet, as soon as any community feel that they can support a pastor of their own, there is a natural and universal desire to have one; and thus stations grow up in our towns and cities in answer to a demand from the people. In older communities a minister's influence depends largely upon his personal acquaintance, and not simply upon his ministerial character. This is especially true in cities; and hence a growing desire for lengthening the term of the pastoral relations.

During the preceding year, the Church in Indiana had suffered the loss of one of her ablest ministers, Rev. William Beauchamp, Presiding Elder of Indiana District, Missouri Conference, which event took place at Paoli, Orange County, Indiana, October, 1824, in the fifty-third year of his age. Mr. Beauchamp was a native of Delaware; was converted in early life, and, in 1794, joined the itinerancy. His first appointments were Alleghany Circuit, Pittsburg, New York, and Boston. He located in 1811. In 1815, he removed to Chillicothe, Ohio, and took the editorial charge of the *Western Christian Monitor*—the only periodical at that time in our Church. He discharged his editorial duties with conspicuous ability. Mr. Beauchamp had previously published a volume of "Essays on the Truth of Christianity," a work of considerable merit. In 1817, he removed to Mt. Carmel, Illinois, and superintended the formation of a new settlement. In 1822, he again entered the traveling connection, and was stationed in the city of St. Louis. In 1823, he was appointed presiding elder of Indiana District, which included Charlestown, Flat-rock, Blue-river, Bloomington, Honey-creek, Vincennes, Patoka, Mount Sterling, Corydon, Indianapolis, and Eel-river—eleven large circuits—embracing one-third of the territory of the state of Indiana. He was the same year elected a delegate to the General Conference, which met in Baltimore; and such was the impression made by him upon the members of that body that he lacked but two votes of being elected to the episcopal office. Had it not been for the fact that so large a portion of his ministerial life had been spent out of the itinerancy, his name would doubtless have honored the history of our episcopacy. On his return to his district he was seized with an affection of the liver, and, after suffering for about six weeks, fell asleep in Jesus, in the full prospect of a glorious immortality.

Mr. Beauchamp was one of nature's noblemen, a man of true greatness. He was often styled the "Demosthenes of the West." His manner was plain, and his style easy and natural. His sermons made a lasting impression. His standard of Christian character was high. Holiness was his favorite theme. When holding forth the promises and invitations of the Gospel, there was a gentleness and tenderness in his manner and in the tones of his voice, that was sure to touch the sympathies of his hearers; but when he became argumentative, and discussed doctrinal points, and especially when he denounced dangerous errors, his voice would become elevated, his whole system nerved, and the tones of his voice and the flash of his keen eye would startle his hearers like peals of thunder. On one occasion the force of his eloquence was fully demonstrated. It was on a subject of controversy. His antagonist, who had sat and listened for some time to his arguments, too powerful for him to answer, began to look as if the voice which he now heard came from another world through the shadow of a man. He rose, apparently with a view to leave the house; but, being overcome, he staggered, caught by the altar-railing, and fell into his seat, and there sat overwhelmed and confounded until the discourse closed, when he quietly left the.house. The death of such a minister is deeply felt; but God watches over his Church, and " the gates of hell shall not prevail against it."

The second session of the Illinois Conference was held in Bloomington, Monroe County, Indiana, beginning September 28, 1826. There were returned to this Conference members as follows: In Madison District,

4,352; in Charlestown District, 4,443; and in those portions of the Wabash and Illinois Districts lying in Indiana, 2,045; making a total membership in Indiana of 10,840; while that portion of the Illinois Conference lying within the state of Illinois only included a membership of 2,595. The appointments to the work in Indiana, made at this Conference, were as follows:

MADISON DISTRICT—JOHN STRANGE, Presiding Elder.

Madison Station—C. W. Ruter.
Madison Circuit—James Scott and Daniel Newton.
Lawrenceburg—James L. Thompson and George Randle.
Whitewater—James Havens and John F. Johnson.
Connersville—Robert Burns.
Rushville—N. B Griffith.
Flat-rock—Abner H. Cheever.
Indianapolis—Edwin Ray.

CHARLESTOWN DISTRICT—JAMES ARMSTRONG, Presiding Elder.

Charlestown—Allen Wiley and James Garner.
Corydon—George Locke and Samuel Low.
Paoli—W. H. Smith and Smith L. Robinson.
Eel-river—Daniel Anderson and Stith M. Otwell.
Crawfordsville—Henry Buell.
Bloomington—A. Wood.
Salem—Wm. Shanks and John Hogan.
Washington—William Moore.

WABASH DISTRICT—CHARLES HOLLIDAY, Presiding Elder.

Vincennes—Stephen R. Beggs.
Patoka—Asa D. West.
Booneville—Thomas Davis.
Mount Vernon—Thomas Files.

The tide of emigration was extending northward, and as the Church kept even pace with the population the names of the charges indicate very clearly what portions of the state were being settled by white men, and the plans of these early circuits give a clearer idea of the physical toil and personal hardships of the itinerancy of that day, than any mere verbal description, however graphic it might be. Indianapolis Circuit, in 1825, comprised the following preaching-places : In the county of Marion : Indianapolis, Headley's, M'Laughlin's, and Lamaster's; in the county of Madison : Pendleton, Shetterley's, and Smith's; in Hamilton County: Danville, Wilson's, and Claypool's; in Hendricks County and in the county of Morgan: Matlock's, Barlow's, Booker's, Martinsville, Culton's, and Ladd's; at Hough's, in Johnson County, and Ray's and Rector's, in Shelby County. In 1825 Honey-creek Circuit included the following appointments : Carlisle, Johnson's, Robbins's, Wall's, and Wear's, in Sullivan County ; Jackson's, Jr., Jackson's, Sr., Ray's, and Barnes's, in Vigo County; and Wilkens's, Merom Bond's, and Graham's, in the county of Sullivan. Paoli Circuit, in 1826, embraced the following appointments : In Orange County : Paoli, Vawter's, Little Orleans, and De Pew's ; in the county of Lawrence: Irving's, Fingir's, and Sewell's Meeting-house; in the county of Martin : Bruner's, the Widow Shelmyer's, M'Gaw's, Nellam's, Father Hall's, and at Hall's, Jr. ; Brider's and Springer's, in Perry County ; and in the county of Crawford : Leaton's, Fredonia, Leavenworth, M'Grew's, Sherwood's, and Riley's. The roads were merely bridle-paths, the streams were unbridged and without ferries, meetings were mostly in private houses. School-houses and churches were few and far between.

The third session of the Illinois Conference was held at Mt. Carmel, Illinois, September 20, 1827. At this Conference, the appointments for the work in Indiana were as follows :

MADISON DISTRICT—JOHN STRANGE, Presiding Elder.

Madison Station—Edwin Ray.
Madison Circuit—James Garner and Abner H. Cheever.
Lawrenceburg Circuit—Allen Wiley and D. Newton.
Lawrenceburg Station—James L. Thompson.

Whitewater Circuit—Thomas S. Hitt and James Scott.
Wayne—S. R. Beggs and William Evans.
Connersville—Robert Burns.
Rushville—James Havens.
Columbus—C. B. Jones.
Indianapolis—N. B. Griffith.
Vernon—Henry Buell.

CHARLESTOWN DISTRICT—JAMES ARMSTRONG, Presiding Elder.

Charlestown Circuit—G. Locke, C. W. Ruter, Supernum., and E. G. Wood.
Corydon—J. W. M'Reynolds and S. Low, Supernumerary.
Paoli—William Moore and James M'Kean.
Eel-river—William H. Smith and Benjamin Stevenson.
Crawfordsville—Eli P. Farmer.
Bloomington—Daniel Anderson and S. M. Otwell.
Salem—William Shanks and John Hardy.
Washington—Thomas Davis.

WABASH DISTRICT—CHARLES HOLLIDAY, Presiding Elder.

Vermilion—John Fox.
Vincennes—J. Miller and Asahel Risley.
Patoki—Charles Slocum.
Booneville—William Mavity.
Mount Vernon—Thomas Files.

Edwin Ray found the Church in Madison greatly excited over what was known as the Radical Controversy. Ray did what he could to reclaim the disaffected brethren, and to disabuse the public mind by publicly vindicating the economy of the Church; but his efforts apparently hastened the crisis. During the year quite a number withdrew, and organized a separate Church. They built a respectable house of worship on Third Street, and flourished for some years; and their Church, at one time, numbered some three hundred; but they soon began to decline, and the greater part returned to the old Church again, and appeared satisfied that, while there might be a difference of opinion as to the rights and powers of bishops and presiding elders, that difference of opinion did not justify schism in the Church. In 1828, the Illinois Conference met in Madison, Indiana, Bishop Roberts presiding. The members reported in that part of the work lying in Indiana were: Madison District, 5419; Charlestown District, 6700; and in that part of Wabash District lying in Indiana, 3974. Madison District began at Madison, on the Ohio River, and extended north of Randolph County, and thence west to White River, and down White River, including Andersontown, Noblesville, Indianapolis, and Martinsville; from thence south-east to the east fork of White River, called Driftwood, some distance below Columbus, in Bartholomew County, and from thence to Madison, embracing all of the intermediate country, except a narrow strip of country extending from Paris to Versailles, called Vernon Circuit, which was included in Charlestown District. Extensive revivals prevailed throughout most of the Conference. Lawrenceburg Circuit, under the labors of N. B. Griffith and E. G. Wood, was in a blaze of revival. A number of young men were received into the Church, in the bounds of this circuit, during the year, whose names have been since identified with the history of the Church. Of these we mention J. V. Watson, subsequently of the Michigan Conference, sometime editor of the *North-western Christian Advocate*, and author of several good books; a remarkably gifted preacher, and although a great sufferer from asthma, and for several years a confirmed invalid, yet such was his strength of will that he accomplished more than most robust men would have thought possible for them to have done; he was a man of brilliant imagination, had a remarkable command of language, and while he was naturally a true genius, he depended on the genius of hard work for success,—Edward Oldham, who labored for some years as a faithful and efficient minister in the Indiana Conference, and F. C. Halliday. Indianapolis appears on the list of appointments, for the first time, as a station, and James Armstrong was

pastor. Wisely and well did he lay the foundations of
Methodism in the capital of the state. Fall-creek appears for the first time on the list of appointments, with
Charles Bonner as the preacher. During the year there
was a glorious camp-meeting held in the vicinity of Pendleton, within the bounds of Bonner's circuit, at which
fifty souls were converted to God and added to the
Church. The following incident, in connection with this
meeting, is from the pen of Wiley: "A part of the session, at the middle of the day, on Sabbath, was devoted
to the subject of Baptism, and at the close of the service
some forty or fifty adults and children were baptized.
After the public baptism was over, the elder was informed
that there was a poor, afflicted man in a wagon, whose
body was, to a considerable extent, decayed by some kind
of abscess or ulceration; but there was yet body enough
left to hold the soul, which could not stay much longer on
the earth, as disease was rapidly encroaching on the vital
parts of the system. This poor Lazarus, with all his
stench of disease, heard the sermon, and felt its force,
and was desirous to be baptized before he died; and his
wish was met in the wagon. His meek, penitent, weeping countenance is still fresh in my memory. If baptism
were confined to immersion alone, this poor man must
have died unbaptized; for I suppose the most zealous im-
mersionist in the world would not have attempted to put
the fragments of his decaying body under the water. To
my mind this fact is a most powerful argument against
the absolute necessity of immersion to constitute valid
baptism; for if that be the case, this penitent believer
must have died unsealed with God's sign of the Christian
covenant; but if pouring or sprinkling be valid baptism,
while the head and heart are alive, and reason and feeling continue, the penitent may be baptized. This poor

man felt that it was valid, and in a few days left the remains of a loathsome carcass, and went to rest." .

In September, 1829, Illinois Conference met in Edwardsville, Madison County, Illinois; Bishop Soule presiding. The following charges appear for the first time in the list of appointments: Washington, in Wabash District; Franklin and Vernon, in Madison District; and Logansport Mission, which was included in Charlestown District; Stephen R. Beggs, missionary, and John Strange, Presiding Elder.

How a man could make four rounds in a year, on a district extending from Charlestown, on the Ohio River, to Logansport, on horseback, without improved roads, with few ferries, and no bridges across the streams, is marvelous. But Strange was a man of one work, and, although of a delicate constitution, he was lion-hearted. He had threaded his way through the forests in Eastern Indiana, from one settlement to another, and from one block-house to another, carrying a trusty rifle to protect himself from the Indians, that he might preach the Gospel, and carry the consolations of religion to the first pioneers of civilization. Such heroism greatly endeared him to the people, and his visits to the block-houses and forts were hailed with delight. He had a remarkable trust in Divine providence. When on a visit to some of his old friends in Lawrenceburg, in 1816, he had a severe attack of fever. Toward the close of his sickness, the horses which he and Mrs. Strange rode got out of the stable and strayed off. The family with whom he stayed, and other friends, having made an unsuccessful search for the horses, seemed quite uneasy about them. Strange said to them, in a mild, chiding way: "Why are you so uneasy about the horses? All the horses in the world belong to the Lord, and he will give

me just as many as I need." At another time his horse
strayed away from him at Cincinnati; but he seemed
perfectly unconcerned, and borrowed another to go to
his appointments. Some one said to him, "Brother
Strange, are you going without your horse?" He replied, "There are hundreds of persons here who can
hunt a horse as well as I can, who can not preach one
word, and I shall go to my work." But the toil and
exposure necessarily connected with traveling a district
extending from the Ohio River to Logansport, told
rapidly on his constitution. Allen Wiley was presiding
elder on Madison District, and George Locke on Wabash
District.

In September, 1830, Illinois Conference met in Vincennes. Bishop Roberts was to have presided; but he
was detained at St. Louis by sickness, and Samuel H.
Thompson was chosen to preside. Bishop Roberts did
not reach the seat of the Conference until after its
adjournment. Members reported at this Conference,
15,205. At this Conference, Indianapolis District was
organized, with James Armstrong presiding elder. The
district embraced Indianapolis, Franklin, Fall-creek,
White-lick, Greencastle, Rockville, Crawfordsville, and
Logansport. Seventeen young men were admitted on
trial; one of whom was E. R. Ames, now one of the
honored bishops of the Church. This year Fort Wayne
Mission was organized, and N. B. Griffith was the missionary. Fort Wayne Mission was in Madison District,
of which A. Wiley was presiding elder.

The next session of the Conference was held in
Indianapolis, October 4, 1831. At this Conference,
Crawfordsville District was organized, and James Armstrong was the presiding elder. The work in Indiana
was included in the Madison, Charlestown, Indianapolis,

Crawfordsville, and Wabash Districts. The Church had extended northward as far as St. Joseph County. In 1830, Erastus Felton, who had been sent by the Ohio Conference to St. Joseph Mission, had formed some societies in the north part of Indiana. In 1831, N. B. Griffith was sent to South Bend Mission. He organized a society in South Bend, of which Samuel Martin was the leader. But the only charges lying in the north part of the state were Greencastle, Crawfordsville, Lafayette, Pine-creek, Rockville, Logansport, South Bend, and Fort Wayne.

In 1832, Illinois Conference was divided, and Indiana constituted. Indiana Conference embraced the whole of the state of Indiana, except a small strip included in Illinois Conference; the Wabash River being its western boundary, from its mouth as far up as Pine Creek, in Warren County.

The first session of the Indiana Conference was held in New Albany. There were reported at this Conference 19,853 white members, and 182 colored. At this Conference sixty preachers were appointed to charges, and four charges were left to be supplied. There were five presiding elders' districts, as follows: Madison, James Havens, Presiding Elder; Charlestown, William Shanks, Presiding Elder; Indianapolis, Allen Wiley, Presiding Elder; Vincennes, James L. Thompson, Presiding Elder. Missionary District, James Armstrong, Superintendent. The Mission District included the following charges and ministers:

MISSIONARY DISTRICT—JAMES ARMSTRONG, Presiding Elder.

Upper Wabash Mission—Samuel C. Cooper.
St. Joseph and South Bend Mission—R. S. Robinson and G. M. Beswick.
Kalamazoo Mission—James T. Robe.
Fort Wayne Mission—Boyd Phelps.
Laporte Mission—James Armstrong.

In 1831, Fort Wayne was included in Madison District. There was a large wilderness, uninhabited save by savage Indians and wild beasts, lying between the settlements on the Upper Whitewater and Fort Wayne, requiring the presiding elder each round to lie out one night in the woods. Wiley would take off his saddle, and construct a bed out of his saddle and saddle-blanket, tie his horse's bridle around his waist, and get what rest he could with the wolves howling around him. During one of his visits to Fort Wayne, this year, he was accompanied by R. S. Robinson, and during their stay they held a series of meetings in Masonic Hall, which exerted a salutary and powerful influence on the minds of the people. Wiley preached in the morning and Robinson at night, for several days in succession; and it was Wiley's opinion, if the meetings had continued a few days longer, that nearly the whole community would have professed religion; but the preachers had to leave to attend a camp-meeting in Wayne County. Wiley often remarked that he never thought of their leaving Fort Wayne when they did without feelings of regret.

CHAPTER V.

Retrospective View—First Settlers—First Preachers—Settlement of
Clarke County—Quaker Settlements—Vincennes District in 1811—
Rangers of 1812—New Harmony Colony—First Methodist Preach-
ing in Vigo County—Incident—Introduction of Methodism in Harri-
son County—Early Men of Note—Dennis Pennington—" Uncle
Walter Pennington "—" Uncle Billy Saffer "—Edward Pennington—
Early Methodists in New Albany—Peter Stoy, Aaron Daniels, and
Others—First Society in Jeffersonville—Societies in Charlestown
and Madison—Methodist Preaching in Rising Sun—First Class
formed—Lawrenceburg Circuit organized—Mr. Bartholomew—Isaac
Dunn—Rev. Elijah Sparks—Mrs. Amos Lane—Isaac Mills—Jacob
Blasdell—Rev. Daniel Plummer—Rev. A. J. Cotton—Samuel Goodwin—Rev. Augustus Jocelyn—Hugh Cull—Whitewater Circuit
formed—Israel Abrams—Camp-meeting near Saulsbury—Methodism established at Moore's Hill—Adam Moore and Others—John C.
Moore—Moore's Hill—Influence of Local Preachers—Names of
Noted Local Preachers—" Sketch of Early Society in Indiana," by
Rev. A. Wood—The Missionary District in 1832—First Camp-
meeting in Laporte County—Introduction of Methodism in Elkhart County—Local Preachers in Connersville and Whitewater Circuits—James Conwell and Others—An old-fashioned Quarterly-
meeting—Dr. Benjamin Adams—John Strange—Account of his
Labors—Letter of John Schrader—Facts in the Early History of the
Church in Indiana—Preaching in Bar-rooms—Incident—" Characteristics of the Early Indiana Settlers," by Rev. A. Wood.

HAVING traced the expansion of the Church from the
first introduction of Methodism into the state until
the organization of the Indiana Conference, it is proper to
take a retrospective survey of the field, the condition of
society, and notice some of the local agencies and less
prominent instrumentalities by which the Church had
achieved success hitherto. The seat of the Territorial
Government, first at Vincennes, and then at Corydon, attracted settlers, at an early day, to the south-western

part of the state. Knox County was organized in 1802. Vincennes was the seat of the Territorial Government, as well as for the county. The original settlers were French; but, in addition to these, at a very early day there were a number of families from Maryland, Virginia, and Pennsylvania. The French society ranged all the way from the half-savage up to the polished deist and the learned priest. The Virginia element ranged from the fugitive cut-throat up to the chivalrous governor, always including a large adventurous element, composed of young men who, as yet, were sowing their wild oats. Religious services were conducted, from the beginning of the settlement, by the Romish priests. Joseph Oglesby and Jesse Walker, as missionaries from the Illinois Conference, preached the Gospel in the settled portions of Knox County, in an early day. A Presbyterian preacher from Kentucky, by the name of James M'Cready, settled in the county, and preached with efficiency. Clarke County was organized in 1801, and its first settlers were families from Virginia, who were of Scotch or German origin. The spirit of independence was carried into their religious views, and whether they were Baptists, Presbyterians, or Methodists, they were very nearly congregational or independent in their notions of Church government. Prelacy and apostolic succession had no place among them. That portion known as Clarke's Grant was settled by soldiers, irrespective of religious profession. The first Methodist preachers came over from Kentucky; occasional preaching was had, as early as 1802, in what was known as the Robertson and Prather Settlements, and in 1807, Silver-creek Circuit was organized. The Virginians who settled in Clarke County were not as well educated as some from the same state who settled in Knox, but they were more homogeneous, and more opposed to slavery. There were a few Quaker settlements in the south-west part of the state, at an early day, and they disseminated a strong anti-slavery sentiment; and where there were isolated Quaker families, they welcomed Methodist preachers and Methodist preaching. There were no settlements formed by Methodists, as a body of emigrants, but occasionally a few Methodist families would be found contiguous to each other. Emigrants from England settled in a body in the counties of Dearborn and Franklin. Scotch Covenanters settled in a body in Gibson County. The Friend Quakers settled in a body in Wayne, Washington, and Orange Counties. In 1811, Vincennes Circuit embraced the country from the Ohio River on the south, to the farthest point of white population on the east side of the Wabash, north. There were settlements in the forks of White River, now Davies's County; at Patoka, now Gibson County; and on Honey Creek, in what is now Sullivan and Vigo Counties. The settlements were visited by Methodist preachers, at that early day, and there were, in all these early settlements, persons who had been converted in the great revivals in Kentucky and Tennessee, and who hailed with pleasure the appearance of evangelical ministers among them. At the commencement of the War of 1812, the moral and religious condition of the settlers on the Wabash was, perhaps, as good as that of any other new country; but there was sent into those frontier settlements a class of soldiers called "Rangers," who were supported by Government, and lived in idleness and dissipation. And while they afforded protection to the settlers from the Indians, they exposed them to many temptations, and not unfrequently corrupted their morals. The leisure and the opportunities afforded by the officers of the army, and of the new Territorial Government, for dissipation, exerted a pernicious influence upon the general population.

From 1814 to 1820, the south-western part of the state settled rapidly. Frederick Rappe settled his colony at New Harmony. The emigration was chiefly from the Southern States—South Carolina, Tennessee, and Kentucky, and a few from Southern Ohio. Among these emigrants were some Methodists. These, of course, formed the nucleus of societies when the itinerants came among them, and they were never far behind the front wave of emigration. The first Methodist preacher that visited the county of Vigo, was Jacob Turman, who preached at the cabin of John Dickson, near Rogers's Spring, and organized a class, consisting of Dickson and wife, J. Lambert and wife, and William Winters; the last-named being the class-leader. At one time a company of hostile Indians came near the house, with the intention of murdering the congregation; but as they drew near the house, the congregation was engaged in singing, and such was the influence of the music on them that they quietly retired. They reported to the interpreter, at the treaty, not long afterward, that they retired out of veneration for the Great Spirit.

Methodism was early introduced into Harrison County. Silver-creek Circuit, which was the first regular charge in Indiana, included the settlements in Clark, Floyd, Harrison, and Washington Counties. Harrison County was subsequently in Indian-creek, and, at a later period, in Corydon Circuit. Methodism, in Harrison County, had some noted representatives in early times. Among these was Dennis Pennington, who was a member of the first Convention that formed the Constitution for the State,—he was several times elected a member of the State Legislature, and exerted a good influence,

both in public and private life,—Uncle Walter Pennington, a famous, though illiterate local preacher, who was
extensively known, and "Uncle Billy Saffer," a local
preacher of remarkable eccentricity, and without doubt
the greatest wag in all the land. A number of his
speeches found their way into the newspapers of the
day on such themes as, "How I got my Education;"
"My Second Courtship," etc. Edward Pennington was
also a prominent and active steward in the Church in
that county in an early day. Among the early Methodists in New Albany, Floyd County, are the names
of Peter Stoy, a ship-joiner, whose influence was good,
and who is worthily represented by a pious posterity;
Aaron Daniels, father of Rev. Wm. Daniels, now an old
and highly respected minister in Indiana Conference, and
Rev. John Daniels, of California Conference; Matthew
Robinson, John Evans, and Daniel Seybrook; Thomas
Sinex, father of Rev. Thomas H. Sinex, an educated
and able minister of the Gospel; Edward Brown, Isaac
Brooks, Benjamin Blackstone, and Obadiah Childs. The
first organized society in Jeffersonville was in 1810,
under the ministry of Rev. Selah Payne, who traveled
Silver-creek Circuit that year. The first society was
composed of: Mr. Beman and wife, Stephen Beman,
Lyman Beman, and Amanda Beman, and children; Mary
Toville, afterward Mary Taylor; Davis Floyd, Mary
Floyd, Richard Mosley, Samuel Lampton, Charlotte
Lampton, and Mrs. Leatherman. Societies had been
previously formed in the neighborhood of Charlestown,
in the Robinson and Prather Settlements. Madison had
preaching at an early day, and was included in the old
Whitewater Circuit.

Methodist preaching was introduced into Rising Sun
by John Strange, in 1814 or 1815. The services of Mr.

6

Strange were procured in the following manner: Mrs. Elizabeth De Coursey, learning that he had an appointment two miles below the town, at the house of Mr. Goodin, in company with another lady, walked to the place of preaching, heard the sermon, and solicited an appointment for Rising Sun. The preacher consented, and left an appointment, to be filled on his next round. At the appointed time a small congregation assembled in the woods, where the foot of Main Street now is, seating themselves on logs and the limbs of trees that had been felled by the new settlers. The preacher was on time. He stood on the trunk of a fallen tree, and sounded the Gospel trumpet into the listening ears of his attentive and delighted hearers, and left another appointment. Mr. Strange preached three or four times. A Mr. Craft, who had opened a house of public entertainment, offered his bar-room for preaching, which was accepted. Rev. Joseph Oglesby succeeded John Strange, and, during a brief stay, gathered up some six names, preparatory to the organization of a class. Rev. Daniel Sharp succeeded Oglesby. Sharp organized the first class in the town, and put it on the plan of the circuit. The class consisted of nine persons, namely: Elizabeth Craft, John Gordon, Nancy Gordon, Henry Hayman, Elizabeth Howlit, Jane Fulton, Azariah Oldham, Rachel Oldham, and Elizabeth De Coursey. The class was formed, and the meetings held in a school-house on the north-east corner of Main and High Streets.

Lawrenceburg Circuit was organized as early as 1813. It included the present territory of Dearborn and Ohio Counties, and portions of Ripley and Franklin Counties, and several appointments in the state of Ohio. Lawrenceburg, Aurora, Elizabethtown, Hardentown, Manchester, the Smith Settlement, where Mount Tabor

Church now stands, Moore's Hill, Eubank's, and Judge Louden's, were prominent appointments on the circuit. A Mr. Batholomew, in Aurora, was one of the early Methodists in that town, and his house was a home for the preachers for many years. Among the early Methodists in Lawrenceburg were Hon. Isaac Dunn, who was an associate judge for a number of years. He was among the first settlers at the mouth of the Great Miami, was early converted, opened his house for public worship and for the entertainment of the itinerant preachers. He remained a citizen of Lawrenceburg until the day of his death, which occurred in 1870, when, at the ripe age of eighty-two, he exchanged a home in the Church militant for one in the Church triumphant. Rev. Elijah Sparks was a talented and educated local preacher, who early settled in Lawrenceburg. He was a practicing attorney, and yet maintained a true Christian and ministerial character. Mrs. Lane, the wife of Hon. Amos Lane, a prominent lawyer, and for some time a member of Congress from that district, deserves mention among the early Methodists of Lawrenceburg. She was a lady of fine personal presence, of cultivated manners, of superior intellectual endowments, and remarkable force of character. Her influence was valuable in the Church and in the general community. Isaac Mills was one of the early Methodists at Elizabethtown, and his house was a home for the preachers, whose society he and his family greatly prized. On the occasion of a quarterly-meeting, his house was thronged with company; for the early quarterly-meetings were signals for the gathering of Methodists throughout a distance of forty or fifty miles. It was customary on these occasions for persons who would entertain company to announce, at the close of eleven o'clock preaching on

Saturday, how many persons and horses they could entertain; for nearly every body came on horseback. On one of these occasions, when the presiding elder was done preaching, and had dismissed the congregation, the preacher-in-charge' requested those who could entertain company to announce how many they would take. Father Mills cried out, "I will take all of the preachers and their families," when Major M'Henry, who was a worthy Methodist pioneer in that locality, thinking that Father Mills's invitation was rather exclusive, got on a bench and called out, "I will take Lazarus and all his family." As might be expected, the Major had the larger crowd. Jacob Blasdell, who resided on Tanner's Creek, a few miles above Lawrenceburg, was an early Methodist, and a staunch advocate of temperance. His son, Hon. Henry G. Blasdell, for some years the popular and worthy Governor of Nevada, has been a worthy pioneer of Methodism in that new mountain territory. Rev. Daniel Plummer, an able local preacher from the state of Maine, early settled at Manchester; and "Plummer's Chapel" was one of the earliest and best brick churches built within the bounds of the old Lawrenceburg Circuit. Mr. Plummer was an able preacher and an enterprising citizen. He represented his county several years in the State Legislature. Rev. A. J. Cotton was also a prominent local preacher in the old Lawrenceburg Circuit. He taught school in the county for many years, was also a probate judge, and married more persons and preached more funeral sermons than any other man in his day. He wrote a good deal of poetry, chiefly of a local and ephemeral character, and was author of a volume entitled "Cotton's Keepsake."

The house of Samuel Goodwin was one of the earliest houses for Methodist preachers at Brookville, and continued to be such until the day of his death. He has given two sons to the ministry: Rev. T. A. Goodwin, for some time a member of the Indiana Conference, and subsequently President of Brookville College, and editor of the *Indiana American,* which he first published at Brookville, and then at Indianapolis; in the relation of local preacher he has always been industrious, and his ministrations have been acceptable in any pulpit,—Rev. W. R. Goodwin, for some years a member of the South-eastern Indiana Conference, and then of the Illinois Conference. Mr. Goodwin gave his sons a collegiate education, and was one of the founders and early patrons of Indiana Asbury University. Rev. Augustus Jocelyn was an able local preacher at Brookville, in an early day.

Rev. Hugh Cull, a local preacher, and one of the members of the Convention that framed the first Constitution for the State, settled in the Whitewater country, a few miles south of Richmond, in 1805, and was, doubtless, the first Methodist preacher that settled in the state. He resided on the farm where he first settled for a period of fifty-seven years. He died on the 1st of August, 1862, in the one hundred and fifth year of his age. He retained both his mental and physical vigor, in a remarkable degree, until near the close of life. A few months before his death his physical strength gave way, and he gradually descended to the tomb. His death was triumphant. His last whispers were, "Glory, glory, glory!" Father Cull was a man of medium size, black hair, remarkably heavy eyebrows; he had a pleasant voice and a very sympathetic nature. His preaching was very acceptable. His house was a home for the traveling preachers for many years, and few men relished preaching more than he. His interest in the sermon often proved a help to a young or timid preacher. He had no children. For many years his family consisted of himself and wife, and a niece of his wife's, whom they had adopted as a daughter. Father Cull served for a few months in the War of the Revolution, just at its close, and also in the War of 1812. He was a man of simple tastes and temperate habits. There was no acidity in his nature. He used no stimulants; he drank but little tea or coffee; sweet milk, from the spring-house, and honey from his own hives, usually adorned his table in the Summer-time. He made a profession of religion in early life, and preached it for many years, and, although subject to occasional spells of melancholy in his later years, was, for the most of his life, a happy Christian. He lived to see "the wilderness blossom as the rose."

Whitewater Circuit was formed in 1807, and lay partly in Ohio and partly in Indiana. In 1808, a meeting-house was built about a mile and a half south-east of the old town of Salisbury, the first seat of justice for Wayne County, and was situated about half-way between Centerville and the city of Richmond. It was called "Meek's Meeting-house." Of course it was built of logs, but God honored it with His presence, and the humble worshipers often felt, "Master, it is good to be here." Not long after this, a second meeting-house was built in Wayne County, on the farm of John Cain, about three miles north-west of the city of Richmond. It was built of logs, eighteen by twenty-two, with a chimney in one end. The third meeting-house in the county was called "Salem," and was built where the town of Boston now stands. It was larger than either of the others, and it, too, was built of logs. The first frame meeting-house built by the Methodists, in Wayne County, was erected under the administrations of Rev. James Havens, in the town of Centerville. The largest subscription was by Israel Abrams, a converted Israelite, who gave fifty dollars, which was then really a large donation. Abrams loved God and the Church, and through a long life he showed his faith by his works, always setting an example of liberality. In 1810, there was a camp-meeting held just south of the old town of Salisbury, in Wayne County. John Sale was the presiding elder; Thomas Nelson and Samuel H. Thompson were the circuit preachers. It was a profitable meeting, and its fruit is all garnered above.

Methodism was early planted at Moore's Hill, in Dearborn County. The early settlers in that neighborhood included a number of excellent Methodist families from the state of Delaware and the eastern shore of Maryland, among whom was Adam Moore, a local preacher, after whom the village was named; John Dashill, who was also for many years a local preacher; Charles Dashill, and Ranna Stevens. These men and their families gave a moral impress to society, in that part of the country, that is permanent and valuable. No part of our state maintains a higher standard of morals, and no community has been less cursed with intemperance and its kindred vices. John Strange once held a glorious camp-meeting on the ground now occupied by the flourishing town of Moore's Hill. The blessing of a covenant-keeping God has rested upon the descendants of these early Christian families. Their sons and daughters have come to honor. Moore's Hill college is a monument to the intelligence and Christian liberality of John C. Moore, one of the sons of Rev. Adam Moore, the original proprietor of the town. And although he has been gathered with his father to his heavenly home, his works remain, and the college that was founded chiefly through his instrumentality, it is hoped, will continue to bless the world through the ages to come. The village of Moore's Hill, now noted for the moral and literary tone of its society, and for the college of which it is justly proud, owes its name to the following blunder: Mr. Moore had erected a mill that was driven by horse-power, as water-power could not be commanded in that vicinity; and as the early settlers, from a considerable distance, brought their corn to be ground, it occurred to some one that it would be a good idea to have a post-office established in the vicinity of the mill; and accordingly a petition was sent to Washington, praying for the establishment of a post-office at Moore's Mill. The Postmaster-General, mistaking the M for an H, located the post-office at Moore's Hill, and that gave name to the village that subsequently sprang up, and to the college that has been founded, chiefly through the exertions and liberality of one of the sons of the original proprietor of Moore's Mill.

Among the agencies honored in the early planting of churches in Indiana, and in carrying forward revival efforts, local preachers and exhorters occupied a prominent place, and are worthy of honorable mention. Many of the former had been traveling preachers, who had been compelled to locate for want of a support, and who continued to labor with efficiency. Such was Moses Ashworth, the apostle of Methodism in Southern Indiana. He settled in Posey County, where he labored as a local preacher for a number of years. These located preachers usually acted in concert, and kept up a regular plan of appointments. Of these, Garnett, Wheeler, Schrader, and Ashworth, who labored in Posey, Vanderburg, and adjoining Counties, were prominent; and at camp-meetings and two-days' meetings they were a power. Daviess County had four local preachers of note, in an early day, namely: James M'Cord, Elias Stone, John Wallace, and Ebenezer Jones. M'Cord, Stone, and Wallace traveled some; Jones remained local, and raised a large family. These were all useful men in their day. Wallace and Stone both died away from home, on circuits; M'Cord removed to Crawford County, Illinois, where he lived to a good old age. The names of Joseph Pownell, Jacob Lapp, John Lowry, Stephen Grimes, John Fish, Richard Posey, John Collins, Richard Browning, Isaac Lambert, Jacob Turman, William Medford, Samuel Hull, Job M. Baker, Wesley Morrison, William Bratton, Hezekiah Holland, Joseph Freeland, and Jesse Graham, deserve honorable mention. Augustus Jocelyn, of Brookville, was a giant among the local preachers of his day. He was a man of culture and of extraordinary ability. James Garner settled in Clarke County soon after the Robertsons came there. He was a great help in building up the Church. He was a total abstinence man, notwithstanding the prevalent custom of using whisky in nearly every family. He raised a large family, and two of his sons were preachers. He was a revivalist, and gathered many into the Church. Barzillai Willey and Cornelius Ruddle were also efficient local preachers in Clarke County. Davis Floyd was also an efficient local preacher at Corydon. He was a practicing lawyer, and for some time Judge of the Circuit Court. Walter Pennington, familiarly called "Uncle Watty," was a licensed preacher, but his talent lay in exhortation. He was a natural wit, and, withal, something of a wag, but nevertheless a useful man. John Jones, who resided in the village of Elizabeth, in Harrison County, a shoemaker by trade, was also a useful local preacher. Jones came from Baltimore, and was for many years recording steward on Corydon Circuit. George Prosser was a local preacher and a physician, in Orange County. Jacob Bruner was a local preacher of considerable usefulness among the hills of Martin County. Joseph Arnold, Isam West, and William Webb were useful local preachers in Warwick County. At Evansville, Robert Parrott was prominent both as a citizen and a local preacher. Richard and Joseph Wheeler were also prominent local preachers in the vicinity of Evansville. They were from England, and had been familiar with Methodism in the old country, having sat under the ministry of Dr. Adam Clarke.

The following sketch of early society in Indiana is from the pen of Rev. A. Wood, D. D., than whom few men have seen more of Indiana, or observed it more closely:

"In 1816, the season was very cold. In the western part of New York, and the north-western part of Pennsylvania, they raised no grain for bread. This caused many who had tried that country to move further south. Hence, in 1817, large numbers built family boats at Orleans, on the Alleghany, and floated down the Ohio. They settled in Dearborn, Switzerland, Jennings, and Washington Counties, forming neighborhoods of their own. In many respects, they differed from the Kentuckians, especially in the arts of labor for opening a new farm in the forest. These brought the Yankee ax, with the crooked helve; they used oxen for rolling logs, and built their cabins square, instead of oblong, with the chimney in one end, having a fifth corner, like the letter V, as the Virginians and Kentuckians did. These Yankees and Pennsylvanians sought out the mill-sites, as they were called, and erected water-mills on the streams. I never knew a Kentuckian in those days build any thing better than a horse-mill. During the Territorial Government, the offices were filled by Virginians; but from 1816 to 1820, the State Government was in the hands of Pennsylvanians. There was never a sufficient foreign immigration from Europe to make a political power; yet there were local settlements of English direct from old England in Franklin, Dearborn, and Vanderburg Counties; the Swiss at Vevay, and the French at Vincennes. These, however, were contented with the home influence, and did not aspire to the offices of state. Not so, however, with the New Yorker, Pennsylvanian, Jerseyman, Virginian, or stray Yankee. A desire for office prompted some of them to remove to the new country, as was confessed by one of the associate judges, who, on returning to his old home, said: 'Do you think I would stay here and be a *common man*, when I can go there and be a judge?'

"An unfortunate occurrence took place at Vincennes, in the early history of Methodism there, that left a bad impression for some time. Thomas A. King, a member of the Tennessee Conference, who had traveled Patoka Circuit, and was very popular at Vincennes and in all that region of country, went into mercantile business, and, as his capital was limited, he bought largely on credit. A great change occurring in the condition of currency, causing a heavy reduction in prices, he failed to make payment, but sold his goods to William and Henry Merrick. The goods were enjoined; they were all three arrested for fraud, and, as the law then was, sent to jail by the creditor. The last mention of King's name in the Minutes of the Conference is the record of his location in the Tennessee Conference, in 1817. He was a talented and popular young minister, but unfortu-

nately yielded to the spirit of speculation, often so rife
in a new country; and, whether guilty of intentional
fraud or not, his course blighted the remainder of his
life, and involved his two friends.

"In 1832, James Armstrong was appointed superintendent of the Missionary District, and missionary on
Laporte Mission. The district embraced Upper Wabash
Mission, S. C. Cooper; St. Joseph and South Bend Missions, R. S. Robinson and George M. Beswick; Kalamazoo Mission, James T. Robe; Fort Wayne Mission,
Boyd Phelps; Laporte Mission, James Armstrong.

"The first meeting-house was built this year at Door
Village, by James Armstrong, who secured a subscription of three hundred dollars at one of his quarterly-
meetings there. The first camp-meeting held in Laporte
County was on the farm of J. Osbon, while Armstrong
was on his death-bed. He was unable to leave his room,
but gave directions for the management of the meeting.
The preachers at the meeting were Boyd Phelps, A.
Johnson, and E. Smith. About this time some influential local preachers moved into the county. There
was quite an emigration from Clarke County, and F.
Standiford and Stephen Jones came from Ohio.

"Methodism was introduced into Elkhart County in
1830, under the following circumstances: James Snyder,
residing on Elkhart Prairie, went to Michigan to hear
E. Felton preach at the village of White Pigeon, and invited him to his cabin, which was taken into the mission, and a class formed at his house, of which Azel
Sparklin was the leader. The same year a class was
formed on Pleasant Plain, at Jacob Roop's, consisting of
nine members, of whom Samuel Roop was the leader.
The first quarterly-meeting in the county was held by
Erastus Felton, assisted by a local preacher by the name

of James Hellman, from Fort Wayne. Elkhart County
was included in the St. Joseph Mission for some years.
In 1832, there were societies organized at Roope's, Tib-
betts's, and Frear's. Richard S. Robinson organized
the first class in Goshen, and Robert P. Randell was the
leader. The class consisted of about twenty members,
and met in a log-house on Fifth Street. The first camp-
meeting in the county was held on the farm of James
Frian. Connersville and Whitewater Circuits were
favored with the labors of a large number of talented
and industrious local preachers. Prominent among these
was James Conwell, who came from Maryland, and settled near where the town of Laurel now stands, of which
he was the proprietor. He built a meeting-house a mile
and a half above Laurel, some years before that town
was laid out, called Boachim. Mr. Conwell was a man
of large wealth, owning a great deal of land. He also
conducted a dry-goods store, and annually drove a great
many hogs to Cincinnati; for that was the only way of
getting live-stock to market, there being neither railroads or canals in the state. Mr. Conwell was the first
man ever known to keep the Sabbath while driving hogs
to market; and no matter what was the condition of the
weather, the roads, or the market, when Saturday night
came, he stopped with his hogs, and rested until Monday.
He usually went in advance of his drove, made arrangements for resting over the Sabbath, and generally had
an appointment for preaching to the people; and he
had the pleasure of knowing that he had some seals
to his ministry as the result of these labors. Mr. Conwell was one of the early and zealous advocates of a
system of internal improvement in Indiana. The Whitewater Canal owed its construction to his influence; and,
although the work has proved a financial failure, Mr.

Conwell showed, by his devotion to that and other public works, that he was a public-spirited and useful citizen. Mr. Conwell served as a member of the State Legislature, and, by his ability and public spirit, commanded the respect of his fellow-members. Mr. Conwell was a very sympathetic man. He cried a great deal while he was preaching, and usually made his hearers cry before he was done. From 1824 to several years afterward, James Conwell, John Havens, Joel Havens, Thomas Silvey, John Morrow, Charles Morrow, John Gregg, James Gregg, John Linville, James Linville, Robert Groves, and Thomas Leonard, were all within the bounds of Connersville Circuit."

Dr. A. Wood remarks:

"Every variety of gifts were exemplified in these men. They were strong in doctrine, wise in discipline, critical in letters, bold in reproof, and pathetic in exhortation; and at a camp-meeting their labors were very efficient for lasting good on the entire community. John Morrow was a scholarly man, and spent most of his life as a school-teacher. Joel Havens was chiefly noted for his wonderful gift of exhortation. Few men knew how to play on the emotions and passions of an audience as did he. The two Greggs and John Linville embraced some heresy, and were led away from the Church. Charles Hardy, William Patterson, and William Hunt were also talented local preachers within the bounds of the old Connersville Circuit. Patterson had traveled extensively in the South-west previous to his location. Thomas Milligan and Thomas Hewson were local preachers residing in the bounds of Bloomington Circuit, in 1826. They had both been traveling preachers. An old-fashioned quarterly meeting, in a new country, on one of these large four-weeks' circuits, with the circuit preachers, presiding elder, and this large array of local preachers, with the exhorters, class-leaders and stewards, made an occasion of interest, and often marked an epoch in the history of some neighborhood or village."

Dr. Aaron Wood, in a letter under date of May 10, 1871, says of Dr. Benjamin Adams, who resided for some time in the bounds of Corydon Circuit:

"I hope some one will give you an account of Dr. Ben. Adams. He was the first male child born in Louisville, and was a rude boy, the son of a widow. He had a log roll over him when a boy, that put out one of his eyes and left a scar across his forehead and nose, down to his chin. He was a shoe-maker when he was converted and began to preach. His preaching in the market-house of Louisville attracted the attention of some rich men, who furnished him money to go to Philadelphia and study medicine. He was the only man I ever knew that was a great doctor, a great preacher, and a great politician, at the same time. He was connected with Corydon Circuit when it had one thousand members and twenty local preachers. Our acquaintance, up to that time, was mostly a conference acquaintance. On an appeal by T. Highfield, who was accused by Adams, and found guilty by the society of Corydon, John Strange was in the chair, and Wm. Daniels, Secretary. Appeals were very common in those days on those large circuits. Highfield had been expelled by Thomas Davis at the close of the year, who had kept no minutes of the trial. I took the ground, in his defense, that, as there was no minute or proof of the specification before the Conference, he should be restored to the Church, or at least have a new trial. After a half-day in debate, Adams beat me, and the

Conference affirmed the decision of the society. This acquaintance made us true friends ever afterward."

John Schrader was a pioneer itinerant, and, after his location, an efficient local preacher for many years. He was born in Baltimore, 1792; emigrated with his parents to Knoxville, Tennessee, in 1795. He was converted and joined the Church in 1810; was licensed to exhort in 1811, and to preach in 1812. He was admitted into the Conference in 1814, and appointed to Greenville Circuit, in Kentucky, which had ten appointments, and was four hundred miles around. Peter Cartwright was his presiding elder. In 1815, he was sent to Vincennes Circuit, with twenty appointments, and three hundred miles around it. Jesse Walker was his presiding elder. In 1816, he was sent to St. Charles, Missouri, where there were twenty appointments, and the circuit was three hundred and fifty miles in circumference. Samuel H. Thompson was his presiding elder. In 1817, he was sent again to Vincennes Circuit, with King and Davis as colleagues. The circuit had been enlarged until it was five hundred and fifty miles around it. Jesse Walker was the presiding elder. In 1818, he was sent to Blue-river Circuit, which was supposed to lie somewhere between Corydon and the mouth of the Wabash River, stretching along the Ohio, and extending north no one knew how far. After the most diligent search, he failed to find any circuit within the prescribed limits, and reported the facts to his presiding elder, who sent him for the third time to Vincennes Circuit. In 1819, he was sent to White-river Circuit, Arkansas, which had ten appointments, and was four hundred miles in circumference. In 1820, he was sent to Corydon Circuit, Indiana, where he remained two years. At the end of the second year he located. He married Pamelia

Jacquess in the Fall of 1822, shortly after his location. He was ordained deacon by Bishop Asbury at Lebanon, Tennessee, in 1816, and ordained elder by Bishop Roberts at Olwell's Camp-ground, below Alton, Illinois, in 1818.

The following letter from Father Schrader, in answer to one of inquiry, under date of March 10, 1871, will be read with interest by many who have known him:

"DEAR BROTHER,—Yours of February 9, 1871, is before me. Some years have passed since I sent you an account of my travels in the Church, from the time of the first Missouri Conference to the time of my settlement in Poseyville—in all eight years—all of which I have now forgotten. The date of my location, and the list of my appointments in the work, you can find in the Minutes of the Conference much better than I am able to give them. Next October I shall be seventy-eight years old. My mind is truly superannuated. I am worn out, and am of no use in the Church. Whether you will be able to read this scrawl or not, I can not tell. The Lord is my only hope. In Him I will trust until my end shall come, which I think will not be long. I will be glad to get one of your books, when you have completed your work.

"I remain yours,   JOHN SCHRADER."

Several facts in the early history of the Church in Indiana deserve special notice, and call for a word of explanation. The first societies, as a general rule, were formed in the country, and the first circuits were named after rivers or creeks. The town sites were located either with reference to commercial advantages or as expected seats of justice for counties, in many cases yet to be organized. In many of the towns the property-holders, and the incumbents and seekers for office, were not only irreligious, but opposed even to the forms of religion, and made no provision for Christian worship. In such cases, the villages were unpromising fields for Christian effort, while those who settled in the country were not only less exposed, but also less inclined to vice. The moral impress of the first settlers in many of the towns in Indiana remains to the present day. Connersville, Vevay, Salem, Terre Haute, and Vincennes were for many years unpromising fields of labor, because the influence of wealth and of official and social position were all against Christianity. The same, to a great extent, was true in Jeffersonville and Rising Sun. In many cases, the proprietor of the town, the clerk of the court, or the landlord of the tavern, gave tone to the morals of the village. In other cases, some man of capital, or some family of culture, made an impress that was not only abiding, but reproducing; for society, like the individual, has its formative state, its educational period, when it takes on, with more or less distinctness, the characteristics that are likely ever afterward to adhere to it. Brookville, Corydon, Charlestown, Bloomington, and Indianapolis were fortunate in this respect. Their early and more influential citizens were, many of them, professors of religion, and those who were not professors of religion respected it, and recognized the importance of its influence upon society; and the good resulting to these respective communities from the character and position of their early settlers, is incalculable.

But "honor to whom honor is due." The bar-room, although saturated with whisky and tobacco, was nevertheless often the first place thrown open for preaching, in a Western village, and the landlord would pride himself in maintaining good order during the services. The first sermons preached in New Albany and in Rising Sun were preached in bar-rooms. A preacher on one of our Western circuits had, in his monthly rounds, to pass a village in which there was a tavern, a blacksmith-shop, a store, and a few other buildings. As he had to pass the tavern about the middle of the day, he concluded to leave an appointment and preach them a sermon, while his horse was eating. He accordingly left word that, at his next round, he would preach at 12 M., in the bar-room. The landlord circulated the appointment far and wide. When the preacher came in sight, quite a company of men had gathered, and were busy pitching quoits until the preacher should arrive. The preacher dismounted, gave his horse in charge of the hostler, walked into the bar-room, followed by the crowd of men, and began services immediately. After singing and prayer, he took his text: "Seek first the kingdom of God and his righteousness, and all these things shall be added unto you." He endeavored, in plain words, to show them the absurdity and folly of serving the devil. "Now," said he, "if you want to be happy, the devil can't make you happy. He is the most wretched being in all the universe; and, as misery loves company, he will drag you down to his own fiery abode. If you are seeking for honor, the devil has none to bestow: he is the most dishonorable being that lives. And if you are seeking for wealth, the devil has none of it; if you were to sweep hell from one end to the other, you would not get a sixpence." A large, honest, but coarse-looking fellow, sitting right before the preacher, with eyes and mouth wide open, exclaimed, unconsciously, "God! money is as scarce thar as it is here!" Seed thus sown by the wayside sometimes produces permanent fruit. A sermon preached under somewhat similar circumstances, by James Conwell, of Laurel, led to the conversion of a tavern-keeper, who disposed of his liquors, and opened his bar-room for preaching, and it remained the permanent place of worship until the erection of the village church.

Rev. A. Wood, D. D., whose opportunities for observation have been unequaled, gives the following sketch of the characteristics of the early settlers in Indiana:

"The most liberal and hospitable were those who came from Virginia and Maryland; the most economical and tidy came from New Jersey; the most enterprising and commercial came from Pennsylvania and New York, with here and there a stray Yankee; the least enterprising and uneducated came from South Carolina and East Tennessee. Kentucky sent two characters: the one a lazy hunter, who had neither enterprise nor education; the other, industrious farmers, who moved away from slavery, or sought county offices. These last were educated, and very hospitable.

"During territorial times, Virginians and Marylanders had nearly all the offices. The contest at the first state elections, while the seat of Government was at Corydon, was between the Virginians and Pennsylvanians. After it went to Indianapolis, it was between the Kentuckians and the Indianians of the older counties—Franklin, Dearborn, Harrison, and Knox having, by that time, produced their own aspirants.

"And it is remarkable that, down to 1825, Ohio sent very few emigrants who stopped in Indiana. There were interspersed, in all the towns, a few educated men from England, Ireland, Germany, and the older states; and the peculiar, personal, magnetic power wielded by individuals, is felt to this day; and the present characteristics of the county towns may be traced back, good or bad, to the influence of a few men. The Methodists, as an organized power, did not have an even start with other denominations, among the first settlers. The Presbyterians, Baptists, and Quakers all had their neighborhoods, houses, preachers, and schools in advance of us. True, they have had more offshoots, or divisions; for, be it known, all who are now here in the state went from them, not from us. The New-lights were from the old Kentucky Synod; the Disciples from the old Baptists; the Cumberlands, from the Presbyterians; the United Brethren in Christ began by a union of Presbyterians and Baptists: they never were Methodists. Otterbein was a Presbyterian, and Bœhm was a Menonite. These offshoots from the old Churches, in differing from the parent stock, took shape and color from the Methodists, doing all they could to absorb from our soil. It is matter of rejoicing that there never was an offshoot from us but our colored brethren, and they are none the less Methodists by their present organization."

CHAPTER VI.

IN 1831, the Church in Indiana lost an able and zealous
minister, in the person of Rev. Edwin Ray. He was
born in Montgomery County, Kentucky, July 26, 1803;
made a profession of religion at a camp-meeting in Clarke
County, July 26, 1819. His father, Rev. John Ray,
was for many years a noted Methodist preacher in Kentucky, Tennessee, and North Carolina: a man of remarkable personal courage and Christian zeal. In 1793, we
find him appointed to Green Circuit, in East Tennessee.
The three following years he labored in Virginia. From
1797 to 1800, he traveled extensively in North Carolina,
and from excessive toil and exposure, he broke down,

and had to retire from the effective ranks of the ministry, where he had been an honored instrument in the hands of God, of doing much good. In 1801, he located, and returned to Montgomery County, Kentucky, where his family resided until 1831, when, in consequence of his opposition to slavery, he emigrated to Indiana. Although his family remained on his farm near Mt. Sterling, he re-entered the itinerancy in 1819, and for two years traveled Lexington Circuit, after which he successively traveled Limestone, Madison, Danville, and Hinkstone Circuits. Mr. Ray settled some seven miles north of Greencastle, in Putnam County, where he died in 1837, in the sixty-ninth year of his age, esteemed and beloved by all who knew him. Edwin Ray had inherited the personal courage and moral heroism of his father. He was received into the Kentucky Conference in 1822, where he labored with diligence and success for two years. In 1824, he volunteered for, and was transferred to, Illinois Conference. He labored with zeal and marked success in Vincennes, Bloomington, and Indianapolis Circuits, and in Madison Station, where he had to check the tide of radicalism, that for a time threatened to sweep all before it. In the conference year of 1829 and 1830, his health having failed, he received a superannuated relation; but such was his zeal for God that he labored half of that year in Terre Haute, notwithstanding his impaired health. The following year, though still sustaining a supernumerary relation, he was stationed in Terre Haute, where he labored beyond his strength, and with marked success; and notwithstanding Methodism was feeble, he drew to his ministry the most intelligent and thoughtful, and made a profound impression in favor of religion. Having finished his labors for the year, he started for conference, but had traveled only

a few miles when he was taken severely sick, and
stopped at the house of Mr. I. Barnes, where, after an
illness of eleven days, he closed his earthly pilgrimage.
His death was triumphant. He said: "Tell my brethren in the ministry that the religion I have professed and
preached to others, has comforted me in life, supported
me in affliction, and now enables me to triumph in
death." A letter from his then venerable father, under
date of November 11, 1831, only a short time after Edwin's death, contains the following paragraph: "When
I was told that Edwin was praying in another tent, I
was much affected, and solemnly promised God, if he
would convert him, I would give him up to Him all his
days. The good Lord heard my request, and answered
my prayer. The news of his death was not so affecting
to me as a location. I would willingly supply his place
with another son, if I had one, only to live as long and
useful as Edwin. But the Lord has taken him home;
bless the Lord!" Edwin Ray was an honor to so noble
a father. A man of sound judgment, deep religious experience, and well versed in the doctines of the Bible;
open and frank in his manner, he found ready access to
the hearts of the people in social life; earnest and impassioned in the pulpit, his ministry was both popular and
effective. Colonel John W. Ray, only surviving son of
Edwin Ray, is widely known throughout the state as an
efficient Sabbath-school worker, and an eloquent lay
preacher.

Rev. Benjamin C. Stevenson, who had just been appointed to Indianapolis Station, died in the Fall of 1831.
He was a young man of marked ability and great promise. Dignified in his deportment, cultivated in his manners, eloquent in the pulpit, and devoted to the work of
the ministry, the Church had much to expect from him.

He was converted at the age of sixteen. In 1827, he joined the Illinois Conference, and traveled successively Eel-river and Carlisle Circuits, and Galena Mission. In 1830, he was stationed in Madison, and in 1831, was appointed to Indianapolis Station; but before he had entered upon his new field of labor, only a few weeks after his marriage, the Master called him from labor to reward.

In 1833, the Indiana Conference met in Madison, Indiana. At this Conference there were reported 23,617 members; eighteen preachers were received on trial, and sixty-eight preachers were appointed to charges. John Strange and Anthony F. Thompson had been called during the year from labor to reward.

Strange died in Indianapolis, on the 2d day of December, 1833. He was in many respects a remarkable man. He evinced a singular deadness to the world, and a remarkable trust in Divine providence. He was a man of slender form, black hair, keen, penetrating eyes, a rich, musical voice, clear and distinct in its tones, rising from the lowest to the highest key without the slightest jar. He was a charming singer. Graceful in manner and eloquent in the pulpit, he was a recognized power in the Church. Strange entered the ministry in the old Western Conference, in the state of Ohio, in 1810, when he was not quite twenty-one years of age, and spent his ministerial life in Ohio and Indiana. In 1812, he traveled Whitewater Circuit, which extended from the neighborhood of Lawrenceburg, on the Ohio River, to where the city of Richmond, in Wayne County, now stands. One of his appointments was at a fort on Clear Creek, a few miles north-west of where the city of Richmond now stands. Mr. Strange was a very punctual man. Once every four weeks he made his appearance at the fort, with his rifle on his shoulder.

The country was at war with Great Britain. The Indians were hostile, and it was very dangerous for a solitary man to travel through the country; but, trusting in Divine providence, and not forgetting his rifle, and keeping a sharp look-out for the Indians, Mr. Strange passed through the dense woods from one appointment to another, unharmed. His self-denial, and entire devotion to the work of the ministry, greatly endeared him to the people. His power over an audience was wonderful. In voice and gesture he was faultless. Oratory was native with him. No man was ever more truly born a poet than John Strange was an orator. Often, in his happiest flights of eloquence, he would lift his audiences from their seats, and hundreds would find themselves unconsciously standing on their feet, and gazing intently at the speaker. His descriptive powers were fine. When he was preaching the funeral of Edwin Ray in Indianapolis, who had been his intimate friend and associate, toward the close of his sermon, while describing the second coming of Christ, he represented him as descending in the clouds, bringing the saints with him. He stood erect for a moment, and, looking upward, cried out, "Where is Edwin Ray?" Still looking upward, he exclaimed, in a voice that thrilled his audience, "I see him; I see him!" And then, with both hands raised, as if welcoming him, and with a voice that seemed to reach the heavens, he cried, "Hail, Edwin! Hail, Edwin! Hail, Edwin!" The effect was thrilling, and will never be forgotten by those who heard it. Strange was then sinking under pulmonary consumption, and in a few months he joined Edwin Ray "on the evergreen shores." The mortal remains of Strange sleep in the old cemetery at Indianapolis.

Anthony F. Thompson was a young man of promise.

He entered the ministry in 1829, and closed his labors and his life May 19, 1833.

In 1834, the Indiana Conference met in Centerville, Wayne County. Members reported, 24,984 whites, and 229 colored. The missionary collections for the whole Conference amounted to $152.50. Three preachers located during the year, namely: Lorenzo D. Smith, Thomas S. Hitt, and Isaac N. Ellsbury; and three preachers had died during the year: George Locke, Nehemiah B. Griffith, and James Armstrong.

George Locke was born in Cannonstown, Pennsylvania, on the 8th of June, 1799. His parents were David and Nancy Locke. His great-grandfather and grandfather were both clergymen in the Church of England, and his father was educated in reference to the ministry in the Presbyterian Church; which design, however, he abandoned, and engaged in teaching. The mother of George was a lady of superior endowments, and a pious member of the Presbyterian Church. The family came to Kentucky in 1798, and settled in Mason County, but, two years afterward, removed to Shelbyville. Young Locke was converted in a revival that occurred under the labors of a local preacher by the name of Edward Talbott. In 1817, he was licensed to exhort, and, shortly after, to preach. At the session of the Tennessee Conference for 1818, he was admitted on trial, and appointed to Little-river Circuit, and the next year to the Powell's-valley. In 1820, he was sent to the Bowling Green Circuit, as the colleague of Benjamin Malone, and with Charles Holliday as his presiding elder. During the year he was married to Miss Elizabeth B. M'Reynolds, a lady of fine cultivation and deep piety, and belonging to one of the best Methodist families in the state, and the following year he located.

But, not satisfied in a local relation, his name reappears
the next year in the list of itinerants, from which it
is never after to be stricken until he is called to his
reward.   His fields of labor in Kentucky, after his
return to the Conference, were the Jefferson and Hart-
ford Circuits; on the latter of which he remained two
years.   Beyond the Ohio River, the country was filling
up with remarkable rapidity.   Not only from Virginia and
Tennessee, but also from Kentucky, hundreds of families, attracted by the cheap and fertile lands of Indiana
and Illinois, had sought homes within their rich domain.
Mr. Locke, believing that a wider field for usefulness
presented itself in this new country, in the Autumn
of 1825, requested to be transferred to the Illinois Conference, then embracing the states of Illinois and Indiana.   His first appointment was to Corydon Circuit,
where also he continued the following year.   In 1827,
he was appointed to Charlestown Circuit.   His labors on
Corydon Circuit had been crowned with signal success;
but on Charlestown Circuit he was privileged to witness
one of the most remarkable awakenings with which
Southern Indiana has ever been visited.   He remained,
however, on this circuit but about six months.   The
General Conference of 1828 elected Charles Holliday,
then presiding elder of the Wabash District, Agent for
the Book Concern at Cincinnati; and George Locke was
appointed to fill the vacancy on the district.   This district, at that time, extended from Shawneetown, on the
Ohio River, up the Wabash, on both sides, above Terre
Haute some twenty or thirty miles, embracing an area
of territory in Indiana and Illinois of at least a hundred
miles from east to west, by two hundred miles from
north to south.   He traveled this district four years,
receiving, much of the time, scarcely enough to pay

traveling expenses. His wife, who had been engaged in teaching from the time he re-entered the traveling connection, supported the family, and rejoiced that in so doing she could enable her husband to preach the unsearchable riches of Christ. His slender constitution gave way under the labors and exposures endured upon that district, and, though he completed the usual term of service, it was about the last of his effective labor.

Some time in the Winter of 1831–32, one of the severest Winters ever known in the West, Mr. Locke was returning home, after an absence of several weeks. When he reached the Wabash River, he found it gorged with ice. He and another traveler waited at the house of the ferryman, three or four days, for a change in the weather, or in the condition of the ice; but as no change came, and as they were impatient to proceed on their journey, they resolved on breaking a channel through the ice, for the ferry-boat. Accordingly, the next morning, they addressed themselves to the work with all diligence, and at sunset found themselves within a rod or two of the opposite shore. Mr. Locke was standing on the bow of the boat, fatigued and tremulous, breaking the ice with a rail. Striking a piece with all the force he could command, it suddenly gave way, not making the resistance he had anticipated, and precipitated him into the river. As he arose, and was just drifting under the ice, his companions rescued him. Though the shock was a fearful one, and he was not only thoroughly drenched but thoroughly chilled also, he resolved to persevere in his work, and actually did persevere till the shore was reached. He then mounted his horse, and rode ten miles to the next house; but when he reached there, he was frozen to his saddle, and speechless. The horse stopped of his own accord, and the family, coming to the door, and perceiving his condition, lifted him from his horse, and cared for him very kindly, until, after a day or two, he was able to resume his journey. Mrs. Locke had, for days, been anxiously awaiting the return of her husband, and finally yielded to the appalling conviction that he was frozen to death. A friend who was with her tried to assuage her grief by inducing her to look more upon the hopeful side, but she refused to be comforted. When he suggested to her that he should not be surprised even if she should see her husband that very night, she besought him not to trifle with her feelings by endeavoring thus to make her credit an impossibility. He had scarcely had time to assure her that he was far from trifling with her feelings, when the latch of the gate was lifted, the well-known footstep of her husband was heard, and instantly she was well-nigh paralyzed with joy in his arms.

Amidst all his manifold and self-denying labors, he never abated his habits of study. He redeemed time, not only for the study of systematic theology, but for general reading. He acquired some knowledge of Greek and Latin, and made considerable proficiency in the higher branches of mathematics. He continued his studies until a few weeks before his death, and had his books brought to him, even after he was confined to his bed. The General Conference of 1832, of which Mr. Locke was a member, divided the Illinois Conference, and constituted a separate conference of the state of Indiana. In the Autumn of that year he was transferred to Indiana, and was returned to Corydon Circuit. Here his health became much reduced, which led him to remove to New Albany, and engage with his wife in school-teaching. In the Autumn of 1833, he took a superannuated relation, and on the 15th of July, 1834, he died.

He never recovered from the cold contracted from falling into the Wabash River. He died of consumption, after much patient suffering, and in the full confidence of being welcomed to the joys of the Lord. His last words, which were uttered with his last breath, were, "Glory! Glory! Glory!"*

James Armstrong was a native of Ireland, and was brought by his parents to America when but a child. He was converted when about seventeen years of age, and attached himself to the Methodist Church, in the city of Philadelphia. He was licensed to preach in the city of Baltimore, in 1812. He emigrated to Indiana in 1821, and in the Fall of the same year joined the itinerant connection, in which he continued an able and efficient minister till the close of life, which occurred at his own residence, in Laporte County, on the 12th of September, 1834. Of him, Hon. R. W. Thompson says, in his "Fallen Heroes of Indiana Methodism:" "Armstrong was a man of immense power—strong, logical, and conclusive. He threw his whole soul into his work; and if, sometimes, he was not altogether precise in his style, yet at others he seemed almost moved by inspiration, so completely were his words expressive of his correct thoughts. When he intended to strike a hard blow, he never failed to make it terrific, shivering the helmet of whatsoever adversary dared, in his presence, to assail the citadel of Christianity." (Indiana Methodist Convention, 1870.) Mr. Armstrong's ministry was very successful. God gave him many seals to his ministry in Indiana, and honored him, as an instrument in His hands, with laying deep and broad the foundations of the Church, in this new and growing state.

Nehemiah B. Griffith was a native of the state of

* Sprague's "Annals," p. 610.

New York. In the eighteenth year of his age, he came with his father's family to the state of Ohio. When about eighteen years of age, he was led to Christ, and into the Methodist Church, chiefly through the instrumentality of Rev. W. H. Raper. He entered the ministry in 1822, and continued, with great zeal and efficiency, until the day of his death, which occurred in St. Joseph County, August 22, 1834. Mr. Griffith was a very successful preacher. He was a clear doctrinal preacher; and he preached the doctrines of the Bible so practically and experimentally, and withal with such an unction, that his ministry was generally attended with extensive revivals of religion. His last words were, "Sweet Heaven, I am coming!"

"Previous to 1832, all the settlements of Northern Indiana were visited by missionaries from Michigan, which was then in what was called North Ohio Conference. Erastus Felton, in 1830, and L. B. Gurley, in 1831, preached in Laporte County. But, in 1832, there was made an Indiana Conference, and James Armstrong was appointed missionary, and superintendent of a mission district. He settled on a farm near Door Village. James Armstrong was the evangelist of our Church in this country, influencing many Church members to move to it from the older parts of the state, and remaining in the country, as an enterprising missionary, until his death. Armstrong was a man of medium weight; his chin, lips, and nose sharp; eyes small, eyebrows heavy, forehead square and high, and hair thickset and dark. He was always neatly dressed in plain black. He had a good voice, with a free use of plain English words of Saxon origin; nothing of the Irish brogue, but much of the fire which, as he felt himself, he failed not to impart to others who gave him audience, until the bond became so strong between the speaker and hearer, that both were carried along with the force and beauty of the subject before them. He was called a topical preacher; and before a promiscuous congregation, his memory, his imagination and tact, enabled him to conduct a controversy with great ingenuity, for success to any cause he espoused. As a man and a minister, he attached personal friends, who liberally sustained his enterprises, and boldly defended his measures. Having been presiding elder over all the state of Indiana, from the Ohio to the Lakes, he was a herald of the Gospel whom God owned and blessed; and his untiring industry and influence, devoted as they were entirely to the organization of the Church in the new settlements, place him on the page of our history as the leading evangelist. In order of time the societies were formed: first, at Door Village; second, at Laporte; third, Union Chapel; fourth, Michigan City. At all these there were societies and stated worship before the year 1837. The first meeting-house was at Door Village; the second, at Laporte; the third, Union Chapel; and the fourth, Michigan City; and from these there branched off societies in every direction." (Sketches by A. Wood.)

Elkhart Circuit was organized in the year 1836. S. R. Ball was the preacher. The first quarterly-meeting was held in the village of Goshen, January 9, 1836. The following were the preaching-places, as entered on the steward's book: Elkhart, Conley's, Warner's, Shelley's, Goshen, Gormell's, Elkhart Prairie, Wood's, Hawpatch, Burton's, Little Elkhart, Shaky Creek, Cross's, and White Plains.

In October, 1835, the Indiana Conference met in Lafayette. At this Conference twenty-three preachers were admitted on trial. There were sixty-five pastoral.

charges, divided into seven presiding elder's districts, as follows:

Madison—A. Wiley, Presiding Elder.
Charlestown—C. W. Ruter, Presiding Elder.
Bloomington—Joseph Oglesby, Presiding Elder.
Vincennes—A. Wood, Presiding Elder.
Crawfordsville—J. L. Thompson, Presiding Elder.
Laporte—Richard Hargrave, Presiding Elder.

Of the sixty-five pastoral charges, nine were stations, namely: Madison, New Albany, Jeffersonville, Indianapolis, Bloomington, Vincennes, Terre Haute, and Crawfordsville. Six of the charges were missions, namely: Otter-creek, in Vincennes District; Cole-creek and Lebanon, in Crawfordsville District; and Fort Wayne and Deep-river Missions, in Laporte District.

Edward R. Ames was agent for the Preachers' Aid Society, which originated as follows:

At the Conference in New Albany, in 1832, it was announced that Colonel James Paxton, of Indianapolis, deceased, had bequeathed a portion of his property to the Methodist Episcopal Church in the state of Indiana, "to be employed in extending the work of the Lord in the bounds of the state of Indiana, helping the most needy preachers belonging to that Church, whether effective or superannuated." James Armstrong was appointed an agent on behalf of the Conference to receive the same. Allen Wiley was also appointed an agent on behalf of the Conference to receive a similar bequest for the same purpose, made by Samuel Swearingin. These, with one or two other small bequests, laid the foundation of the Preachers' Aid Society of the Indiana Conference—the Society having been properly chartered by an act of the Legislature. With a view to increase its funds, in 1835, E. R. Ames was appointed its agent.

In October, 1836, the Indiana Conference held its

REV. E. R. AMES, D. D.

ONE OF THE BISHOPS OF THE METHODIST EPISCOPAL CHURCH

session in Indianapolis, Bishop Roberts presiding. At this Conference, Indiana Asbury University was located at Greencastle. The Conference, having determined, for reasons that are stated at length under the head of "Educational Institutions," etc., to establish an institution of high grade under the authority of the Church, did, in 1835, agree upon a plan for founding a university. Subscriptions were taken up, and proposals made from different points in the state, with a view of securing a location for the university. Lafayette, Rockville, Greencastle, Putnamville, and Indianapolis were the principal competitors. After receiving proposals, and hearing the representations from different points, the Conference, at its session in Indianapolis in 1836, located the institution at Greencastle. At this Conference twenty-four preachers were received on trial, ninety preachers were appointed to pastoral charges, and two to agencies. E. R. Ames was continued in the agency of the Preachers' Aid Society, and John C. Smith agent for the university.

During this Conference year, in the Summer of 1837, there was a memorable camp-meeting held in the bounds of Rushville Circuit, in what is now the southern edge of Knightstown, on the ground of Mr. Lowry. The attendance was large for that day. F. C. Holliday, then quite a young man, was in charge of the circuit. He had secured the attendance of a strong ministerial force, among whom were James Havens, E. R. Ames, J. C. Smith, Elijah Whitten, Robert Burns, C. B. Jones, Augustus Eddy, and an array of efficient workers of less note. The religious interest of the meeting was excellent from the first. Mrs. Richmond, from Indianapolis, by her remarkable singing, her fervent prayers and exhortations, added much to the interest of the meeting. On Sunday night, just after the lamps had been lit, and the audience called together for public worship, there burst suddenly on the encampment one of those fearful tornadoes with which our country is occasionally visited. In an instant every light was extinguished, and the audience left in perfect darkness, save when it was relieved by the flash of the lightning. The wind leveled a track through the forest, just across one end of the encampment, as effectually as a mower cuts the grass with his scythe. The audience had been gathered just out of the track of the tornado. A beech-tree of considerable size, within the circle of tents, was blown down right toward the altar, which was covered with a frame shed. Large numbers were knocked down, either by the force of the wind or the branches of the tree, but no one was hurt. Two men, who were standing under the tree, fell in the hole where the tree had stood; a falling tree knocked a tent over them, that was just in the rear of where they stood, and yet they were rescued without a scratch. One entire row of tents was prostrated by the falling timber, and yet not a single inmate hurt. A large tree-top was broken off, and lodged right over a tent crowded with people. So numerous and marvelous were the escapes, that they made a profound impression upon the minds of the people. The work of God broke out with increasing power on Monday, and many, doubtless, owed their awakening to the incidents of the tornado.

An amusing fact, worth relating, occurred in connection with the visit of Ames and Smith to this camp-meeting. Smith was agent for the college, and Ames for the Preachers' Aid Society. They left Rushville in company, *en route* for the camp-meeting. They had procured the names of a number of well-to-do farmers, upon whom they proposed to call, on behalf of their respective agencies, on their way to the camp-meeting, each alternately having the right, according to private agreement, to make the first application.

Their first call was on a Pennsylvania German, residing near the village of Burlington. Smith made the first presentation of his cause, showing the advantages of education, and the importance, both to the Church and State, of founding a Christian university. The old gentleman heard him patiently through, and then informed him that he did not believe in college learning. In his opinion it made young men proud and lazy; and being unwilling to work, they would live by cheating their neighbors. Upon the whole, he regarded colleges as rather dangerous institutions, and would give nothing toward founding a college in Indiana. Smith having failed to secure a donation to his enterprise, it was Ames's turn to present his cause. He informed the old gentleman that he was an agent for a very different object; that the preachers, who had planted Churches all through our country, and were really laying the foundations of our Christian civilization, giving security to our homes, and increased value to our property, as well as leading sinners to God, and carrying the consolations of religion to the sorrowing and afflicted, were generally poor men. Their severe labors and exposures either brought them to early graves, leaving their families unprovided for, or left them, in the evening of life, so broken down in health as to be unable, by their personal exertions, to secure an adequate support; that the Church and the country owed these men and their families a debt of gratitude that could never be fully paid; that he was agent for a Society called "The Preachers' Aid Society of the Methodist Church," the object of which was to raise a fund to aid in supporting the broken-down or worn-out preachers and their families, and of aiding such as did not get a support from their circuits. The old man listened attentively, and when Mr. Ames was done, he said, "I believes in your agency." Mr. Ames explained to him that ten dollars would constitute a person a life member of the Society. Said he, "I takes three life memberships in the Society—one for myself, one for my wife, and one for my daughter." He gave his notes, payable in a short time; and when the preacher came around, he requested that preaching be removed to his house, because it was larger; "and," said he, "I want you to put my name and my wife's name and my daughter's name on the class-book; for I bought three life memberships in the Church, of Mr. Ames, and we all want to belong to Church!" Of course their names were put on the class-paper. The old gentleman paid his notes in due time, and, what is better, he and his wife and daughter made good life members in the Church.

In October, 1837, the Indiana Conference met in New Albany, Bishop Soule presiding. There were reported to this Conference, 31,058 members in the Church in Indiana, being an increase, during the year, of 3,138. There were seventy-nine pastoral charges, divided into eight presiding elders' districts, to wit:

Madison District—E. G. Wood, Presiding Elder.
Charlestown District—C. W. Ruter, Presiding Elder.
Indianapolis District—Augustus Eddy, Presiding Elder.
Bloomington District—Henry Talbott, Presiding Elder.
Vincennes District—John Miller, Presiding Elder.
Crawfordsville District—Allen Wiley, Presiding Elder.
Laporte District—Richard Hargrave, Presiding Elder.
Centerville District—David Stiver, Presiding Elder.

E. R. Ames was transferred to Missouri Conference, and stationed in St. Louis. William M. Daily and John

A. Brouse were appointed agents for Indiana Asbury University, and James Havens agent for the Preachers' Aid Society. Ames had a severe attack of fever in St. Louis, and at the end of the Conference year was transferred back to Indiana Conference, and the ensuing year was stationed in Madison, Indiana. Wiley remained but one year on Crawfordsville District, his health having suffered very seriously; and at the ensuing Conference, he was stationed in Indianapolis. Most of the preachers from the eastern part of the state had gone to the Conference, in New Albany, in 1837, by the way of the Ohio River. In returning from the Conference, there were some forty or fifty preachers on board the mail-boat, *General Pike*, bound from Louisville to Cincinnati, among whom was Bishop Soule.

The "Fall races" had by that time just closed at Louisville, and a large number of sporting gentlemen, vulgarly called gamblers, were on the boat, bound for Cincinnati and other points along the river. The boat left the wharf at Louisville a little before noon. As soon as dinner was over, the gamblers took possession of the gentlemen's cabin, which was soon lined with card-tables, plentifully supplied with cards and liquor; and a scene of profanity and drunkenness began, that was remarkable for a steam-boat, even in that day. It seemed as though the lower regions had emptied some of their worst specimens into that company. Bacchanalian songs and coarse jests, interspersed with a great deal of profanity, filled the entire room. The bishop became excited; he arose, and walked from one end of the cabin to the other, closely surveying the scene. It was one of the cases in which open reproof would have caused strife, and perhaps led to serious results. Speaking in a loud voice, that all the preachers might hear him, the bishop said,

"Brethren, can not we sing too?" The preachers gathered together in a group, and commenced singing lustily:

> "Jesus, the name high over all,
> In hell, or earth, or sky;
> Angels and men before it fall,
> And devils fear and fly."

The gamblers paused, listened, and looked astonished. One by one, they began to leave the card-tables, and retire to their state-rooms, or get out on the deck of the boat; and by the time the preachers had sung two or three hymns, there was not a pack of cards to be seen anywhere about; the card-tables were shoved back, and cards and brandy-bottles and gamblers had all disappeared; and, during the afternoon and evening, the company, though large, was as quiet and agreeable as any one could have desired.

George Randle located in 1831. He was an Englishman by birth. Came to this country as a preacher. In 1829, he had traveled Madison Circuit, and, in 1830, Vevay Circuit. Having married a Miss Eubank, contrary to the wishes of her friends, and the alienation increasing, rather than being cured, after the marriage, her father's friends, thinking that the Conference dealt too leniently with Mr. Randle, withdrew from the Church with the "Radical Secession," as it was called, and took two societies in the north part of Dearborn County, including two stone churches, the titles to which had not been properly vested in the Church. The Conference located Mr. Randle in 1831, and in the unfortunate trouble neither of the parties seemed to be satisfied with the action of the Church—doubtless because they were impelled in their actions by passion, that was not shared by those who were called to pass judgment in their case. Mr. Randle settled in the southern part of Dearborn County, accumulated a fine property, and raised a large and respectable family. He left the Church shortly after his location, and never reunited with it, although his family belonged to the Church, and he attended its ministry.

In 1833, John A. Decker and Wm. Evans located.

In 1834, Samuel Brenton, Eli P. Farmer, Asa Beck, and James Scott located. Samuel Brenton will be noticed more especially in connection with the Methodist educators in Indiana. Eli P. Farmer traveled a number of years in the Indiana Conference, either as a supply, under the employment of a presiding elder, or as a member of the Conference. He was an earnest and ready talker, but a rough, uncultured man. After his location he withdrew from the Church, but continued to preach.

Asa Beck was for many years a laborious circuit preacher, and, owing to feeble health, sometimes supernumerary, sometimes superannuated, sometimes effective, and sometimes located; but in whatever relation he sustained to the Church, he maintained the true character of a Christian minister.

James Scott was a man of marked individuality. He was a man of small stature, quick in all his movements, well read in dogmatic theology, rather fond of controversy in his earlier days. He had a keen, incisive mind, that could cut a knotty question right through the core. And when he had closed a conclusive argument with one of his peculiarly culminating sentences, he would pause and look keenly at his hearers, while his countenance wore a self-satisfied expression—as much as to say, "Do you see the force of that?" And, if they were intelligent hearers, they generally did see the force of it.

In 1835, Thomas S. Hitt and Isaac N. Ellsbury located. They were both of them good men and true, eminently useful as itinerants; and their usefulness continued after their location.

In 1836, there were seven locations, namely: L. D. Smith, John I. Johnson, Robert Burns, Joseph Oglesby, Zachariah Gaines, Wm. D. Watson, and James V. Watson. Three of these, Burns, Oglesby, and James V. Watson, were well known throughout the state. Robert Burns was a zealous and successful preacher, and, although never occupying what might be regarded as the more prominent appointments, he was eminently useful. Oglesby entered the itinerancy in the old Western Conference, before the organization of the work in Missouri, Illinois or Indiana. He traveled for many years, and did a great deal of hard frontier work. He studied medicine, and had some skill as a practitioner. He served awhile as presiding elder. In doctrine he was supposed to lean toward Pelagianism. He located because of some reflections upon his opinions or his utterances by the Conference; but, in view of his long and faithful services, and of his undoubted Christian character, in a few years the Conference placed his name on the superannuated list, where it remained till the close of his life. James V. Watson located in consequence of ill-health, but re-entered the Conference again, and, at its session in Lawrenceburg, in 1839, was sent to White Pigeon, in Michigan—one district of the Indiana Conference being included in the territory of Michigan. When the appointment was read out, Watson sprang up on a bench and called out, "Where is White Pigeon? Who can tell me any thing about my White Pigeon?" It was a name he had never heard, and of its location he knew nothing. But Watson found his White Pigeon, and lived to make an impression upon the Church that will not soon be forgotten. He founded a paper, by his own exertions, that grew into the *North-western Christian Advocate,* of which he was the popular and talented editor at the time of his death. Watson was the victim of asthma for many years, and was a great sufferer; but he accomplished what few men of robust health would have thought possible. He was a close student, a remarkably eloquent preacher, and a forcible and perspicuous writer. Besides editing the *North-western,* he was the author of a book of sketches and essays, called "Tales and Takings," and a work on "Revivals of Religion." He participated in two sessions of the General Conference.

At the session of the Conference in New Albany, in 1837, William H. Goode was appointed principal of New Albany Seminary. That was the first literary institution under the care of the Indiana Conference, and William H. Goode was our pioneer educator. In the month of May, 1837, Mr. Goode was elected principal of New Albany Seminary, upon the resignation of Philander Ruter, A. M. By the act of the presiding elder, Rev. C. W. Ruter, who was also President of the Board of Trustees, Mr. Goode was authorized to accept, his place being supplied on Lexington Circuit. The Seminary was in a flourishing condition, with about two hundred students, two male and two female teachers, and had comfortable buildings, for that day, though somewhat embarrassed by debt. In addition to the charge of the Seminary, Mr. Goode was expected to labor jointly with the pastor in New Albany Station. Near the close of the Conference year, Mr. Goode resigned the charge of the Seminary, that he might re-enter the pastoral work; and was succeeded in the Seminary by George Harrison, A. M., who continued in charge of the Seminary for several years. .The entire charge of the station devolved on Mr. Goode, after his resignation of the charge of the Seminary, until the ensuing Conference.

Among the founders of this early institution were the names of Ruter, Wiley, Sinex, Leonard, Brown, Downey, Robison, Evans, Stoy, Childs, Conner, and Seabrook. It was an early, earnest, and, in itself, a successful effort; though, like most of our early enterprises, in the absence of precedents and experience, some errors were committed which proved fatal to its continuance. Still, it accomplished great good, and is now represented in the active departments of life by many men and women, in New Albany and elsewhere, that are ornaments to the Church. One single class of six boys gave to the Church the names of Charles Downey, John W. Locke, Thomas H. Sinex, and George B. Jocelyn. The germ of educational enterprise thus early developed has never been lost, but has culminated in the present highly prosperous condition of our educational work, not only in New Albany, but throughout the state.

In October, 1838, the Indiana Conference held its session in Rockville. Among the appointments made at this Conference, are: Indiana Asbury University— C. Nutt, J. W. Weakley, Professors; Samuel C. Cooper and Zachariah Gaines, Agents. At this Conference, L. D. Smith, Boyd Phelps, Stephen R. Ball, Henry Van Order, and William B. Ross were granted locations. They were efficient preachers; but while some were compelled to retire for the want of an adequate support, and others from impaired health, God raised up others to take their places, and to meet the demands of the rapidly extending work. Thirty-two young men were admitted on trial at this Conference.

The sessions of those early conferences were not only seasons of great interest to the preachers, but the journey to and from the conference was, to many of them, an important affair. The whole state being in one conference, and the chief mode of travel being by horseback, it of course took a number of days to make the journey from the more remote portions of the state.

At the session of the Conference in Rockville, in 1838, the preachers along the Ohio River had to go clear across the state on horseback. Enoch G. Wood, who was then presiding elder on Madison District, and F. C. Holliday, who was stationed in Rising Sun, made the journey to Conference in company, from Indianapolis. Wood came from Madison to Indianapolis, and Holliday went from Rising Sun to Brookville, in one day; the next day, to Centerville; the next, to Knightstown; and the next, to Indianapolis. Wood and Holliday started from Indianapolis on Saturday morning, and reached Danville, in Hendricks County, for dinner, where Wood was taken unwell, and they remained over until Monday, Holliday preaching twice in the court-house on Sunday. Resuming their journey on Monday morning, they reached Greencastle for dinner.

Late in the afternoon, having traveled some distance without seeing a house, and coming across a double log-cabin, and fearing that it might be their only chance, they applied for entertainment for the night. The good woman said her husband was absent to mill, but would be home by dark, and they could stay. During the night there was a tremendous racket in the door-yard, and a severe contest with the farmer's dog, assisted by his master, and what the preachers supposed was some wild animal. They thought of going out and seeing what was the matter, but not being called by the man of the house, and, withal, being tired from their journey, they concluded not to turn out. In the morning the man of the house expressed regret at the disturbance during the night, and feared that their slumbers had been interrupted. Upon inquiry it was ascertained that a large bear had got into the yard, had climbed into the hog-pen, and was trying to carry off one of the hogs. With the help of his dog, the man had saved his hogs, but the bear had escaped. The preachers regretted deeply that they had not been called to his assistance, as the capture of a bear on the way to Conference would have been a romantic incident.

In 1839, the Indiana Conference met in Lawrenceburg, Bishop Roberts presiding, assisted during a part of the session by Bishop Morris.

In October, 1840, the Indiana Conference met in Indianapolis, Bishop Soule presiding. The Conference now numbered one hundred and fifty-three traveling preachers, four hundred and eighteen local preachers, and included 52,626 communicants; being an increase in the membership during the year of 9,116 members.

This year our first German mission was established in Indiana, called Indiana German Mission, and John Kisling and M. J. Hofer were the missionaries. It is interesting to trace the progress of the Church from small beginnings to respectable proportions, not only in numbers, but to note its progress in liberality. We take the contributions to the missionary cause as an example. In 1835, the contributions for missions amounted to $528.50; in 1840, to $1,474.92.

CHAPTER VII.

From 1841 to 1856—Indiana Conference in 1841—George K. Hester—
Thomas Gunn—Isaac Kelso—Indiana Conference in 1842—E. W.
Sehon and Edmund S. Janes address the Conference—Indiana
Conference in 1843—General Conference in 1844—Indiana Dele-
gates—Indiana Conference divided into two Conferences—Indiana
Conference in 1844—John A. Decker—Ebenezer Patrick—North
Indiana Conference in 1845—Peter R. Guthrie and Daniel S. Elder—
Growth of Methodism from 1832 to 1843—Division of the State
into four Conferences—Benjamin T. Griffith—Walter Prescott—
James E. Tiffany—Wm. C. Hensley—Francis F. Sheldon—Emmons
Rutledge—Isaac Crawford—Hosier J. Durbin—Isaac Owen—His
Life and Labors—Calvin W. Ruter—His Character and Services—
James Jones—Seth Smith—Geo. M. Beswick—John H. Bruce—
Statistics for 1856—The early Circuit System—Results of relin-
quishing Week-day Preaching—Effect of Building Churches too
close together in the Country.

IN 1841, the Indiana Conference held its session in
Terre Haute. Twenty-five young men were admitted
on trial, and three located, namely: George K. Hester,
Thomas Gunn, and Isaac Kelso. George K. Hester, besides giving a number of the best years of his life to
the itinerancy, has given three talented and educated
sons to the same work, namely: F. A. Hester, Wm.
M'K. Hester, and Milton Addison Hester—the latter of
whom fell a victim to the cholera while stationed in St.
Louis, in 1850. Thomas Gunn was a faithful minister,
whose labors were blessed in the building up of the
Church; but impaired health induced him to ask for
a location. Isaac Kelso was a man of feeble health,
and of some eccentricity of character. After his location, he preached some for the Christians, or Campbell-

ites, and awhile for the Universalists. He wrote a romance called "Danger in the Dark," directed against Jesuitism in particular and the Papacy in general. The volume was published just as the "Know-Nothings," as a political organization, were exerting a great influence in the Western States; and, although there was no connection between that movement and his book, the former helped to sell the latter. But in a short time both the author and the book seemed to be forgotten.

In October, 1842, the Indiana Conference held its session in Centerville, Wayne County. Thirty-one preachers were admitted on trial. E. W. Sehon and Edmund S. Janes visited this Conference as secretaries of the American Bible Society. They each had a high reputation, both as able preachers and eloquent platform speakers, and both addressed the Conference on the claims of the Bible cause. Sehon made the first address, and fairly captivated the congregation with his eloquence. When Mr. Janes arose to follow him, after a few very pertinent introductory remarks, he seemed to become strangely embarrassed, and, after struggling along for a few minutes, he paused, and, looking over the congregation, said: "Brethren, my position to-day reminds me of an incident in connection with one of Napoleon's generals at the battle of Waterloo. One general accosted another, who, all pale with fear, was, nevertheless, rallying his troops, with the remark: 'General, you are scared!' 'Yes,' said he, 'I know I am scared; and if you were half as badly scared as I am, you would run; but I mean to stand and fight it out.' I am scared," said Mr. Janes, "but I mean to make a speech." That broke the spell; and Mr. Janes made such a speech, both for argument and eloquence, as but few men could deliver.

In October, 1843, the Conference held its session in Crawfordsville, Bishop Andrew presiding. Thirty-one preachers were admitted on trial, and two located; namely, Thomas Spillman and John Richey.

In May, 1844, the General Conference convened in the city of New York. The delegates from Indiana Conference were: Matthew Simpson, Allen Wiley, E. R. Ames, John Miller, C. W. Ruter, Aaron Wood, Augustus Eddy, and James Havens. At this General Conference the state of Indiana was divided into two conferences—that part of the state lying south of the National Road retaining the name of Indiana Conference, and that part of the state lying north of the National Road was called North Indiana Conference. The Indiana Conference held its session in Bloomington, October, 1844, and North Indiana Conference held its session the same Fall in Fort Wayne.

The Indiana Conference contained, as reported at its session in Bloomington, October, 1844, traveling preachers, 105, and 35,971 members. The North Indiana Conference included 101 traveling preachers, and 27,563 members. In Indiana Conference, two members had died: John A. Decker and Ebenezer Patrick. Decker was a native of Tennessee; came to Indiana with his parents when a boy, and was converted at the age of eighteen. He was licensed to preach in the Fall of 1828, and in the Fall of 1829 was received on trial in the Illinois Conference. From this time he continued to travel until the time of his death, with the exception of some five or six years, during which, in consequence of impaired health, he sustained a local relation. He died on the 25th of October, 1843. Ebenezer Patrick died on the 16th of August, 1844. Mr. Patrick was a native of Vermont. He was admitted into the Indiana Conference in 1835, and continued a faithful and useful minister to the close of life. In a fit of delirium, caused by fever, he seized a razor and cut his own throat.

September, 1845, the North Indiana Conference held its session in Lafayette. Burroughs Westlake and Zachariah Gaines had died during the year. Westlake was a man of ability. He was received into the Ohio Conference in 1814. The last nine years of his ministry were spent in Indiana. Mr. Gaines was a native of Virginia. He was admitted into the Ohio Conference in 1832, and the same year transferred to Indiana. In 1836, under the pressure of pecuniary embarrassment, he located; but in 1838, he re-entered the itinerancy, where he labored till the close of life.

In October, 1845, the Indiana Conference held its session in the city of Madison. Peter R. Guthrie and Daniel S. Elder had died during the year. They were both of them young men of ability and promise. Mr. Guthrie entered the ministry in 1839, and Mr. Elder in 1840. Their ministerial career was brief, yet they gathered not a few sheaves for the heavenly garner, and finished their course with joy; witnessing a good confession in death, as they had done in life.

The growth of the Church was constant from 1832 to 1843, having increased in that time from 20,035 to 67,976; and from 1838 to 1843 its increase was almost unparalleled, being, in five years, 32,716.

In 1852, the state was divided into four Conferences, called Indiana, South-eastern Indiana, North Indiana, and North-west Indiana Conferences. The numbers for that year stood as follows: Indiana Conference, 25,412 members, and 84 traveling preachers; North Indiana Conference, 16,747 members, and 72 traveling preachers; North-west Indiana Conference, 19,729 members, and 78 traveling preachers; South-eastern Indiana Conference, 19,367 members, and 100 traveling preachers,—all of the German work in the state being included in the South-eastern Indiana Conference; the German work comprising two entire districts, called, respectively, South Indiana District, and North Indiana District. George A. Breunig was presiding elder on South Indiana District, and John Kisling on North Indiana District; and the German membership amounted to 2,061.

In 1849, South-eastern Indiana Conference suffered the loss of three of its members by death: Benjamin T. Griffith, Walter Prescott, and James E. Tiffany. Griffith was a native of Virginia. He united with the Church in 1830, and soon commenced preaching. He was admitted on trial in the Indiana Conference, in 1831 or 1832, and labored faithfully till the time of his death (with the exception of one year, during which he was superannuated), which occurred August 30, 1849.

Walter Prescott was a native of England, the son of a Wesleyan preacher. He came to America in 1841, and connected himself with the Missouri Annual Conference, with which he remained until the separation of the Southern Conferences from the Methodist Episcopal Church. Determining to continue in the Methodist Episcopal Church, he came to Indiana in 1846, and at the session of the conference that Fall, he was appointed to Jeffersonville. Here he remained two years. He was then appointed to Wesley Chapel, in the city of Madison, where he labored until the 30th of July, when the Master called him up higher. His death was triumphant. When told that he was dying, he replied, "I am glad;" and faintly repeated:

"Preach him to all, and cry in death,
Behold, behold the Lamb!"

He was a superior preacher, and during his brief career made full proof of his ministry.

James E. Tiffany was also a native of England, born near Huddlesfield, in Yorkshire, that great home and hive of Methodism, on the 21st of September, 1820. He came to America in 1829. He made a profession of religion and united with the Methodist Church in 1839, at which time he was a student in Miami University. He died of cholera on the 18th of July, 1849. The midnight cry found him with his lamp trimmed and burning.

In 1850, William C. Hensley, John L. Eagers, Francis F. Sheldon, Emmons Rutledge, and Isaac Crawford were all gathered to their rest. Hensley had been five years in the ministry, and was but twenty-nine years of age; yet his ministry had been blessed to the salvation of many. Sheldon entered the Conference in 1840, and ended his earthly course on the 16th of January, 1850. Rutledge was admitted on trial in the Indiana Conference in 1837, and continued to labor with efficiency till the close of life. He was a useful and faithful minister, and had victory in death.

Isaac Crawford was a native of New York. He came to Indiana in 1835, and in 1837 was admitted on trial into the Indiana Conference, and continued to labor faithfully till the close of life. By his amiability and the faithfulness with which he performed his duties, he secured the confidence and co-operation of the Church, and his labors were usually blessed to the upbuilding of the Church.

The same Conference was called, the ensuing year, to mourn the loss by death of a young minister of more than ordinary ability—Hosier J. Durbin—who, at the time of his death, was agent for the American Bible Society. August 11, 1851, he left Greensburg, for his residence in Madison, designing to take the cars at Vernon; and, although there was the prospect of a severe storm, yet he could not be prevailed on to delay his journey. When a few miles south of Greensburg, the storm increased in violence, and when entering a wood, he hesitated a moment as to whether he should proceed, and, as he was in the act of turning back, a limb fell upon him, causing the injury which resulted in his death, on the ensuing Friday; he having received the injury on Monday. He was licensed to preach, August 26, 1833. In the Fall of 1835, he was admitted on trial in the Indiana Conference, and appointed to Vevay Circuit, with James Jones as preacher in charge. At the end of the year, Mr. Durbin desisted from traveling, and, until 1842, devoted himself to secular pursuits. In 1840, he was a representative in the State Legislature, from Switzerland County. In 1842, he again united with the Conference, and was appointed to Vevay. His subsequent appointments were: Jeffersonville, Canaan, Rising Sun, Connersville. In 1849, he accepted the agency for the American Bible Society for the southern half of the state of Indiana; in which agency he was laboring with great efficiency at the time of his death. He was an able preacher, an amiable man, and respected and beloved in all the relations of life.

REV. ISAAC OWEN.—The life of Isaac Owen is full of instruction. He was a native of Vermont, but came, with his parents, to the territory of Indiana, in 1811. He said: "When I was a boy, we lived in the woods in Knox County. Grist-mills were few and far between. In order to get meal to make our bread, we had to pound the corn in a hominy-mortar, with a pestle. In the Winter season, sometimes having no shoes, I was driven to the expedient of heating blocks of wood to stand upon, in order to keep my feet from the frozen ground, while I pounded the corn to make meal for our bread." His father died in 1824. And yet this boy of the back-woods, fatherless and poor, secured a good education, attained to eminence as a preacher of the Gospel, and did more to found Asbury University in Indiana, and the university in California, than any other man.

At the age of sixteen, young Owen made a profession of religion, and united with the Methodist Episcopal Church; and, in 1834, he was admitted on trial in the Indiana Conference, and sent to Otter-creek Mission. Although he began the active work of the ministry with a very limited education, and an equally limited acquaintance with theology as a science, yet he prosecuted successfully both his literary and theological studies. As soon as he had mastered the grammar of his own language, he took up the study of the Greek, and in a short time his Greek Testament became, and continued to be, his daily companion. He spent fourteen years in the itinerancy in Indiana, four of which were spent as financial agent for Indiana Asbury University; and, during that time, he raised, by the sale of scholarships, over sixty thousand dollars. He was one of the first missionaries to California, and had the honor of preaching, if not the first, among the first, Methodist sermons preached in California. He was the first presiding elder ever appointed in California. Much of Mr. Owens's work was that of a pioneer, and few men were better fitted for such work. His ministry extended through a period of thirty-two years; and in that time he accomplished much for the cause of his Master. As college agent, he not only secured funds for the institution, but he explained to poor young men how they could obtain an education. There are many men in useful and honorable positions, who owe their success to the encouragement they received from Isaac Owen.

Rev. Calvin W. Ruter was among the pioneers of Indiana Methodism. He entered the ministry in the old Ohio Conference in 1818. In the Fall of 1820, he was admitted into full connection, ordained deacon, and transferred to Missouri Conference, and appointed to the charge of Silver-creek Circuit. This was his first introduction to the work in Indiana—a work with which he was to be henceforth identified till the day of his death. Mr. Ruter filled the most important appointments in his Conference through the whole course of his ministry. He was for many years the secretary of his Conference, and represented it in several sessions of the General Conference. He was a man of fine personal presence, dignified and courteous in his bearing. He was an excellent presiding elder, and always popular as a stationed preacher. Impaired health compelled him, on several occasions, to take a supernumerary or a superannuated relation to his Conference. He was postmaster at New Albany for four years, during the administration of James K. Polk; and, at a later period, was Register of the United States Land-office at Indianapolis for four years. But he never compromised his Christian or ministerial character. He died in Switzerland County, in 1859.

Rev. James Jones was a pioneer and hero of early Methodism in the West. He was a native of England, and came to the United States in 1803. In August, 1817, he was licensed to preach by Rev. Moses Crume, Presiding Elder in Ohio Conference. He removed the same year to Indiana, and settled in Rising Sun, where a small class of Methodists had been organized a few years previously, by John Strange. Here he lived and labored as a local preacher till 1820, when he was admitted on trial in the Ohio Annual Conference, and appointed in charge of Whitewater Circuit. After traveling six years, he located, and continued to labor in a local relation until 1834, when he was readmitted into the traveling connection in the Indiana Conference, with which he retained his connection until the time of his death, which occurred on the 7th of November, 1856. He had been attacked by a stroke of paralysis while holding a protracted meeting in 1848, from which he but partially recovered; yet, unwilling to leave the work, he sustained an effective relation until the Fall of 1851, when he reluctantly consented to a superannuated relation, which he sustained until called to his heavenly rest. He was a man of true courage, of indomitable resolution, great perseverance and promptness in filling all of his appointments. He was a man of much prayer and of extraordinary faith. While a local preacher, it was his habit for several years to spend his Winters in New Orleans; and his labors were greatly blessed, on several occasions, in promoting revivals of religion in that city. He was bold in reproving vice. His sympathies were tender as a woman's, and his zeal for the Master's cause was a flame that burned to the close of life.

Rev. Seth Smith died in October, 1843. He had been fifteen years in the ministry, having united with the conference in 1838. The whole of his ministerial life was spent in Indiana. His last appointment was Milton Circuit, in Wayne County. He was blessed with several extensive revivals of religion during his ministry.

In 1853, George M. Beswick closed his ministry. Mr. Beswick was licensed to exhort in his sixteenth year, and to preach in his eighteenth year; and at the age of twenty-two he was admitted on trial in the Indiana Conference, and appointed to Salem Circuit. He traveled circuits in different parts of the state until 1838, when he was appointed to Logansport District. He subsequently traveled Greencastle, Centerville, and Lafayette Districts, and filled several other important appointments in the Church. He was a member of the General Conference of 1852. Of him, Hon. R. W. Thompson said: "He was a man of immense power. Gentle by nature, and accomplished by study and reflection, he bore about him, wherever he went, an air of dignity and decorum which always excited respect; and whatever he said, was uttered with so much propriety and eloquence as to command the closest attention. He always interested and instructed his hearers, and had no superior in the state." At the time of his death he had just been appointed a second time to Greencastle District, after an absence of eight years.

John H. Bruce, of the same Conference, died the same year. At the age of fifteen he was converted, at a camp-meeting, and soon after began to exhort. He was admitted on trial in the Indiana Conference in 1836. He spent seven years on circuits—one as agent of Ft. Wayne College, and the remainder of his ministerial life as presiding elder. He traveled Logansport and Terre Haute Districts. He was a faithful man, and made full proof of his ministry.

The statistics for 1856 were as follows: Indiana Conference, 22,702 members, and 103 traveling preachers; South-eastern Indiana Conference, 19,503 members, and 99 traveling preachers; North Indiana Conference, 20,049 members, and 105 traveling preachers; Northwest Indiana Conference, 14,900 members, and 92 traveling preachers; making a total of 77,154 Church members, and 399 traveling preachers, being an increase in the ministry, in four years, of 65, and a decrease in the membership of 4,301.

The relinquishment of week-day preaching involved the breaking up of the large circuits, and the abandoning of many small societies. Our early circuit system, while it was admirably adapted to carry the Gospel to the whole people, multiplied preaching-places needlessly, and established societies so close together that they must necessarily remain feeble. In many instances they were unwilling to consolidate and unite on some common center of population, where a strong society could be built up; and, as a consequence, during this transition period, many members were lost to the Church. And it is possible that, in some cases, circuits were needlessly reduced, and week-day preaching abandoned sooner than it should have been. But it is an unwise administration that allows churches in the country to be built nearer than four or five miles of each other. With the facilities for getting to church, possessed by our farming population, a mile or two, more or less, in the distance to church, is no object; while, if churches are built closer together, they can not, in the very nature of the case, command congregations of sufficient size to sustain Sabbath preaching, without making church expenses burdensome, or failing to give the ministry an adequate support.

CHAPTER VIII.

Sketch of Samuel C. Cooper—Samuel Brenton—Indiana Conference in 1857—George W. Ames—Transfers—Wm. H. Metts—Time of holding North Indiana Conference changed—Increase in Membership in 1857—North Indiana Conference in 1859—Joseph R. Downey appointed Missionary to India—South-eastern Indiana Conference in 1859—Delegates to General Conference—Indiana Conference Delegates—North-west Indiana Conference Delegates—Churches in Indiana in 1860, from "United States Census Report"—Methodist Liberality—Allen Wiley—His Character and Labors—Sessions of the Indiana Conference down to 1850—Annual Increase of Ministers and Members from the organization of the Conference to 1851—Growth of North Indiana Conference from its organization to 1851—Aggregate Membership in the State in 1850—Number in 1860.

IN 1856, North Indiana lost one of its old and influential members, in the person of Samuel C. Cooper, who closed his earthly pilgrimage on the 19th of July, 1856. Mr. Cooper entered the ministry in 1827. His first appointment was to Cash-river Circuit, in the state of Illinois. The remainder of his appointments were in Indiana. He was for several years an efficient agent for Indiana Asbury University. He was twice a delegate to the General Conference. He was a man of superior business talents, and in secular life would probably have amassed a fortune; but he gave his undivided energy to the Church. His early educational opportunities were poor; but, by reading and observation, he became an instructive preacher. He was a fine executive officer, and a safe counselor.

Samuel Brenton, of the same Conference, died on the 27th of March, 1857. He was a native of Ken-

tucky; born in 1810. He entered the ministry in the
Illinois Conference in 1830, and traveled successively
Paoli, Crawfordsville, and Bloomington Circuits. In
1830, his health having failed, he located, and continued in a local relation until 1841; during which time
he studied law, and was admitted to the bar as a practicing attorney; in which profession he took immediate
rank as an able counselor. In 1844, he re-entered the
itinerancy, and filled important stations, including that
of presiding elder on Fort Wayne District, down to
1848; which year he was elected a delegate to the
General Conference. During this year he had an attack
of paralysis, by which he lost the use of his right side,
and was compelled to resign the pastoral work. And
the same year he was appointed Register of the Land-
office at Fort Wayne. In 1851, he was elected a representative in Congress from the Tenth Congressional
District, and served two sessions. In 1853, he was
elected President of Fort Wayne College, which position
he filled with efficiency. In 1854, he was again elected
to Congress, and re-elected in 1856; but death cut short
his career of honor and usefulness. He was a man of
superior mental power, and his intellectual achievements in his later years, after one-half of his physical
frame was paralyzed, evinced, in a striking manner, the
triumph of mind over matter. He was a true Christian,
and whether in the work of the ministry, or engaged as
a practicing attorney, or as president of a college, or as
a member of the National Congress, he never laid aside
his character, nor compromised his Christian profession.

In October, 1857, Indiana Conference met in New
Albany, Bishop Morris presiding. At this Conference
George W. Ames was entered "withdrawn." He had
been for several years in the ministry, but had not been

especially successful, and, without any avowed change of opinion, but, perhaps, partly from declining health, and partly from not being heartily in sympathy with ministerial work, he withdrew from the connection. Daniel Curry, who had resigned the presidency of Indiana Asbury University, was transferred to New York East Conference. Benjamin F. Crary, who had been elected President of Hamline University, at Red Wing, was transferred to Minnesota Conference. Wm. H. Metts, of the North Indiana Conference, died at Dublin, Indiana, January 20, 1857. He had entered the ministry in 1853. He was a young man of promise, and died in the midst of his usefulness.

In 1856, the North Indiana Conference was changed from a Fall to a Spring Conference—its first Spring session being held in Marion, April, 1857.

In April, 1858, North Indiana Conference held its session in Winchester. The other Indiana Conferences continued to meet in the Fall. The North-west Indiana Conference met that Fall in Valparaiso. Indiana Conference at Mount Vernon, and South-eastern Indiana Conference at Columbus. The increase in the membership during the year had been as follows: North Indiana Conference, 339; North-west Indiana Conference, 2,674; Indiana Conference, 3,509; South-eastern Indiana Conference, 1,599; making a total increase of 8,121.

In the Spring of 1859, North Indiana Conference held its session at Logansport. At this Conference, Joseph R. Downey was appointed missionary to India. In due time he and his young wife sailed for that distant mission field. Downey entered with zeal upon his work, but fell an early victim to the climate. But the graves of Christian missionaries constitute a bond of union between Christian and pagan lands that can never be broken, and enlist the sympathies and efforts of the Church for the universal subjugation of the world to Christ. The dying language of Cox, the early missionary to Africa, "Though a thousand fall, let not Africa be given up," did much toward kindling missionary zeal in the Churches at home.

South-eastern Indiana Conference met in Indianapolis, October, 1859. At this Conference, E. G. Wood, F. C. Holliday, John W. Locke, and John H. Barth were elected delegates to the ensuing General Conference, which was to meet in Buffalo, in May, 1860.

The Indiana Conference held its session in Bloomington, and the delegates elected by the Indiana Conference were: C. B. Davidson, W. C. Smith, John Kiger, and Elias H. Sabin. The delegates from North Indiana Conference were: Cyrus Nutt, John B. Birt, Jacob Colclazer, and Lonson W. Monson. The delegates from North-west Indiana Conference were: John L. Smith, Jacob M. Stallard, Richard Hargrave, and James Johnson.

According to the United States Census Reports for 1860, the churches in Indiana stood as follows:

Baptists—Number of churches, 475; church-sittings, 164,710; value of church property, $430,510.

Baptist (Tunker)—Number of churches, 27; church-sittings, 9,900; value of church property, $25,350.

Christian—Number of churches, 347; church-sittings, 125,600; value of property, $270,515.

Congregational—Number of churches, 11; church-sittings, 5,250; value of property, $42,600.

Dutch Reformed—Number of churches, 6; church-sittings, 1,500; value of property, $7,850.

Episcopal—Number of churches, 29; church-sittings, 10,350; value of property, $117,800.

Friends—Number of churches, 93; church-sittings, 41,330; value of property, $111,650.

German Reformed—Number of churches, 9; church-sittings, 3,800; value of property, $26,600.

Jewish—Number of churches, 2; members, 450; value of property, $8,000.

Lutherans—Number of churches, 150; church-sittings, 46,384; value of property, $237,000.

Moravian—Number of churches, 1; church-sittings, 400; value of property, $3,500.

Presbyterian—Number of churches, 275; church-sittings, 104,195; value of property, $626,435.

Cumberland Presbyterian—Number of churches, 27; church-sittings, 11,270; value of property, $32,200.

Reformed Presbyterian—Number of churches, 8; church-sittings, 3,150; value of property, $16,350.

United Presbyterian—Number of churches, 18; church-sittings, 6,650; value of property, $24,300.

Universalists—Number of churches, 28; church-sittings, 9,130; value of property, $37,850.

Union—Number of churches, 44; church-sittings, 13,022; value of property, $35,804.

Roman Catholics—Number of churches, 127; church-sittings, 57,960; value of property, $665,025.

Methodist—Number of churches, 125; church-sittings, 432,160; value ot property, $1,345,935.

Of the 2,933 churches reported in the state, 1,256 were Methodist churches; and of the $4,065,274 worth of church property in the state, $1,345,935 were owned by the Methodists. A pretty good showing for a denomination that has gloried in preaching the Gospel to the poor, and that had received no foreign aid in the accumulation of its Church property.

The men who, under God, achieved such success for Methodism in Indiana, were, many of them, remarkable men. They were men of large views. They planned for the future, and out of their scanty means they contributed liberally to build up the institutions of the Church; and their example, as well as teaching, encouraged liberality on the part of the Church; and while the Church, as a whole, has, perhaps, failed to come up to the Bible standard of liberality, yet, when we look at the property the Methodist Church has literally created in this comparatively new state, and other annual contributions for Church purposes, it is evident that the upbraidings it sometimes receives for penuriousness is unmerited.

Prominent among those who laid the foundations of Methodism in Indiana, and prominent among its most successful builders, was Allen Wiley. Mr. Wiley was born January 15, 1789, and came to Indiana Territory with his parents in 1804. He joined the Church, as a seeker of religion, in April, 1810, and in the June following obtained the evidence of personal acceptance with God, through faith in Jesus Christ. He was licensed to preach in 1813, and entered the traveling connection, December 1, 1816. He was ordained a deacon by Bishop M'Kendree, in 1818, and an elder by Bishop Roberts, in 1820. He spent eleven years of his ministry in traveling extensive and laborious circuits. He was presiding elder during fourteen years, and a part of that time his district extended from the Ohio River to the vicinity of Lake Michigan, including the present cities of Madison and Ft. Wayne, and required an amount of energy, sacrifice, and toil, of which it is now difficult to conceive. He spent five years as stationed preacher in our larger towns. He served as a delegate in the General Conferences of 1832, 1836, 1840, and 1844. He entered the itinerancy as a married man; he raised and educated a large family; two of his sons became ministers, and one a physician. His early education only included the ordinary branches of an English education, and yet, by continuous study, he became a ripe scholar, familiar with Latin and Greek literature, and a profound theologian. He was an instructive preacher. His sermons were rich in thought, and profound in argument. His voice was heavy and monotonous; and yet, in the days of his vigor, when presiding elder of his large districts, it was no uncommon thing for him, at camp-meetings, to hold an audience of thousands in rapt attention for two hours or more, while he discussed some grand theme of theology. Mr. Wiley planned wisely for the Church. He aided in founding schools; he organized Bible Societies, and labored to promote total abstinence from all intoxicating drinks; he assisted in securing eligible sites for churches, and was one of the founders of Indiana Asbury University. Mr. Wiley owed his great success to his singleness of purpose, his energy, and untiring industry. He evinced, perhaps, more statesmanship in his plans than any of our early preachers. He continued his habits of study to the close of life. Of him, Hon. R. W. Thompson says: " He was unmatched in all those excellences of character which fit a man for the society of the angels. His clear head, sound judgment, great discretion, and acknowledged wisdom, made him like one of the fathers in Israel. And these characteristics were exhibited in all his sermons, which were entirely faultless in style, and distinguished by commanding ability." Mr. Wiley ended his earthly career at Vevay, Indiana, on Sabbath, July 23, 1848, in the fifty-ninth year of his age.

As we have noted elsewhere, Indiana Conference was organized in 1832, being set off from the Illinois Conference by the General Conference of that year. Its sessions, down to 1850, were held at the following times and places:

New Albany, October 17, 1832.
Madison, October 16, 1833.
Centerville, October 22, 1834.
Lafayette, October 14, 1835.
Indianapolis, October 26, 1836.
New Albany, October 25, 1837.
Rockville, October 17, 1838.
Lawrenceburg, October 23, 1839.
Indianapolis, October 21, 1840.
Terre Haute, October 6, 1841.

Centerville, October 19, 1842.
Crawfordsville, October 18, 1843.
Bloomington, October 25, 1844.
Madison, October 8, 1845.
Connersville, October 7, 1846.
Evansville, October 6, 1847.
New Albany, October 4, 1848.
Rising Sun, October 10, 1849.
Jeffersonville, October 9, 1850.
Indianapolis, October 8, 1851.

The following table shows the annual increase in the ministry and the membership, from the organization of the Conference, down to the session of 1851, or to the close of the first half of the present century:

Year.	Members.	Traveling Pr'chers.	Local Pr'chers.	Year.	Members.	Traveling Pr'chers.	Local Pr'ch'rs.
1832	20,035	65	.....	1842	62,942	192	473
1833	23,617	71	.....	1843	67,219	216	488
1834	25,213	73	.....	1844	35,686	110	285
1835	25,476	92	.....	1845	33,673	112	305
1836	28,000	99	333	1846	32,530	119	309
1837	31,058	120	351	1847	30,745	122	309
1838	35,258	139	366	1848	33,262	121	290
1839	43,953	161	412	1849	35,481	137	290
1840	53,033	167	418	1850	37,798	148	290
1841	53,381	177	459	1851	39,271	159	302

In 1844, the Conference was divided into Indiana and North Indiana Conferences, by the National Road, which runs through the center of the state, from east to west. The following table shows the growth of North Indiana Conference, from the time of its organization, down to the session of 1851, that being the last session before the division of the state into four Conferences:

Year.	Members.	Traveling Pr'chers.	Local Pr'chers.	Year.	Members.	Traveling Pr'chers.	Local Pr'ch'rs.
1844	27,343	105	220	1848	27,337	120	282
1845	27,383	110	222	1849	28,683	134	269
1846	27,336	114	267	1850	30,397	149	279
1847	26,302	120	258	1851	32,234	170	288

From these figures, it appears that the growth of the Church was constant from 1832 to 1843; and that from 1838 to 1848, its increase was truly remarkable. From 1843 to 1847, there was a decrease in both of the Conferences, amounting, in the aggregate, to nearly ten thousand. This was doubtless owing in part to the wonderful ingatherings of the few preceding years, and the resulting diminution of effort on the part of the Church.

The aggregate membership in the state, according to these figures, including the preachers, was, in 1850, 72,404. In 1860, the membership was 96,965, being an increase, during the decade, of 24,561

CHAPTER IX.

NOTWITHSTANDING the heavy draft made upon the Church, as well as upon the loyal men of the country at large, by the terrible rebellion and secession of the Slave States, and the consequent civil war that ravaged our country from 1861 until the surrender of the Confederate armies in 1865, the Church in Indiana continued to prosper, and the membership arose from 96,-965 in 1860, to 113,800 in 1870. And the increase in Church improvements, such as churches, parsonages, and school-houses, was even greater than the numerical increase in the membership. Indiana Methodism contributed largely to the suppression of the rebellion. The antislavery doctrines of Methodism, that had been received without dilution or adulteration by the most of our people, would naturally array them on the side of the Government, when the slave power was putting forth all of its efforts for the overthrow of the Government. Loyalty to the civil power, when that power answers the ends for which government is instituted, is a religious duty; and there were but few Methodist pulpits in Indiana but what enforced that duty. Methodist ministers entered the army as chaplains, and some of them as officers and soldiers. The remark of President Lincoln, that "the Methodist Church sent more soldiers into the field, more nurses to the hospitals, and more prayers to Heaven for the preservation of the Union, than any other," was as true of Indiana Methodism as of that of any portion of the loyal states. The resort to arms on the part of the South for the maintenance of slavery, was both unwise and uncalled for. True, the growing opposition of public sentiment in the North to the extension of slavery, taken in connection with the division of the Democratic party, which division was brought about by those who soon became leaders in efforts to divide the Union, insured the election of Mr. Lincoln as a Republican President in 1860, by a plurality 30,000 larger than elected his predecessor. And in the conservative state of Indiana the vote had changed, from a Republican minority of 46,681 to a majority of 5,923. But, although a Republican President was constitutionally elected, the judicial and legislative branches of the Government were in the opposition, and would have continued so throughout his term of office, so that no offensive measures could have passed, and no objectionable Cabinet Ministers be appointed. Even Congress, declared its willingness to incorporate into the Constitution a clause utterly prohibiting interference with slavery in the states. The loyal States, and several of the Slave States, that were as yet hesitating to assume open rebellion, and were trembling in the balance, sent delegates to a Peace Convention, which was presided over by ex-President Tyler, who had betrayed the party that elected him, and afterward obscured his old disgrace by the added crime of treason to his country.

But their efforts were ineffectual. No honorable concessions could satisfy those who had predetermined the destruction of the Government. The South understood better than the North—because it had studied the question more thoroughly—the deep significance of Mr. Lincoln's election. It was an assurance to them that a vitalizing and unifying spirit had moved upon the face of the chaos into which the political parties in the North had crumbled, and that the power of slavery must break, or be broken upon, this new creation. It was an assurance to them that the power, which had not only filled the Presidential chair and courts of law, term after term, but had underreached and overreached, misconstrued and misapplied the Constitution, must go no further. It was an assurance that the proud waves of the barbarism of slavery should roll no further; and here their fury should be stayed. All this was better understood at the South than in the North. For nearly half a century their public men had used every art known to politicians to bring the public into subjection to an oligarchy. Society, through the entire social scale, was prepared for the rebellion, whenever their leaders should say the word. And immediately on the election of Mr. Lincoln that word was said. South Carolina, with assumed dramatic dignity, announced her determination to secede. On the 12th of April, 1861, the telegraph flashed the intelligence through the Union of the bombardment of Fort Sumter. Through the long Saturday that followed, business was at a stand. With bated breath and anxious look all waited for additional news. Telegraph-offices and newspaper bulletin-boards were watched by anxious crowds. Greater events than the bombarding of a single fort, and the capturing of a small but brave garrison, have occurred in the history of our country; but no tidings ever thrilled the heart of the nation like the dispatch that passed along our telegraphic lines at ten o'clock, announcing that "Sumter has fallen." The issue could no longer be evaded—treason or loyalty must triumph. Treason had appealed to the arbitrament of the sword, and from that tribunal loyalty would not shrink; and, though men's faces were pale, and their eyes moist, yet were their hearts brave; and wherever our national banner was unfurled to the sight of our people on that day, it awakened a deeper love for that emblem of liberty and national unity than they had ever felt before. A new meaning seemed to stream from its folds. And when another dispatch came, saying, " Mr. Lincoln will issue a proclamation to-morrow, calling for seventy-five thousand volunteers," wherever the intelligence was received, men cheered and shouted until they were hoarse. Sunday morning dawned; but what a Sabbath! From four hundred Methodist pulpits in Indiana, on that day, prayers went up for the preservation of the Union, the maintenance of the national life, and the suppression of rebellion, at whatever of cost in blood and treasure it might require. And in not a few instances, congregations, pastor and choir, united in singing national songs, which on that day had a sanctity and a significance that they had never possessed before. Indiana's quota of the seventy-five thousand men was six thousand.

Governor Morton's proclamation was the blast of a war-trumpet indeed; and before its echoes had died away along the borders of our state, *fifteen thousand men* stood ready for the war. They were not soldiers, but they were the materials out of which the best class of soldiers were made. Most of them made pecuniary sacrifices, and many of them large ones, to respond to their country's call. They did not stop to count the cost; they stood ready to give all for their country. Among these raw recruits, Methodism was in every regiment, and perhaps every company. But as the war grew in its proportions, and as the draft upon the men and means of the country for the prosecution of the war became greater, religious men in larger proportions gave themselves to the support of the national cause. In many cases, whole Bible-classes from the Sabbath-schools enlisted together. Professors and students left college halls and literary pursuits for the privations of the camp and the perils of the battle-field. While the Churches were generally truly loyal, Methodism was intensely so, and being numerically the largest denomination in the state, contributed more than any other to the strength of the Union cause. The political value of Methodism to the preservation of our national life has not been fully estimated. The Methodist Episcopal Church is in no sense a political Church, and interferes with politics, in any justly objectionable sense, perhaps as little as any of the Churches in the land; and while her members are as free as those of any Church, or of no Church, to declare and advocate their sentiments, yet the Methodist Church has never ignored moral questions because politicians had embodied them in political platforms; and because of her numbers, her antislavery doctrines, and her unswerving loyalty, she has been an important auxiliary in saving the national life; and even her friends have generally underestimated her political value in this respect. Chief Justice Chase remarked, in an address delivered in New York, shortly after the close of the war, that "whatever was valuable or praiseworthy in our institutions, or in our form of government, that survived the Rebellion, was indebted to the Methodist Church." This was uttered in no spirit of disrespect to other Churches, but in view of the facts in the case. Look how this matter stands in our state. There are over 100,000 Methodist communicants in Indiana, including the German Methodists. It is usual, in estimating the whole population, to add three non-communicants for every communicant, as adherents of the Church, and a moment's reflection will convince any one that the estimate is not too high. We then have a Methodist population of 400,000. The proportion of voters to the entire population is as one to six. According to the calculations in the "United States Census for 1860," in the new states and territories, one-fifth of the population were voters. One of the orators of the Revolution said, "We are so many millions—one-fifth of whom are fighting men." The voting population in any community is greater than its fighting population. But that no one may question the basis of our calculation in this estimate, we place the proportion of voters at one in eight of the population, and that gives Methodist voters in Indiana, 50,000. Deduct, for Democrats and possible overestimate, 10,000, and that leaves an unmistakable Union Methodist vote of 40,000. That is to say, take Methodism out of the state, and the election in 1860, when Mr. Lincoln was elected, would have gone against the Union party about 25,000 votes.

On the basis of this same calculation, look at the value of the Methodist Church to the nation. We had in the loyal states, in 1864, one million communicants. Counting non-communicants, we had four millions. This gives five hundred thousand Methodist votes. Mr. Lincoln's popular majority in 1864 was four hundred and six thousand eight hundred and twelve, or less than the Methodist vote by ninety-three thousand one hundred and eighty-eight. Of the more than four hundred pastors in Indiana, there was not one that was not true to the Government during the war. The antagonism of Methodism to slavery, her outspoken testimony on all moral questions, and her numerical strength, constitute her a mighty force in the interests of humanity and of good government. And the loyal men of the nation cheerfully concede the valuable service which Methodism has rendered in saving the life of the nation.

That the Church should have held her own during the terrible years of the Rebellion would have been matter of thankfulness; but her actual progress in all the elements of true prosperity, is an occasion of rejoicing. The drafts made upon the country during the war developed an unprecedented spirit of liberality, which not only carried hospital supplies, sanitary stores, and the ministrations of religion, to the soldiers in the army, but it increased the Churches' contributions in every department of Christian enterprise. The people formed the habit of giving, and of giving with a frequency and a generosity hitherto unknown. And a spirit of Christian activity and zeal was developed by the necessities of the war, as well as a spirit of increased liberality. Christian commissions and Christian associations have been brought into being, or developed into new vigor. Christians of different denominations have been brought into closer union with each other, and denominational jealousies have greatly abated. These are some of the moral compensations of the war.

Methodism has passed through several distinct phases in its progress of development in our state; not in its essential characteristics, but in its modes of operation and its social characteristics, as these have been modified by the improvements of the country and the progress of society. The early circuits were necessarily large, the settlements sparse and often remote from each other, and it was the habit to preach every day in the week. The preacher's duty consisted chiefly in preaching and in meeting the class, which latter duty almost invariably followed that of the sermon. The cabin homes of the early settlers were the only churches, split-bottomed chairs the pulpits, and the mode of worship of the most free and unrestrained character. Our itinerancy brought our preachers in contact with the whole people, and by organizing societies in every neighborhood, as they were enabled to do by the system of week-day preaching, our societies rapidly increased; and while some others were directing their efforts to the towns, and the chief centers of influence, Methodism was spreading over the whole land; and while others were looking after educational trust funds, and the patronage of those in power, Methodism was seeking to get sinners converted, with a single-ness of purpose and a zeal that was truly apostolic. But few of the early founders of Methodism in Indiana took statesmanlike views of the future. They took little thought as to the accumulation of property for the Church. Eligible sites for the erection of churches could have been secured for the asking, or for a nominal consid-eration, from the original proprietors of nearly every town in the state; and yet little thought was bestowed on this subject. The first meeting-houses were built for the accommodation of those who were then members of the societies, with little or no reference to the permanent centers of population; and it so happened that in a few years many of the churches were found to be wrongly located; and as the country became older, and the demand for Sabbath preaching compelled the discontinuance of week-day appointments, many of the churches ceased to be occupied. They were built too close together for Sabbath appointments; and as roads became improved, and farmers found themselves possessed of horses and carriages, as means of conveyance to church, it made but little difference whether the place of worship was one mile or three miles distant from their residence. And yet it was difficult, and in many places impossible, to unite these small country societies and week-day appointments in some common center, for the erection of a larger church, and the permanent establishment of Sabbath preaching. There were sacred associations around nearly every log meeting-house in the land, that made it a sacrifice of feeling to abandon any of them. In them many of the members had been converted; by them were the humble grave-yards, in which their cherished dead slumbered; and there were precious memories that made these rude temples dear to the hearts of the worshipers; and it is not strange that, in the discontinuance of week-day preaching, and the consequent abandonment of some of the country meeting-houses, the Church lost a good many members. But the change was inevitable. Sound judgment is as much needed in the suitable location of churches as in the location of business-houses. As a general rule, it is unwise for any denomination to build its houses of worship in the country, nearer than five miles of each other. If built much nearer, they can not be self-sustaining, and give their pastors a reasonable support, without making the contributions for Church purposes burdensome. In many instances, week-day preaching was doubtless discontinued sooner than it needs to have been, and pastoral visiting did not take the place of week-day preaching as effectively as it should have done, and as was the intention of the Church in making the change; and yet the transition has been made from large pastoral charges to small ones, and from week-day preaching to nearly exclusively Sabbath services, with as little friction as could have been anticipated.

In church architecture, Methodism has undergone a great change. Our first churches, like the homes of the early settlers, were made of logs. The second editions of our houses of worship were usually plain frame or brick buildings, without steeples or bells. Now the finest and most costly Protestant churches in our chief towns are those owned and occupied by the Methodists; their steeples are as high, and their bells as numerous and as rich toned as any; and it is evident that Methodists are investing more money in church-building than the members of any Church among us. And while the Methodist Church has required no high standard of literary qualification as a condition of admittance into the ministry, it has come to pass that in our principal Churches the highest ministerial qualifications are demanded, and that demand is as fully met as in any of our sister Churches. We have also changed our customs in regard to sittings in congregational worship. Formerly the sexes were separated, even of those belonging to the same household, while now not only family, but promiscuous sittings, are allowed, and in many of the churches the seats are pewed. There is a gradual and commendable improvement in the support of the ministry, and in the contributions to the various enterprises of the Church. The vested funds for Church purposes in Indiana amount to $3,650,969.

Each of the conferences has societies for the relief

of superannuated preachers and the widows and orphans of deceased preachers. These societies are in their infancy, and their funds are being rapidly increased. They stand as follows:

Indiana Conference...$15,814
North Indiana Conference... 16,000
North-western Indiana Conference... 10,000
South-eastern Indiana Conference... 12,000

    Total $53,814

PAID FOR MINISTERIAL SUPPORT.

Indiana Conference...$76,203 71
North Indiana Conference.. 88,542 00
South-eastern Indiana Conference..................................... 66,307 04
North-western Indiana Conference..................................... 75,798 00
That part of the Central German Conference included in Indiana 12,003 00

    Total for ministerial support in 1869.........................$318,253 75

BENEVOLENT CONTRIBUTIONS.

Indiana Conference...$11,769 61
North Indiana Conference.. 11,885 48
South-eastern Indiana Conference..................................... 11,080 63
North-western Indiana Conference..................................... 9,701 46
German work in Indiana.. 3,547 20

    Total.. $47,984 38
Ministerial support... 318,253 75

    Total for ministerial support and benevolence.............$366,838 13

METHODISM AND POPULATION.

Population... 1,668,000
Methodists... 113,800

To these are to be added the members of the African Methodist Episcopal Church. Their statistics stand as follows:

Ministers.. 42
Members..2,418
Sabbath-schools.. 31
Officers and teachers... 204
Scholars...1,417

The growth of Methodism among the German population in Indiana has been remarkable. The record of German Methodism in the state is as follows:

Ministers	23
Members	3,214
Churches	47
Value of churches	$83,000
Parsonages	19
Value of parsonages	$22,900
Sunday-schools	42
Officers and teachers	487
Scholars	2,440

The responsibilities of Indiana Methodism, in view of her numbers and resources, are enormous. May she prove equal to her position in the future as in the past!

CHAPTER X.

INDIANA CONFERENCE.

THIS is the Mother Conference in Indiana. It should, in justice, have antedated the organization of the Illinois Conference; but, as we have seen, although the larger share of the membership was in Indiana, the societies in Indiana, Missouri, and Illinois were included in the Illinois Conference, down to 1832. Indiana Conference comprises the south-western part of the state. It numbers 121, of whom fourteen are superannuated. There are seven Presiding Districts, supplied as follows: Indianapolis District—B. F. Rawlins, Presiding Elder; Bloomington District—J. H. Ketcham, Presiding Elder; Vincennes District—John Kiger, Presiding Elder; Evansville District—W. F. Harned, Presiding Elder; Rockport District—W. M. Zaring, Presiding Elder; New

Albany District—John J. Hight, Presiding Elder; Mitchell District—John Walls, Presiding Elder. Members, 25-062; probationers, 3,363; local preachers, 224; churches, 303—value, $614,590; parsonages, 66—value, $117,450; Sunday-schools, 314; officers and teachers, 3,049; scholars, 20,006; volumes in library, 31,730. The superannuated members of the Conference entered the traveling connection at the following dates: John Schrader, 1814; Asa Beck, 1828; W. V. Daniels, 1833; W. C. Smith, 1840; S. Ravenscroft, 1839; C. Cross, 1854; J. C. Smith, 1830; H. S. Dane, 1832; J. Talbott, 1838; E. W. Cadwell, 1842; Silas Rawson, 1837; W. F. Mason, 1850; R. B. Spencer, 1853; M. M. C. Hobbs, 1856.

INDIANA CONFERENCE RETROSPECT.

No.	Date of Session.	Place.	Bishops.	Secretary.
1	October 17, 1832...	New Albany....	J. Soule..........	C. W. Ruter.
2	October 16, 1833...	Madison..........	J. Soule..........	C. W. Ruter.
3	October 22, 1834...	Centerville......	R. R. Roberts...	C. W. Ruter.
4	October 14, 1835...	Lafayette.........	R. R. Roberts...	C. W. Ruter.
5	October 26, 1836...	Indianapolis....	R. R. Roberts...	C. W. Ruter.
6	October 25, 1837...	New Albany....	J. Soule..........	C. W. Ruter.
7	October 17, 1838...	Rockville........	J. Soule..........	J. C. Smith.
8	October 23, 1839...	Lawrenceburg..	J. Soule..........	E. R. Ames.
9	October 21, 1840...	Indianapolis....	J. Soule..........	E. R. Ames.
10	October 6, 1841...	Terre Haute....	R. R. Roberts...	M. Simpson.
11	October 19, 1842...	Centerville......	T. A. Morris.....	M. Simpson.
12	October 18, 1843...	Crawfordsville..	J. O. Andrew...	M. Simpson.
13	September 25, 1844	Bloomington ...	B. Waugh.........	L. W. Berry.
14	October 8, 1845...	Madison..........	T. A. Morris.....	M. Simpson.
15	October 7, 1846...	Connersville....	L. L. Hamline...	M. Simpson.
16	October 6, 1847...	Evansville	B. Waugh.........	M. Simpson.
17	October 4, 1848...	New Albany....	T. A. Morris.....	F. C. Holliday.
18	October 10, 1849...	Rising Sun......	E. S. Janes......	M. Simpson.
19	October 9, 1850...	Jeffersonville...	T. A. Morris.....	M. Simpson.
20	October 8, 1851...	Indianapolis....	B. Waugh.........	M. Simpson.
21	October, 1852........	Bedford..........	O. C. Baker......	L. W. Berry.
22	October 29, 1853...	Evansville	E. R. Ames......	L. W. Berry.
23	September 13, 1854	New Albany....	E. R. Ames......	L. W. Berry.
24	September 12, 1855	Vincennes	M. Simpson......	T. H. Sinex.
25	September 3, 1856	Greencastle.....	B. Waugh.........	Daniel Curry.
26	October 1, 1857...	New Albany....	T. A. Morris.....	W. M. Hester.
27	September 30, 1858	Mount Vernon..	E. S. Janes......	W. M. Hester.
28	October 5, 1859...	Bloomington ...	L. Scott..........	W. M. Hester.
29	September 26, 1860	Sullivan	O. C. Baker......	W. M. Hester.

No.	Date of Session.	Place.	Bishops.	Secretary.
30	September 25, 1861	Rockport	M. Simpson......	W. M. Hester.
31	September 24, 1862	Greencastle.....	E. R. Ames......	John Laverty.
32	September 16, 1863	Washington.....	T. A. Morris.....	John Laverty.
33	September 26, 1864	Princeton	M. Simpson......	B. F. Rawlins.
34	September 14, 1865	New Albany....	L. Scott...........	J. J. Hight.
35	September 12, 1866	Vincennes......	E. Thomson......	S. Bowers.
36	September 11, 1867	Indianapolis....	T. A. Morris.....	S. Bowers.
37	September 16, 1868	Bedford..........	C. Kingsley.....	S. Bowers.
38	September 8, 1869	Evansville.......	E. R. Ames......	S. Bowers.
39	August 31, 1870.....	Bloomington ...	M. Simpson......	S. Bowers.
40	September 13, 1871	New Albany....	L. Scott...........	S. L. Binkley.

NORTH INDIANA CONFERENCE.

This Conference, embracing the north-east quarter of the state, is composed of 153 members, including fourteen superannuates, and eleven probationers. The work is divided into eight presiding elders' districts, with the following elders in charge of them: Anderson District—W. H. Goode, Presiding Elder; Richmond District—M. Mahin, Presiding Elder; Muncie District—N. H. Phillips, Presiding Elder; Logansport District — V. M. Beamer, Presiding Elder; Fort Wayne District—W. S. Birch, Presiding Elder; West Fort Wayne District—H. N. Barnes, Presiding Elder; Warsaw District—L. W. Monson, Presiding Elder; Goshen District—H. J. Meck, Presiding Elder. Besides the ministers appointed to pastoral charges, Rev. Thomas Bowman, D. D., is President of Indiana Asbury University; Rev. J. B. Robinson, President of Fort Wayne College; Rev. R. Toby, Agent for Fort Wayne College; and Rev. C. Martindale, Agent for the State Temperance Alliance. Church members, 24,718; probationers, 6,231; local preachers, 273; Sabbath-schools, 366; officers and teachers, 4,119; scholars, 27,340; churches, 345—value, $762,375; parsonages, 87—value, $122,930. Of the fourteen superannuated

F.E. Jones Sc

Affectionately,

Wm H. Goode

preachers on their list, they entered the ministry as follows: Robert Burns, in 1826; G. C. Beeks, Jacob Colclazer, and H. B. Beers, in 1836; G. W. Bowers, in 1837; Jacob Whiteman, in 1841; E. Maynard, in 1845; B. Smith and J. W. Welch, in 1851; J. Maffit, in 1853; and L. J. Templin, in 1858.

NORTH INDIANA CONFERENCE RETROSPECT.

No.	Date of Session.	Place.	Bishops.	Principal Secretary.
1	Oct. 16–21, 1844............	Fort Wayne....	Waugh...	M. Simpson.
2	Sept. 24–29, 1845.........	Lafayette.......	Hamline	S. T. Gillett.
3	Sept. 16–22, 1846.........	Laporte.........	Morris...	S. T. Gillett.
4	Sept. 15–22, 1847.........	Indianapolis....	Janes.....	S. T. Gillett.
5	Sept. 6–11, 1848.........	Greencastle....	Hamline	S. T. Gillett.
6	Aug. 29—Sept. 4, 1849...	Logansport	Waugh...	John C. Smith.
7	Aug. 21–26, 1850.........	Cambridge City	Janes.....	J. C. Smith.
8	Aug. 20–27, 1851.........	South Bend.....	Morris...	S. T. Gillett.
9	Sept. 20–28, 1852.........	Fort Wayne.....	Baker.....	S. T. Gillett.
10	Sept. 21–24, 1853.........	Richmond......	Ames.....	C. Nutt.
11	Sept. 20–23, 1854.........	Peru.............	Simpson.	C. Nutt.
12	Sept. 14–19, 1855.........	Goshen	Scott......	C. Nutt.
13	Sept. 24–29, 1856.........	Muncie..........	Baker....	H. N. Barnes.
14	April 8–11, 1857...........	Marion	Simpson.	H. N. Barnes.
15	April 7–14, 1858...........	Winchester.....	Ames.....	J. C. Medsker.
16	April 7–11, 1859...........	Logansport.....	Morris...	H. N. Barnes.
17	April 5–9, 1860............	Mishawaka......	Ames.....	A. Greenman.
18	April 3–8, 1861............	Newcastle	Janes.....	H. N. Barnes.
19	April 10–15, 1862.........	Fort Wayne....	Simpson.	M. Mahin.
20	April 9–13, 1863...........	Wabash.........	Morris...	M. Mahin.
21	April 6–11, 1864...........	Knightstown...	Morris...	M. Mahin.
22	April 12–17, 1865.........	Kendallville....	Scott......	M. Mahin.
23	April 5–9, 1866............	Peru.............	Clark.....	M. Mahin.
24	April 10–15, 1867.........	Anderson.......	Ames.....	M. Mahin.
25	April 15–20, 1868.........	Warsaw.........	Thomson	M. Mahin.
26	April 15–19, 1869.........	Richmond......	Simpson.	M. Mahin.
27	April 13–18, 1870.........	Kokomo.........	Clark.....	M.H. Mendenhall
28	April 12–17, 1871.........	Huntington.....	Ames.....	M.H. Mendenhall

SOUTH-EASTERN INDIANA CONFERENCE.

THIS Conference, as its name imports, includes the south-eastern portion of the state. The statistics are as follows: members, 21,118; probationers, 2,235; local preachers, 151; churches, 283—value, $701,938; parsonages, 48—value, $47,900; Sabbath-schools, 293; officers and teachers, 3,285; scholars, 20,105; volumes in Sunday-school libraries, 31,039 ; aggregate of benevolent contributions for the year, $11,080.63 ; traveling preachers, 115, including 17 superannuates. The charges are embraced in five presiding elders' districts, which are in charge of the following elders : Indianapolis District— R. D. Robinson, Presiding Elder; Connersville District—F. A. Hester, Presiding Elder; Lawrenceburg District—J. B. Lathrop, Presiding Elder; Madison District—W. Terrell, Presiding Elder; Jeffersonville District—E. G. Wood, Presiding Elder. Of the seventeen superannuated whose names are on the roll of the Conference, they entered the ministry as follows : John Miller, in 1823; Joseph Marsee, in 1826; Joseph Tarkington, in 1825; John A. Brouse, in 1833 ; Thomas Ray, in 1833; Lewis Hurlbut, in 1834 ; Asbury Wilkinson, in 1840; Elijah Whitten, in 1832; Isaac H. Tomlinson, in 1861; N. F. Tower, in 1846 ; M. A. Ruter, in 1841 ; H. Richardson, in 1850; D. Stiver, in 1832; Samuel Weeks, in 1838; A. Kennedy, in 1859; W. Long, in 1849; John W. Dole, in 1835. But few of these entered the ministry in Indiana, but by the working of our itinerant system they became members of the Southeastern Indiana Conference, and they are beloved for their work's sake.

SOUTH-EASTERN INDIANA CONFERENCE RETROSPECT.

No.	Date of Session.	Place.	Bishops.	Principal Secretary.
1	October 6, 1852.....	Rushville........	O. C. Baker...	F. C. Holliday.
2	October 5, 1853.....	Brookville	E. R. Ames...	S. P. Crawford.
3	September 28, 1854	Greensburg	M. Simpson...	J. W. Locke.
4	September 27, 1855	Shelbyville......	L. Scott........	T. H. Lynch.
5	September 17, 1856	Madison..........	B. Waugh.....	J. W. Locke.
6	September 23, 1857	Aurora...........	T. A. Morris..	W. W. Hibben.
7	September 22, 1858	Columbus.......	E. S. Janes...	W. W. Snyder.
8	September 28, 1859	Indianapolis....	L. Scott........	W. W. Snyder.
9	September 20, 1860	Lawrenceburg..	O. C. Baker...	T. G. Beharrell.
10	September 18, 1861	Jeffersonville ...	T. A. Morris..	T. G. Beharrell.
11	September 17, 1862	Greensburg.....	E. R. Ames...	J. W. Locke.

No.	Date of Session.	Place.	Bishops.	Principal Secretary.
12	September 16, 1863	Columbus........	O. C. Baker...	J. B. Lathrop.
13	September 21, 1864	Shelbyville......	M. Simpson...	J. B. Lathrop.
14	September 20, 1865	Madison..........	T. A. Morris..	J. B. Lathrop.
15	September 19, 1866	Aurora............	E. S. Janes...	Geo. L. Curtis.
16	September 11, 1867	Connersville.:...	L. Scott.......	Geo. L. Curtis.
17	September 10, 1868	Franklin.........	D. W. Clark..	Geo. L. Curtis.
18	September 15, 1869	Indianapolis. ...	M. Simpson...	Geo. L. Curtis.
19	September 7, 1870	Brookville	L. Scott.......	Geo. L. Curtis.
20	September 6, 1871	Jeffersonville..	L. Scott.......	Geo. L. Curtis.

NORTH-WEST INDIANA CONFERENCE.

The North-west Indiana Conference comprises, as its name imports, the north-west portion of the state. The Conference was organized in 1852, when the state was divided into four conferences, and held its first session in Terre Haute, in September, 1852, at which Bishop Baker presided. The Conference numbers 133, including those on trial, and those on the superannuated list. The superannuates are : Jacob M. Stallard, George Guild, Moses Blackstock, G. W. Hamilton, H. S. Shaw, W. J. Forbes, J. White, H. Smith, J. Ricketts, J. Edwards, W. Copp, P. I. Beswick, D. Shankwiler, John Leach, Miles H. Wood, W. H. Smith, J. B. Gray, David Crawford, John S. Donaldson, Michael Johnson, B. W. Smith. For 1871, the work was comprised in the following districts, which were under the care of the following elders : Lafayette District—J. H. Hull, Presiding Elder ; Terre Haute District—William Graham, Presiding Elder ; Greencastle District—S. Godfrey, Presiding Elder ; Crawfordsville District—John L. Smith, Presiding Elder ; East Lafayette District—I. W. Joyce, Presiding Elder ; Battleground District—J. W. T. M'Mullen, Presiding Elder ; Valparaiso District—W. R. Mikels, Presiding Elder ; Laporte District—L. Nebeker, Presiding Elder ; communicants, 19,531 ; local preachers, 198 ; Sunday-

schools, 285; officers and teachers, 2,916; scholars, 19,-
835. Besides the interest the Conference has in Asbury
University, it has under its care, Stockwell Collegiate Institute, and Battleground Institute, besides a good school
at Valparaiso, more or less under the care of the Conference. Two members of the Conference, to wit, H. B.
Jackson and Thomas B. Wood, are missionaries to South
America.

NORTH-WEST INDIANA CONFERENCE RETROSPECT.

No.	Date of Session.	Place.	Bishops.	Secretary.
1	September 8, 1852	Terre Haute....	Baker............	Luther Taylor.
2	September 7, 1853	Attica............	Ames.	Wm. Graham.
3	September 6, 1854	Laporte..........	Simpson	Wm. Graham.
4	August 28, 1855....	Delphi............	Ames.............	B. H. Nadal.
5	October 8, 1856....	Crawfordsville..	Janes	B. H. Nadal.
6	October 1, 1857.....	Lafayette........	Waugh	Joseph C. Reed.
7	September 29, 1858	Valparaiso	Ames.............	J. C. Reed.
8	September 29, 1859	Greencastle	Morris	J. C. Reed.
9	October 11, 1860...	Terre Haute....	Simpson.........	J. C. Reed.
10	October 10, 1861...	South Bend.....	Simpson.........	Clark Skinner.
11	October 9, 1862...	Lafayette	Scott.............	J. C. Reed.
12	September 30, 1863	Michigan City..	Morris	J. C. Reed.
13	September 7, 1864	Delphi	Baker............	Wm. Graham.
14	September 6, 1865	Attica............	Scott.............	Wm. Graham.
15	August 29, 1866....	Laporte..........	Ames	Wm. Graham.
16	September 11, 1867	Danville	Janes	Wm. Graham.
17	September 30, 1868	Valparaiso......	Thomson........	Clark Skinner.
18	September 8, 1869	Lafayette	Clark	C. Skinner.
19	September 7, 1870	Terre Haute....	Simpson	J. C. Reed.
20	September 6, 1871	Crawfordsville..	Ames.............	J. C. Reed.

CHAPTER XI.

Sabbath-school Cause—Sabbath-school organized by Bishop Asbury in 1786—Resolutions passed by the General Conference of 1824—Organization of the "Sunday-school Union of the Methodist Episcopal Church"—"Sunday-School Advocate" established—Sunday-school Convention in 1844—Superintendents admitted into the Quarterly Conference—Rules of the Discipline on Sunday-schools in 1861— Sunday-schools in Indiana—Statistics.

SABBATH-SCHOOL CAUSE.

METHODISM early fostered the work of Sabbath-school instruction, both in England and in America. It is interesting to note the growth of the Sunday-school idea in the Church, and to mark the different stages of its development. The Methodist Episcopal Church was the first to give the Sabbath-school cause a distinct and direct ecclesiastical recognition in this country. This she did only six years after her organization. In 1790, we find this question asked in the Minutes of the Conference: "What can be done in order to instruct poor children, white and black, to read?" The answer was, "Let us labor, as the heart and soul of one man, to establish Sunday-schools in or near the place of public worship; let persons be appointed by the bishops, elders, deacons, or preachers, to teach gratis all that will attend, and have a capacity to learn, from six in the morning till ten, and from two o'clock in the afternoon till six, where it does not interfere with public worship." Previous to this date, children's classes for religious instruction were authorized. In 1784, in the first Discipline in our Church, the question is asked, "What shall we do for the rising generation?" and one of the answers given was, "Where there are ten children, whose parents are in the Society, meet them at least one hour each week." In 1786, Bishop Asbury organized a Sabbath-school in the house of Thomas Crenshaw, in Hanover County, Virginia. This was, perhaps, the first regularly organized Sabbath-school in America.

To what extent the official exhortation of 1790 was heeded, we can not say; but for teachers to volunteer to teach on the Sabbath, from six until ten in the forenoon, and from two until six in the afternoon, would be more than could be reasonably expected; and the confinement was such that but few children would submit to it, who were allowed any discretion in the matter at all. The schools were intended, chiefly, for the benefit of the poor, and for their instruction in the rudiments of secular learning. The Sunday-school idea was being gradually developed in the mind of the Church, and accordingly we find that the General Conference of 1824 passed three resolutions on the subject of Sunday-schools. It was made the duty of each preacher to encourage the establishment and progress of Sunday-schools. Arrangements were made for the compilation of a catechism for the use of Sunday-schools, and of children in general. The Book Agents were instructed "to provide and keep on hand a good assortment of books suitable for the use of Sunday-schools." By this time the Church had outgrown the idea that Sunday-schools were intended for the instruction of the children of the poor. The schools had lost much of their secular character, and were gradually assuming that religious cast by which they are now chiefly distinguished. All limitations were taken off, and it was made a part of every traveling preacher's official duty to encourage the organization of Sunday-schools.

In 1827, the Sunday-school Union of the Methodist Episcopal Church was organized in the city of New York; and henceforth the Sabbath-school institution with us assumes more of a Churchly character. The preachers are charged " to aid in the instruction of the rising generation, particularly in the knowledge of the Scriptures, and in the service and worship of God." These schools are no longer devoted, chiefly, to imparting secular instruction, nor for the exclusive benefit of the children of the poor; but they are still schools for children. In 1828, the Discipline made it the duty of every preacher, to form Sunday-schools. In 1832, it was made the duty of presiding elders to "promote Sunday-schools, and of the preacher in charge to report the statistics of his Sunday-schools to the last quarterly conference of the conference year, and also to the annual conference." In 1840, the rules relating to Sunday-schools were entirely remodeled. It was made the duty of the presiding elder carefully to inquire, at each quarterly conference, if the rules for the instruction of children have been faithfully observed. The preachers are charged to visit the Sabbath-schools as often as practicable; to preach on the subject of Sunday-schools and of religious instruction in each congregation, at least once in six months, and to form Bible classes " for the instruction of larger children and youth." Sunday-school teaching was no longer confined to little children. " Larger children and youth" are now included, and Bible-classes are organized for their instruction. In 1840, the Sunday-school Union was reorganized, and brought more directly under the control of the Church. In 1841, the child's paper, now so widely known as the *Sunday-School Advocate*, was established. During the session of the General Conference, in 1844, a Sunday-school convention met in the city of

New York, "for the purpose of adopting measures more efficiently to advance the cause of Sabbath-school instruction throughout the Methodist Episcopal Church." This convention recommended to the General Conference the organizing of "a distinct and separate department for the editing and publishing of Sunday-school books." It recommended a competent editor for the Sunday-school department, and requested that the Discipline be so amended as to make Sunday-school superintendents members of the quarterly conference. All of the recommendations but the last one were adopted. In 1856, Sunday school superintendents were, by the Discipline, recognized as members of the quarterly conference. In 1852, male superintendents, being members of our Church, were admitted to the quarterly conferences, "with the right to speak and vote on questions relating to Sunday-schools, and on such questions only." It was not until 1856 that these restrictions were taken off, and the Sunday-school became fully incorporated into the working forces of the Church. In 1860, the addition of a single word in the Discipline shows the further progress of the Sunday-school idea in the mind of the Church. The word "adults" was now added, so that the rule should read, "to form Bible classes for the larger children, youth, and adults." This marks an advance worthy of special notice. At first, Sunday-schools were intended for the children of the poor; next, they were to include all of the children, whether rich or poor; after the lapse of a few years, "larger children and youth" are considered worthy of special mention; and at last the Sunday-school idea becomes so expanded as to embrace adults as well as children and youth; and now the recognized idea of the Sunday-school is, the Bible school for the whole congregation, parents as well as children.

The Sunday-school movement has not only created a juvenile literature of the most instructive and attractive kind, but it has modified the general literature of our times, and is training 1,220,000 scholars, in connection with our own Church, in the lessons prepared by our Sunday-school Union for the training of our Sunday-schools. And the prevalence of Sunday-school institutes, and the extent to which maps and the blackboard are used in our schools, shows the substantial progress that is being made in this department of religious culture.

From this brief survey of the history of the Sunday-school cause among us as a denomination, it is seen that the institution was in vigorous growth at the time when Methodism was being introduced into Indiana. But where the societies where small, the population sparse and poor (as was the case with most of the early settlements in Indiana), Sabbath-schools could not be readily kept up. But as soon as towns sprung up, and permanent societies were formed, Sabbath-schools were organized, and Sabbath-school instruction became a legitimate part of Church work. In the country, the organization of Sunday-schools dates with the discontinuance of week-day preaching, as a general rule. As the large circuits were divided, pastoral charges made less, and preaching confined to the Sabbath-day, the preachers had more leisure for pastoral duties; and in obedience to the instructions of the Church, they bestowed increased attention upon the religious instruction of the children, and upon establishing and building up the Sabbath-schools. At an early day in the history of Sunday-schools, the needed requisites, such as class-books, question-books, books of instruction, maps, and suitable library-books, could not be obtained; but now they are abundant and cheap, and the Methodist Churches in Indiana pay annually, for the maintenance of their Sabbath-schools, more than $20,000; and few investments pay so well. The Sunday-school statistics for the year 1870 were as follows: Schools, 1,312; officers and teachers, 13,996; scholars, 92,223.

CHAPTER XII.

Methodism in some of the Principal Towns—JEFFERSONVILLE ; by Rev. R. Curran, M. D.—First Society formed—First Quarterly Meeting held—First Church built—Celebration of the Centenary of Methodism—Present Statistics—NEW ALBANY—First Church built—Number of Churches at present—De Pauw College—RICHMOND ; by Rev. Thomas Comstock—Settlement of Wayne County—Whitewater Circuit formed—First Church built—First Camp-meeting—Introduction of Methodism into Richmond—Present State of the Churches—INDIANAPOLIS—First Place of Worship in Indianapolis—Mention of Prominent Methodists—Relative Strength of the Churches in the City—List of Appointments from 1821 to 1842—WASHINGTON, Daviess County—First Church built—LAFAYETTE ; by Rev. N. L. Brakeman—First Methodist Sermon—Church organized in Lafayette—Present Strength of Methodism—SOUTH BEND—Account of John Brownfield, Esq.—First Prayer-meeting—First Sunday-school—Church built—Enterprise of "Ladies' Mite Society"—Value of Church Property—ANDERSON ; by Rev. W. H. Goode, D. D.—First House of Worship—Present Church Buildings—PERU—First Class formed—First Church built—TERRE HAUTE—First Mention in the Minutes—Anecdote of Mrs. Locke—METHODISM IN TERRE HAUTE ; by Col. Thomas Dowling—First Church Organization—Present Church erected—Early State of Society—Present Statistics—MADISON—Early Methodists—Church Statistics—VINCENNES—Value of Property—Number of Members—FORT WAYNE—First Class formed—First Sunday-school—Fort Wayne College—Names of Presidents—EVANSVILLE—Circuit Preaching established—Present Charges—Statistics.

HISTORY OF METHODISM IN SOME OF THE TOWNS AND CITIES OF THE STATE.

JEFFERSONVILLE.

BY REV. R. CURRAN, M. D.

THE first society seems to have been organized about A. D. 1807, by some minister, or perhaps a local preacher, from Kentucky. The first official recognition of this society seems to have occurred about A. D. 1810, under the ministry of the Rev. Sely Payne, who traveled Silver-creek Circuit that year, which embraced Jefferson-ville. The first society in Jeffersonville was composed of the following persons, to wit: Mr. Beman, L. P., class-leader; Mrs. Beman, Stephen Beman, Lyman Be-man, Mary Toville, afterward Mary Taylor, Davis Floyd, Mary Floyd, Richard Mosely, Samuel Lampton, Charlotte Lampton, Mrs. Leatherman. There may have been other names on the old class-paper at that time, but that important document having long since disappeared, with other records, the above are all the names which can be identified at this late day. Father Beman seems to have been an earnest, humble Christian; a good represent-ative of the Methodists of his time. The old members, two or three of whom lingered among us to a late period, spoke with enthusiasm of the happy times their little band enjoyed under his faithful leadership. Thus the good seed was sown which has since sprung up, resulting in a glorious harvest.

In consulting the old records of the Silver-creek Cir-cuit, the following items were thought worthy of being transcribed: At a quarterly meeting held at Charles-town, January 10, 1810, the Jeffersonville society is credited with fifty cents quarterage. At the first quar-terly-meeting in 1811, the amount was $1.25. At the first quarterly-meeting in 1812, it had advanced to the sum of $2. The first quarterly-meeting for Jefferson-ville was held March 11 and 12, A. D. 1815. Charles Holliday was presiding elder, and Shadrach Ruark and James Garver were circuit-preachers. The circuit-preachers at this quarterly-meeting received each $15.97, and presiding elder nothing. This was truly the day of small things. Still the holy men labored on through poverty and obloquy, rejoicing in their work, and contented if they might win souls for Christ. They have entered into their reward, and we are still enjoying the blessed fruits of their self-sacrificing and faithful labors.

The spirit of primitive Methodism was well represented for many years in this society, especially by the female members, who had united with the society in its infancy. Among these may be mentioned Anna Tuley, who still lingers on the shores of time, standing as a way-mark—a bright example of Christian meekness and patience, like her ancient namesake, waiting in the temple, looking for the appearing of her Lord. There were also Polly Taylor, Anna Wright, and Elizabeth Jackson. These three sisters lived in the enjoyment of glorious religious experience to the close of life. For a long series of years, on entering the Wall-street Methodist Episcopal Church, the first object that greeted the sight was these three sisters, attired in costume severely plain, occupying a slip near the pulpit; and they were rarely absent from the house of God. Their tender, sisterly love for each other, no less than their constant Christian zeal and exemplary walk, was a sight beautiful to behold. Many a minister has been made to feel the cheering and sustaining influence of their presence and intercessions while delivering his Gospel message. They have passed from the Church militant to the Church triumphant. Among the earlier class-leaders, we find the names of Andrew Fite, James Keigwin, Charles Sleed.

HISTORY OF CHURCH PROPERTY.

THE first record or notice of Church property belonging to the society, is found in a letter, on file, from Rev. William Shanks, Presiding Elder, to James Keigwin, Charles Sleed, Andrew Fite, David Grisamore, Aaron

Applegate, and Nelson Rozzle, dated at New Albany, Indiana, June 22, 1833, as follows:

"DEAR BRETHREN,—Being informed by Brother Ames that it is necessary to appoint trustees for the Church in Jeffersonville, and the Discipline making it the duty of the presiding elder or preacher-in-charge to appoint trustees when and where the Church may need them, I do appoint you to fill the office of trustees, according to the Discipline of the Methodist Episcopal Church.

"WILLIAM SHANKS, Presiding Elder."

The certificate on the back of this paper runs thus:

"Came into the office June 25, 1833; recorded in book A, 2d volume, page 254, number 28.

"JOHN DOUTHETT, R. C. C.

["*Gratis.*"]

Two of these trustees lived in the country, as there were not a sufficient number of male members in town to constitute a board.

The time of the building of the first church on Wall Street will be indicated by the following memoranda. Having been informed that James Keigwin, one of the trustees, had done most of the work on the Church, and perhaps had full knowledge of all the particulars, I addressed a note to him, a short time before his death, asking him to communicate any information he might possess upon the subject. The following is a copy of the letter, in reply to my inquiries:

"LOUISVILLE, *September* 10, 1860.

"DR. CURRAN,—*Dear Sir:* At your request, I herewith submit a statement of facts in regard to the Methodist church in Jeffersonville, of which I agreed to do the brick-work as my subscription toward building the same, which, at the customary prices of the time, amounted to $516.28; but after the foundation was laid, ready for the joists, I found the building would be stopped unless I procured them myself, which I did. Below, you will find a statement.

"AMOUNT OVER REGULAR SUBSCRIPTION.

1833. November 13—To Mr. Young's Bill	$48	03½
" 13—To James Ridge, for Plank	5	28
" 13—To two boxes Glass	8	00
1834. December 9—To turning Column and Plank	10	15
1835. June 22—To making five Window-frames	6	56¼
" 30—To Messrs. Ames and King's Bill	19	20
Recording Deed	1	00
One-third of E. Tulley's Carpenter's Bill	16	00
	114	22¾
Add amount for Brick-work	516	28½
Total	$630	51¼

"JAMES KEIGWIN."

This record shows that the old church was not finished until the Summer of 1835. When the question of building the present church was first agitated, there was a conflict of opinion about the place of its location. After a free discussion of the subject by the whole Church, the present location was unanimously agreed upon; the ground being doubly consecrated, having been occupied by the private residence in which the first society was organized and afterward met. The lecture-room of this church was dedicated to the service of Almighty God by the Rev. Thomas Bowman, D. D., President of Indiana Asbury University, April 22, 1860. On the 16th day of July, 1865, the main audience-room of the Wall-street Methodist Episcopal Church was dedicated to the service of God, by the Rev. T. M. Eddy, D. D., in the use of our beautiful ritual. The Wall-street Church, true to her traditional loyalty to the advice and counsel of our highest Church authorities, with regard to the celebration of the Centenary of American Methodism, labored to carry out the programme as nearly as possible. It is well known we have no rich men in our Church here, and yet we think the offering was not to be despised. We here give a statement of the aggregated amount:

For Centenary Educational Fund	$40 00
Garrett Biblical Institute	10 00
Irish Connectional Fund	25 00
Sunday-school Children's Fund	16 00
Indiana Asbury University	1,012 00
Moore's Hill College	147 00
Public Collection	7 25
Total	$1,259 25

PRESENT STATISTICS.

Population of Jeffersonville	7,209
Full Members in Wall-street	425
Probationers	75
Port Fulton Population	649
Full Members	72
Probationers	14

NEW ALBANY.

METHODISM was organized in New Albany in 1817. The first church was built in 1818, and dedicated by Rev. John Schrader. The sacrament of the Lord's-supper was administered, for the first time in New Albany, by Rev. John Schrader, in 1817. The service was held in a tavern kept by Mrs. Hannah Ruff. Now the Methodists have the following churches: Wesley Chapel, Centenary, Roberts, M'Kendree, and John-street, with an aggregate membership of over 1,400. De Pauw College, for young ladies, is an ornament to the city, a credit to Methodism, and an honor to the large-hearted Christian gentleman whose name it bears. New Albany Methodism is more expansive at present than at any former time. She is now establishing three mission churches in the city—one under the care of Wesley Chapel, to cost $1,200, and two under the care of Centenary Church. Hon. W. C. De Pauw, to whom the Church is indebted for numerous liberal donations, has recently purchased the old St. Paul's Episcopal Church, removed it to the eastern part of the city, and refitted it, at a cost of $2,500, including the lot. The Churches give indications of growing zeal, and a prosperous future.

METHODISM IN RICHMOND AND VICINITY.

BY REV. THOMAS COMSTOCK.

At the treaty of Greenville a large portion of territory was purchased from the Indians, extending from the mouth of the Kentucky River (opposite Madison) to Fort Recovery, now situated in the edge of Ohio, about midway of the eastern boundary of the state—all of which territory belonged to Dearborn County, Indiana Territory. The first settlement in that portion of it which was afterward Wayne County, began in 1804.

Methodism, "the child of Providence," anticipating the moral necessities of the people, as well as the permanent growth of the country, recognizing the voice of the living God in the "Go ye into all the world," of Jesus, kept pace with the westward march of empire.

Rev. Hugh Cull, a local preacher, born of Roman Catholic parents in Havre-de-Grace, Maryland, October, 1757, removed, with his father, to the Redstone country, Pennsylvania, in 1763, and to the place on which Lexington, Kentucky, now stands, in 1777; thence to Henry County, Kentucky, in 1785, where he married Miss Rachel Meek, a devoted Methodist girl of sixteen, through whose consistent Christian life, under Christ, he was brought to feel the need of a Savior, found peace in believing, and in a few months was licensed to preach. Feeling the wrongs and oppression of slavery, and

having no hope that Kentucky would ever become a
free state, he resolved to go North, and, if possible, either
get beyond the latitude where the institution would be
profitable, or where the moral atmosphere would extir-
pate the evil.   In 1804, he entered one hundred and
sixty acres of land four and a half miles south of where
Richmond now stands; and, in 1805, moved his family,
consisting of his wife and Patience, her niece, upon it;
where they all sojourned until, one by one, the Master
called for them.

A few months afterward, he dreamed that a Methodist preacher rode up to his tent; and, on the following day, while he and his wife were picking and burning brush, they saw a stranger approaching on horseback.   Mr. Cull said to his wife, "Rachel, there's the
preacher;" and throwing down his load of brush, he
made for the stranger, grasped his hand, and inquired
if he was not a Methodist preacher.   It was no other
than Rev. Arthur W. Elliott, who had heard that there
was a settlement forming somewhere in the upper Whitewater country, and had come across from Hamilton,
Ohio, through the woods, without a road, to spy out the
country for Christ.   Though they were strangers in the
flesh, the meeting was not unlike that of Jonathan and
David.   Providentially, Mr. Elliott was directed through
the wilderness to a Methodist family singularly prepared
by the Lord to receive him, whose expectation being
that of the righteous, could not perish.   He was welcome to their hospitalities, and invited to share a place
in their earthly mansion, which never lacked room and
other accommodations for a servant of God, though it
was only six feet high, covered with bark, without
window or floor, Brussels carpet, or even a split-bottomed chair, or any other furnishing or furniture, which

"she that layeth her hands to the spindle, and her hands hold the distaff," or the woodman with his ax, had not made, with only three sides, sugar-camp like, having an open front; yet it contained all the essentials of an earthly paradise, made and fashioned after the pattern of the heavenly, "the light of the world" shining into it, being filled with the love of Christ in the hearts of its possessors. Mr. Cull, after providing for his guest and weary creature, hastened over the settlement and announced the "glad tidings" of preaching at his house on the next day. His neighbors came from several miles around, to the number of twelve or fifteen, and listened to the first sermon ever preached in that region of country. After preaching, there being no class to lead, and believing in sowing with one hand and reaping with the other, he proceeded, in apostolical, Methodistic style, to organize a Church out of the handful of hearers. The invitation was given, and six persons came forward, and were formed into a Church-class, with Mr. Cull as their leader. They were, Rev. Hugh and Mrs. Rachel Cull, Peter and Mrs. Martha Weaver, Jacob and Mrs. Nellie Meek; and afterward met regularly for preaching, class and prayer meetings, at Mr. Cull's.

The new society, thus formed, was favored with regular preaching, at rather long intervals, if judged by the present, from Mr. Elliott, during his stay on the circuit, in which Hamilton, Ohio, was situated. The next year Mr. Cull was apprised of the time when the new preacher would be at Hamilton, and, fearing that he could not readily find his way to the new appointment, met him there, and conducted him to his cabin home. Mr. Cull, from the organization of the class, preached also regularly, in his own house and at other places.

In 1807, Whitewater Circuit was formed, with Rev. Thomas Hellums as preacher; but, as far as can be ascertained, he confined his labors to the southern part of the strip of territory, where he was quite successful, and reported, at the close of the year, sixty-seven members.

In 1808, Rev. Joseph Williams was appointed to the Whitewater Circuit, and took in the class at Mr. Cull's, which was given up by the Ohio preachers on his coming to the circuit. Circuit preaching was kept up at Mr. Cull's for nineteen years, from 1805 to 1824, when it was removed to the house of James P. Burgess, afterward a local preacher, about a mile north, where it was continued until 1848, when a neat, commodious brick church was erected in the neighborhood. Mr. Cull, in speaking of Mr. Elliott's first coming, said to a friend: "Uncle Jim, you don't know how my soul jumped; for as far as I could see him coming through the woods, I knew he was a preacher."

Father Cull, as he was called in later life, was a devoted disciple of Christ, and traveled somewhat extensively as a local preacher, sometimes supplying the place of the itinerant for a round, or a part of the year. He was acceptable wherever he went, and was known as the weeping preacher. At Concord camp-meeting he was to preach at 9 o'clock A. M., on Sabbath. After singing and prayer, he announced for his text Job xix, 25, and commenced to read it. "I know," and then said, "Glory!" Repeating, "I know," he said, in a louder tone, "Glory!" Again repeating "I know," he shouted, at the top of his voice, "Glory, glory, glory!" and, covering his face with both hands, wept like a child. The presiding elder, Rev. Robert Burns, asked him if he should read the text, to which he assented. He then introduced his subject by saying that, "Job was no Campbellite—glory!—for he knew—glory!—that his Redeemer lived—glory!" and preached a melting sermon to a weeping congregation.

In view of his stern integrity, ability, and moral uprightness, clearly discerning the evils of slavery, he was elected to the Constitutional Convention, in 1816, which place he filled with true Christian dignity, and to the honor and satisfaction of his constituents.

He continued to preach within a year of his death, and fell asleep in Jesus—whispering the oft-repeated words, "Glory, glory, glory!"—August 30, 1862, "in a good old age, an old man, and full of years," aged one hundred and four years and ten months, in the sixty-fifth year of his ministry; and was buried in the Methodist Episcopal Church-yard, where a most beautiful marble monument marks the resting-place of himself, wife, and niece.

The Lord graciously honored the members of this first Methodist class with a good old age, and peaceful, if not triumphant, death. Mrs. Weaver was the only one that died comparatively young, being about fifty-five, while Mrs. Meek and Mrs. Cull bordered on ninety. Mr. Weaver was in his ninety-seventh year, and Mr. Meek was nearing his ninety-ninth birthday. They were permitted to look far down the stream of life, and share in the triumphs of many a long and hard-fought battle.

During Rev. Mr. Williams's conference year, in 1808, Meek's Meeting-house was built, about four miles southwest from Richmond, and was among the first in Indiana. The total membership, from the Ohio River north, on the eastern boundary of Indiana Territory, to a few miles above where Richmond is located, was one hundred and sixty-five whites and one colored.

In 1810, a camp-meeting was held near Meek's Meeting-house, John Sale, Presiding Elder; Thomas Nelson and Samuel H. Thompson, preachers on the circuit, which was one of the first, if not *the first*, ever held in Indiana.

In 1819, James P. Burgess, seeing the growing evils of intemperance, wrote a temperance pledge, signed it himself, and solicited his neighbors to do likewise. Its provisions would be somewhat novel in these days of tee-totalism, when we have learned better how to treat the wily foe, and were as follows:

1. Beer was not considered intoxicating, hence not mentioned.

2. Wine, rum, gin, brandy, and all other foreign liquors, were left out of the schedule of prohibited drinks, because they cost *money;* and there being so little of that commodity in the country, there was little danger of becoming intoxicated on beverages so *costly*.

3. The only prohibited article was *whisky*, and of that they were at liberty to take a dram every morning.

It created quite a stir in the neighborhood, and many saw that, in signing the pledge, their social and national liberties would not only be abridged but jeopardized; and others refused because there was no exception in harvest; so that, between the two, only a few pledged themselves to *total abstinence*.

The work enlarged, and from the small beginning of the local preacher, with a class of five other members, in 1805, we see the meeting-house erected in 1808; the camp-meeting in 1810, where the multitudes worshiped in the temple not made with hands; the temperance movement, inaugurated in 1819, but as yet no gathering of the children and adults into the Sunday-school. This was not long to continue. In 1822, an itinerant Sunday-school, or rather, Bible-class, was formed (it being exclusively for adults) in the neighborhood of Mr. Cull's, by Rev. James Martin, a Baptist minister, and James P. Burgess, the latter being superintendent. It continued only a part of the Summer. In 1825, J. P. Burgess organized a regular Sunday-school for adults, and children that could read in the New Testament; which was not only the first Methodist Sunday-school in that region, but the first real Sunday-school of which children formed a part. It was organized in a school-house, two and one-half miles south of Richmond. People came to this Sunday-school, on pleasant days, from eight to ten miles around, and from Ohio. They often had to take the benches out of the school-house, and place them on either side of some logs near by, when the superintendent would open the school by singing out of the Church hymn-book, and praying. After that, there being no infant classes, all were put into one class, with the superintendent as the only teacher. They read sometimes one, two, or three chapters, and closed with singing and prayer.

The organization of the first class and Church, and other unpublished facts stated in the foregoing, were received personally from Rev. James P. Burgess and wife, who were married fifty years ago, and are living on the old homestead which her father, Jacob Meek, entered, who was one of the members of the first class, she being then (in 1805) only three years old. A sister, seven years older, also corroborates the above statements.

We have thus casually noticed the beginnings of Methodism in Wayne County, and now turn our attention especially to the cause in Richmond.

In 1806, Andrew Hoover, John Smith, and Jeremiah Cox, members of the Society of Friends, having emigrated from North Carolina a few years before, with some others, who were chiefly Friends, settled permanently in the immediate vicinity where Richmond is located, and John Smith entered the land south of Main Street. A number of wealthy families having settled within a few miles, they formed a nucleus for a Quaker settlement. Emigration set in rapidly, and it was but a short time until the country was, what was then termed, *filled* with the friends of peace. With increased emigration, and the rapid improvement of the country, a Quaker town was a necessity. Hence, in 1816, John Smith and Jeremiah Cox laid off the village of Richmond, which grew rapidly for those days, and soon became, what it continues to be, the largest town or city in that part of the state.

From 1805, when the first Methodist Church organization was effected, until 1822, there had been regular Methodist preaching in Wayne County, and the membership had been many times multiplied at compound rates; but as yet no special effort had been made to introduce Methodism into Richmond. Indeed, the ground seemed to be so preoccupied by the Friends, that there was but little left uncultivated, and that little was so completely under their influence, that it seemed almost impossible to get a foot-hold.

Another reason why special efforts had not been made before, was the Macedonian cry that was heard from "the region beyond," calling for laborers, where there were no Church privileges, and among many families who were without, and never had, a copy of the Bible. The voice of the Master was, "Go ye into all the world," which had been paraphrased and incorporated in their Book of Discipline thus: "Go always, not only to those that want you, but to those that want you most." Believing that Methodism, in its essential principles, was to take the world for Jesus, and the surrounding country having been faithfully cultivated, Rev. Russel Bigelow, in 1822, introduced it into Richmond. The opposition was intense, the Friends considering that any of their families would be disgraced by attending Methodist meeting; others participated in kindred feelings, and there being no Methodist families in the place, no private house could be obtained in which to hold services. There remained only one chance, which was, to get the school-house. After considerable delay, with great reluctance, permission was granted to occupy the little school-house, where, in a short time, a class of seven members was organized, composed of George Smith, Sarah Smith, Mary B. Smith, Rachel S. Smith, Stephen Thomas, Margaret Thomas, and the Widow Pierson, of which George Smith was the leader. The opposition to the work of the Lord through the Methodists, from the Friends and infidels, became so powerful that, in a little while, they were prohibited from using the school-house, when, for a short time, they occupied the house of Mrs. Pierson, until she left Richmond; and then, there being no other place which could be obtained, preaching, as well as other Methodist meetings, were discontinued for the time being.

The spirit of vital Christianity could not long endure the restrictions placed upon it by its erring friends, or avowed enemies. Hence, during the conference year of 1825, under the leadership of Rev. James Havens, the residence of Isaac Jackson was secured for Church services, preaching was resumed, another class organized, and services have continued without interruption to the present.

On the reorganization of the class, and the re-establishing of regular preaching, hostilities commenced anew against what many were pleased to call "a hireling ministry" and a "shouting membership." But the Lord owned and blessed the labors of his servants to such an extent that in 1828 they were able to sustain a two-days' meeting. The influence of Methodism on the morals of the people in the surrounding country had been such as by this time to allay somewhat the intense opposition of a few of the more liberal-minded Friends, as well as others, and permission was obtained to hold the two-days' meeting, and to continue regular services, in the brick school-house. Rev. S. H. Beggs was on the circuit, and the meeting was a glorious success for the cause of Christ, such as had never before been witnessed by the Richmondites; but which, through the grace of our Lord Jesus Christ, was to be repeated time and again, until there should be a shaking among the dry bones of a dead, formal Church, as well as among the open adversaries of a Bible Christianity. The more the Lord manifested his power in saving souls, the more intense was the opposition, especially from infidels and Hicksite Friends—the Friends' Society having divided in 1827—with but few exceptions even among the orthodox Friends. Infidelity and the world united, on the one hand, with a formal Christianity on the other, as a bulwark, behind which the former could take refuge, marshaled such a combination of forces as to be almost irresistible. These forces were publicly and privately brought to bear on the occupation of the school-house by the Methodists, who were the first among the Churches to invade the quiet of Quakerism by seeking to establish themselves in their midst. And they were again left without a home. Truthfully they could say: "We are troubled on every side, yet not distressed; we are perplexed, but not in despair; persecuted, but not forsaken; cast down [out], but not destroyed." Nothing daunted, with prayerful hearts they took the case to the Lord; and a building, not very suitable, was obtained from James Henry, which was made to answer the purpose, until it became too small for a family of one of the tribes of Israel to inhabit.

Necessity was upon them. They could not expect any favors from the authorities, neither were they disposed to ask any, having been so summarily dealt with on former occasions. Hence they determined to build a house of their own for the Lord. They secured the lot on which Pearl-street Methodist Episcopal Church now stands, and proceeded at once to erect a frame church, with stone basement in the rear, which, after subscribing and re-subscribing on the part of all the members, and the few friends who were favorably disposed, they succeeded in finishing so far that they could occupy it for a two-days' meeting; and these were the only dedicatory exercises for the first church built in Richmond, aside from the Friends.

This was in 1831, and Revs. Asa Beck and Richard S. Robinson were on the circuit. The latter was the junior preacher, and it fell to his lot to be at Richmond and carry on the services, with the help of local brethren, who were always on hand at such special occasions. Arrangements had been made with Rev. Mr. Baughman to come over from Eaton and assist. The opposers of Methodism in Richmond had not forgotten the former two-days' meeting, held in the brick school-house, when the truth preached as it was in Christ, became as fiery bomb-shells, disturbing the quiet, formal worshiper, sitting "at ease in Zion," as well as waking up the sinner, sleeping in his sins on the verge of perdition; and they resolved, if possible, to prevent the like occurrence; but had to devise other means than formerly, as they had no power to close the doors of those who worshiped "under their own vine and fig-tree." As Mr. Baughman was to come from Eaton, Ohio, it was currently reported by a few leading infidels, then heralded by others throughout the community, that "the small-pox was raging there," and that it would be at the risk of introducing that loathsome disease should he be permitted to come. A "Board of Health" was hastily appointed, in view of two such fearful visitations as the *small-pox* and a *Methodist two-days' meeting;* and the families who were expected to entertain guests coming from a distance were informed of the sad state of affairs, while the road from Eaton to Richmond was duly guarded. These reports were rife throughout the town; and on Saturday morning, with sad hearts, the few Methodists of Richmond met those from the country, who came to attend the meeting at the new church, and talked over the situation. Mr. Robinson, nothing daunted, preached in the morning and evening, with extraordinary unction from on high, and held the love-feast Sabbath morning, expecting to preach the morning sermon, when, to the surprise of all, Mr. Baughman made his appearance. The effect was electrical, and went like wild-fire through the community. Satan outdid himself, "the wrath of man" was made to praise God; for the house was soon filled with friend and foe to overflowing, regardless of small-pox, Methodist meeting, or any thing else; and the power of God was revealed, while his servant preached, "with the Holy Ghost sent down from heaven," on Isaiah liii, 1: "Who hath believed our report, and to whom is the arm of the Lord revealed?" The gates of infidelity were carried away; a Samson had taken hold of its "middle pillars," while the children of God wept and "rejoiced with exceeding great joy." The masterly effort in the morning brought the crowd to hear the Gospel message at night, when both the power and glory of God were manifested in the conviction and conversion of souls, resulting, at the close of the meeting on Monday, in the accession of thirty-two members to the Methodist Episcopal Church, most of whom had been converted during the meeting. The meeting, with its glorious results, created a great commotion among the infidel portion of community and the staid Friends, who thought the work was too speedily accomplished to be from God, or to be countenanced by his people. The latter have since learned, by a better acquaintance with Methodists and their usages, and the teachings of the Gospel, the truth taught by the Master, "Other sheep I have, which are not of this fold," and rejoice in the prosperity of Zion among the other formerly unrecognized tribes of Israel.

The most determined, yet not exclusive, opposition to Methodism, during these years of struggle for a bare existence in Richmond, was from infidels and Hicksite Friends, or those sympathizing with their views—the latter being only a stepping-stone to the former, while both united in rejecting the atonement, with all the essential principles growing out of and clustering around the same. The Sabbath, never very sacredly guarded, even by the old or orthodox Friends, fared badly at the hands of the Hicksites, as may be seen from the following incident: Mr. C., a Methodist, settled in their midst, and, desiring to raise his family to have due respect for the Sabbath, he was troubled on account of his Hicksite Friends hauling saw-logs through his place on the Sabbath. After praying over the matter, and reflecting upon it, he said to his neighbors that he wanted to live peaceably among them, but if they continued to haul logs through his land on that day, he would feel under the necessity of reporting them to the proper authorities. They responded: "We also want to live peaceably, and on friendly terms with thee; and if it is against thy principles that work should be done on the First Day, we will desist hauling logs through thy place on that day; but thee must remember that we do so, not because we regard the day, but because it is annoying to thee."

To return to our subject. The second two-days' meeting in its own house was the crossing of the Rubicon for Methodism in Richmond, from which it never went back. It was to it the day of Pentecost—to be repeated until, by the power of God, it stood head and shoulders above its enemies, who were compelled ever afterward, though in heart they despised it, to have some respect for it, by recognizing it as a power for good in the community, and according it at least an existence. In the same year (1831) the first Sabbath-school ever organized in Richmond was organized by the Methodists in their own church. The Orthodox Friends followed with a Bible-class, which they termed a Sunday-school, in 1832—afterward taking the regular form of a Sunday-school.

By the blessing of God, Methodism grew and waxed strong in the (un)friendly soil of Richmond, until the frame church must give way to something better, larger, and more durable. In 1851, a new brick building was erected, on the same ground, superior to any other in the city, and one among the largest and finest churches then in the state; with stone basement for Sunday-school and class-rooms, over which was a fine audience-room—all of which were tastefully finished.

The vine of Methodism had taken such deep root,

and its leaven had so permeated community, that its spacious building was not sufficient to accommodate all who desired at least to be under its influence in the services of the sanctuary. This, with the growth of the city, and the somewhat diversity of tastes, led to the withdrawal of forty-two members from Pearl Street, and the formation of a second Methodist charge. They purchased Star Hall, on Main Street; had it refitted, and took the name of Union Chapel, in September, 1858. The chapel was dedicated by Dr. D. W. Clark, in October, and in the latter part of the month Rev. J. V. R. Miller, a transfer from the South-eastern Indiana Conference, was with them as their first preacher.

The new charge, composed of a few leading men, as William G. Scott, Isaac D. Dunn, A. A. Curme, William Bayless, G. Price, Douay M. M'Means, and others, went to work in earnest for their Master. Some of them being Eastern people, they adopted their own peculiarities, and had their church-pewed family sittings, and instrumental music.

From the number of members in Pearl Street, and their devotion to Christ, they were able to move on without embarrassment, and soon filled up the places of those who, though they had gone out from them, yet were one with them in cultivating the vineyard of the Master.

The vine planted by the Lord in Union Chapel, so grew in devotion to God, numbers, and wealth, that in the Spring of 1867, they proceeded to erect a new church building, called Grace Church, on the corner of Seventh Street and Broadway, in the heart of the finest part of the city, which was duly finished, and dedicated to the worship of Almighty God, near the close of 1869. When completed, it was not only the most conveniently arranged, with basement and audience-room, and the

13

finest church in the city, but was excelled only by a few in the state.

During this time, prosperity had also attended the old hive at Pearl Street, and their numbers had so increased that a portion of her members were contemplating a new swarm, out of which to make a third charge. At this juncture, a discussion arose in reference to instrumental music being introduced into the congregation, which had already been introduced into the Sunday-school. It was eventually brought in, and some who opposed it took exceptions, not so much to the music as to the manner in which it was voted in, being by the trustees, instead of leaving it to the vote of the entire membership. Consequently, David Sands, Barton Wyatt, D. D. Lesh, Rev. George W. Iliff, William Gersuch, James Hamilton, William Byers, and thirty-six others, withdrew from Pearl Street, in 1867, and were formed into a new charge, called Third Charge. Their organization being completed, they secured the German Methodist Episcopal Church building to worship in, and Rev. George W. Iliff was sent to the session of North Indiana Conference, at Anderson, in April, 1867, to request the appointment of a minister. Rev. J. C. R. Layton was appointed, came on to the work in good spirits, labored faithfully for a time, then became discouraged, in view of opposition to the cause, and the unsettled financial condition of the charge, and resigned at the close of six months. Rev. P. Carland, a member of the South-eastern Indiana Conference, who had been in the service of the country, had just returned; and desiring to be transferred to North Indiana Conference, was appointed pastor, and remained as such for six months, until the conference in 1868. During the fore part of the session of this conference, David Sands and Barton Wyatt bought Union Chapel, the Third

Charge having been notified that they could only occupy the German Methodist Episcopal Church a few months longer; and Mr. Sands appeared at the seat of Conference, greatly encouraged, to make known the fact, and ask for the continuance of the charge, under the name of Central, it occupying a central position on Main Street. Rev. C. W. Miller was appointed pastor, and during his second year, in view of pewing Grace Church, seventy-seven members, a number of whom were earnest workers, withdrew because the trustees would not leave the question to the vote of the entire membership, and united with Central, thus making it almost equal to Grace Church in numbers, and equal to either in a devoted, earnest, working membership. The three charges in Richmond are in a prosperous condition, steadily progressing, each containing an active, devoted membership, with faithful pastors leading on the hosts of Israel.

From the little band of seven members, in 1822, with staff in hand, sojourning from house to house, sometimes without any home (until 1831), with the enemy pressing hard from all quarters to destroy, Methodism, under the guidance of the "Captain of Salvation," steadily progressed, surmounting difficulties of almost every kind, until—changing the words but little—her votaries may say, with Jacob (Genesis, xxxii, 10): "We are not worthy of the least of all the mercies and of all the truth which thou hast showed unto thy servants; for with our staff we passed over into the city, and now we are become three bands," numbering over eight hundred communicants, with three Sabbath-schools, numbering nearly one thousand attendants, well organized, with energetic officers and an efficient corps of teachers,—all worshiping God under their "own vine and fig-tree," with a Church property worth over seventy thousand dollars.

Methodism, as represented by the Methodist Episcopal Church, leaving out the other two organizations, has not only kept pace with the material growth and numerical population of the city, and other Churches, but has surpassed both city and Churches. With a city of less than ten thousand census inhabitants, over one-twelfth of them are in the yearly census of the Methodist Episcopal Church, and over one-eleventh of her population are members of her Sunday-school organizations, all of which, meeting at the same hour, none of them are duplicated in the enumeration. Behold, "what hath God wrought!"

INDIANAPOLIS.

INDIANAPOLIS CIRCUIT was organized by Rev. William Cravens in the Fall of 1821, he having received his appointment from the Missouri Conference, at its session in Cape Girardeau, Missouri, in October, 1821; Samuel Hamilton being the presiding elder. There is no record of the metes and bounds of the circuit as it was organized by Cravens, but it included all the settlements in Central Indiana. He was succeeded, in the Fall of 1822, by James Scott; and, in the Fall of 1823, Jesse Haile and George Horn were appointed to Indianapolis Circuit. The circuit then extended east to the Ohio Conference boundary, which was a line due north from the city of Madison. Greensburg, in Decatur County, and the settlements on Flat Rock and Blue River, from the vicinity of Columbus as far north as any settlements extended, were all in Indianapolis Circuit, and also the settlements on Fall Creek and White River.

Rev. Joseph Cotton, of South-eastern Indiana Conference, who was raised on Blue River, in the northern part of Shelby County, and whose parents were Baptists, attributes the fact of his being a Methodist to a visit of Jesse Haile's to his father's house in 1824, when he was a small boy. Mr. Haile came across his father's cabin in the woods one forenoon. His father was out in the clearing. Haile entered into conversation with his mother on the subject of religion; inquired if they were religious, and if there was any preaching in the neighborhood. Mrs. Cotton informed him that she was a member of the Baptist Church, but that her husband was not a professor of religion. She proposed to blow the horn and call her husband to the house; but the preacher objected, saying he did not wish to call him from his work, but if the little boy would go with him to the clearing, he would go out and see him. Accordingly, little Joseph accompanied the preacher out to the clearing, and the preacher talked to him so kindly and tenderly, explaining to him how to be good, that he felt to love him. Finding Mr. Cotton engaged in chopping up a tree-top, instead of asking him to sit down and talk with him, the preacher picked up and piled the brush, while Mr. Cotton cut it off; meanwhile telling him who he was, and talking to him about personal religion, until the horn blew for dinner, when of course the preacher was invited to dinner; and, as a matter of course, before dinner, was presented with the whisky-bottle; and his refusal to take a dram nearly broke the friendship so suddenly formed. Kindly, but firmly, the preacher declined the bottle. He asked a blessing at the table; the first that young Cotton had ever heard. After dinner he asked for a Bible, read a chapter, giving a brief commentary upon it as he read; making it a sort of family sermon. He then prayed with them, and for each member of the family; and when he bade them farewell, he left his blessing with them, and, putting his hand on the head of little Joseph, said, " God bless you,

and may you be a good boy and a good man." That
visit made a Methodist of the little boy, who has for
many years been an efficient minister, although his
father's family, and all his relations, continued to be
Baptists.

The first place of worship in Indianapolis was a log-
house; used, also, as a school-house, and situated on
Maryland, between Meridian and Illinois Streets. In the
Fall of 1824, John Miller was appointed to Indianapolis
Circuit.

The first society that was organized in Indianapolis
was composed of the following members: Robert Brenton, Sarah Brenton, Mary Brenton, James Given, Margaret Given, Mrs. Dan. Stevens, and Elizabeth Paxton.
Mr. Brenton was the class-leader. He was also a
licensed exhorter, a man of character and ability. He
was the father of Rev. and Hon. Samuel Brenton, whose
character and services are elsewhere noticed. This
society was organized in 1821, by Rev. William Cravens. The first Gospel sermon ever preached in Indianapolis was preached by Rev. Rezin Hammond, a local
preacher from Clarke County. It was preached under a
Walnut-tree, just south of the state-house. The first
Sunday-school was a Union School, organized in 1822,
and conducted in a cabinet-maker's shop, owned by Mr.
Scudder, situated on Washington Street, opposite the
state-house. The teachers were, Mr. Scudder, James
M. Ray, J. N. Phipps, John Wilkins, Samuel Brenton,
C. J. Hand, Samuel Merrell, Lismond Bassey, Elizabeth
Paxton, and Margaret Given. The school was divided
in 1825, and the Methodists organized theirs in their
place of worship. Wesley Chapel was built in 1826, on
the corner of Meridian and Circle Streets, where the
Sentinel building now is. It was taken down, and a

larger church erected in 1845, which continued to be occupied until 1870, when it was sold, and the present stone church erected, on the corner of Meridian and New York Streets; and the charge has taken the name of Meridian-street Church.

At the session of the Indiana Conference in Centerville, in 1842, the Church in Indianapolis was divided into two charges. The second charge was organized in the court-house, and had John S. Bayless for its first pastor. The charges were designated as Western and Eastern, and were divided by Meridian Street. L. W. Berry was pastor of the Western charge, and John S. Bayless of the Eastern. Asbury Church, situated on New Jersey Street, near South Street, was the third charge. Strange Chapel, whose history has been a remarkably strange one, was the fourth charge. For some years it was a part of West Indianapolis Circuit. The church stood on the west side of the canal. It was finally made a separate charge, the church building moved on to North Tennessee Street, refitted, and a comfortable parsonage built on the same lot with the church. In 1869, the church and parsonage were sold, and a larger brick church built on the corner of Tennessee and Michigan Streets. This church was consumed by fire in 1871; and with that conflagration ends the name and legal existence of Strange Chapel. In 1870, Indiana Conference appointed Rev. L. M. Walters to that charge. A majority of the Church declined to receive him as their pastor. The Church authorities failing to interfere for their relief, and make any change, they organized themselves into an independent, or congregational Church, rented the Universalist church building, just across the street, and called Rev. J. W. T. M'Mullen as their pastor, who served them for a few months; but not being willing to sever his connection with the Methodist Episcopal Church, he declined to remain. The most of them resumed their places in the Methodist Episcopal Church; attaching themselves to such charges as suited their convenience. Those who accepted Mr. Walters as their pastor, having obtained a part of the value of the Strange Chapel property that was consumed by fire, purchased an eligible site on the corner of California and North Streets, and have erected a good church; the new organization taking the name of California-street Church. The other charges have been organized in the following order: Trinity, Third-street, Ames, Grace, Massachusetts-avenue.

Grace was organized by a division of Roberts Chapel, in 1869. Massachusetts-avenue Church was organized in 1870, and was composed chiefly of members from the United Brethren in Christ, who were dissatisfied with the action of their Church in prohibiting their members from belonging to secret societies, as Masons, Odd-fellows, and Sons of Temperance. Rev. A. Hanway, their first pastor, also came from the United Brethren. The charge has been continuously prosperous since its organization. They have built them a neat frame church, and have a well-organized Church and Sabbath-school.

The German Methodist Church was organized about 1850. John B. Stump, Austin W. Morris, William Hannaman, Henry Tutewiler, and another German brother, constituted the first Board of Trustees. They built a small, one-story brick church on East Ohio, between New Jersey and East Streets, which was subsequently enlarged; and in 1870, was superseded by the present spacious and elegant church on the corner of East and New York Streets. Including two Colored Methodist Churches, there are, in Indianapolis, twelve self-sustaining charges, with a membership of 3,200, a Church property worth $283,785, and 4,000 Sabbath-school scholars.

Of the first society that was organized in Indianapolis, there are but two survivors: Isaac N. Phipps and Elizabeth Paxton, both of whom have been useful and active members in the Church since their first connection with it. Colonel Paxton—the husband of Mrs. Paxton— who has been dead for many years, donated the lot on which the Wesley Chapel parsonage was built, and left a legacy for the support of superannuated preachers, and the widows and orphans of deceased preachers, which formed the foundation of the Preachers' Aid Society of the Indiana Conference, which, in the course of time, became the foundation of similar societies in each of the Indiana conferences, and has been the means of accomplishing a large amount of good, and of preventing untold suffering. Mrs. Paxton has abounded in good works all through her life. She has been an active worker in the City Bible Society, the City Benevolent Society, and all of our public charities have been benefited by her contributions and her personal efforts. I. N. Phipps continues an active steward in the Church.

Margaret Given was a truly remarkable woman. She was the first President of the Indianapolis Female Bible Society, and continued to hold the office and efficiently discharge its duties till the day of her death, extending through a period of nearly fifty years. She had a remarkably clear and vigorous intellect, and a capacity for business that many a statesman might covet. She was always busy and always cheerful, giving most of her time to the public, and when nearly eighty years of age would do more walking, uncomplainingly, than most young women of twenty.

John Wilkins, who joined the first class, not long

after its organization, lived to a good old age, and was all through life a model man, "diligent in business, fervent in spirit, serving the Lord." He was liberal to the Church and the poor, and a generous patron of education, being, for a number of years, one of the trustees of Indiana Asbury University.

Among the "elect ladies" that have been ornaments to Methodism in Indianapolis, and who have gone to their reward, are the names of Margaret Given, Mrs. Alfred Harrison, and Mrs. Richmond, the latter of whom, like Mrs. Given, was for many years a widow. Mrs. Richmond was a woman of strong faith. She was gifted in prayer and conversation. She was a very active Christian, a lady of agreeable manners, and her consistent piety gave her great influence in society. Mrs. Harrison was less prominent in spiritual matters, but equally useful in the community. She abounded in good works. She gave liberally and constantly to the relief of the needy around her. She gave much time and attention, and contributed freely, to the founding and building up of the Orphan Asylum, in our city. These ladies left the savor of a good name, and their instructive example is not lost upon those that have come after them; for in no community, of the same numbers, can there be found a larger number of equally active, intelligent, and earnest female workers, in all appropriate departments of Christian work. Indianapolis is eminently fortunate in this respect.

Among the early and faithful workers in the Sunday-school cause in Indianapolis, is the name of Calvin Fletcher, Esq. Mr. Fletcher was among the early settlers in Indianapolis. He was a remarkably industrious and energetic man, accumulated a large property, raised a large and most estimable family, several of whom are widely known. One of his sons, Rev. James C. Fletcher, is the author of the "History of Brazil." Rev. E. T. Fletcher, for a number of years, occupied a front rank among eloquent preachers in the Methodist Episcopal Church. Prof. M. I. Fletcher, who was Superintendent of Public Instruction for the State at the time of his death, was a gifted and accomplished man. Dr. W. B. Fletcher ranks high as a skillful and accomplished physician; and the other sons are distinguished in their vocations, as bankers, farmers, etc. Notwithstanding Mr. Fletcher's numerous and pressing engagements, he bestowed great attention upon the culture of his family, and gave much time to the Church, especially to the Sunday-school cause.

Rev. Joseph Marsee, a superannuated member of South-eastern Indiana Conference, who entered the ministry in Kentucky, in 1826, came to Indiana in 1840, settled in Indianapolis, was superannuated in 1858, and died January 20, 1872. He was for many years an efficient preacher. After his superannuation, he was successful in business, and was an example of liberality. He was a grand specimen of a useful, happy Christian, whose evening of life was as rich in heavenly radiance as an autumnal sunset.

Among the early settlers in Indianapolis was Morris Morris, who removed from Kentucky to the vicinity of Indianapolis in 1821. Mr. Morris served several terms in the Legislature, and two terms as Auditor of State. His son, Hon. Austin W. Morris, was for a number of years a leading politician of the Whig school, and an eminently useful man in the Church. Father Morris and his estimable wife, and Austin Morris, some years since, were gathered to their heavenly home; but their names are familiar as household words in Methodist circles, and their memories are gratefully cherished by those who knew them. General T. A. Morris, a son of Morris Morris, was educated at West Point Military Academy, resigned his position in the army, and, as a civil engineer and a capitalist, has had much to do in building up the railroad system in Indiana; and although a member of a sister Church, yet, as the son of worthy Methodist parents, and himself an honored Christian citizen, is worthy of mention in this connection.

RELATIVE STRENGTH OF THE CHURCHES.

THE following exhibit of the relative strength of the several religious denominations, will be read with interest, and will be found convenient as a matter of reference:

The Protestant Episcopal numbers 582; Methodist Episcopal, 3,219; Presbyterian, 1,736; Baptist, 1,093; Papist, 4,000; Congregationalist, 235; Christian, 900; Lutheran, 810; German Reformed, 300; German Evangelical Association, 118; United Brethren, 42; Unitarian, 500; Friends, 246; Jewish, 58.

In Church property they stand: Protestant Episcopal, $168,000; Methodist Episcopal, $391,000; Presbyterian, $320,117; Baptist, $116,000; Papist, $300,000; Congregationalist, $43,000; Christian, $53,000; Lutheran, $93,000; German Reformed, $21,000; German Evangelical Association, $9,000; United Brethren, $5,000; Unitarian, $6,000; Jewish, $27,000; Friends, $20,000.

The following is a list of the appointments made to Indianapolis, down to the division of the first charge:

1821, William Cravens; 1822–23, James Scott; 1823–24, Jesse Haile and George Horn; 1825, John Miller; 1826, Thomas Hewson; 1827, Edwin Ray; 1828, N. B. Griffith; 1829, Thomas Hitt; 1830–31, Thomas

Hitt; 1832–33, Benjamin C. Stevenson; 1833–34, C. W. Ruter; 1834–35, E. R. Ames; 1835–36, John C. Smith; 1836–37, A. Eddy; 1837–38, John C. Smith; 1838–39, A. Wiley; 1839–40, A. Wiley; 1840–41, W. H. Goode; 1841–42, W. H. Goode. In 1821, the district was called Indiana, and Samuel Hamilton was presiding elder. In 1824, William Beauchamp was presiding elder. Down to this time, the work in Indiana was included in Missouri Conference, and John Strange was appointed to the district. In 1825, Missouri Conference was divided, and the work in Indiana was included in the Illinois Conference, and John Strange was appointed to the district. In 1829, Indianapolis was included in Madison District, and Allen Wiley was presiding elder. In 1832, Indianapolis District was formed, and John Strange was presiding elder. This year, the Indiana Conference was organized. In 1833, A. Wiley, Presiding Elder; 1834, James Havens, Presiding Elder; 1838, A. Eddy, Presiding Elder; and in the Fall of 1840, James Havens was again appointed to the district.

WASHINGTON, DAVIESS COUNTY.

THE Methodist Episcopal Church in Washington, Daviess County, Indiana, was organized in 1816. The population of the village at that time did not exceed seventy-five. The meetings were held in the private residences of Samuel Miller and Thomas Meredith. The society was organized under the ministry of Rev. John Schrader, who was in charge of a large four-weeks' circuit. The only members of the Church now living, whose membership dates back as far as 1822, are, Elizabeth Meredith, Robert Stephens, Rebecca Raper, and William Bratten. Mr. Bratten was the class-leader. About that time, Dr. Holland, a physician, and a local preacher of considerable ability, was connected with the class. The society continued to worship in private residences, in the school-house, and in the court-house, until 1827, when a small, one-story brick was inclosed, near where the Cumberland Presbyterian Church now stands. The congregation was soon sadly disappointed, by the walls of the building gathering dampness, and threatening to crumble to ruins. They were again compelled to worship in private houses, in the school-house, and in the court-house, until in 1837, when Lewis Jones, William Bratten, and John Fryer purchased a residence where the Methodist Episcopal Church now stands. The building was enlarged and converted into a church, received by the trustees, and paid for by donations.

The prospects of the Church were now greatly brightened; and, in the midst of sincere rejoicings, the church was formally dedicated to the worship of God by Rev. A. Wood. The membership had increased to one hundred and twenty-five, and the appointment was made a station; but, after two years, was again connected with the circuit. For several years the Church was blessed with prosperity; and, in 1858, under the labors of Rev. James F. M'Cann, the present house of worship was built, and dedicated by Rev. Calvin Kingsley. In 1859, the charge was again made into a station, and has so continued until the present time. The membership at present is two hundred and fifty-one, including fifty-one probationers.

The charge has been favored with special revivals as follows: In 1845, under the labors of Rev. J. R. Williams, when about forty-five professed conversion; in 1858, under the labors of Rev. J. F. M'Cann, when fifty professed conversion; in 1859, under the labors of Rev. H. B. Hibben, when about fifty made a profession of

religion; in 1863, under the labors of Rev. Stephen
Bowers, when two hundred conversions were reported;
in 1866, under the labors of Rev. W. F. Harned, when
seventy-five conversions were reported; and in 1870,
under the labors of Rev. Aaron Turner, when sixty-five
conversions were reported. In Church music, Sabbath-
school work, and general Christian enterprise, the congregation is alive and progressive.

METHODISM IN LAFAYETTE.

BY REV. N. L. BRAKEMAN.

FROM a variety of sources—mainly from the earliest
settlers—we gather the following facts concerning the
history of Methodism in Lafayette, Indiana:

As early as 1825, Rev. Hackaliah Vredenburg, who
then lived on the Shawnee Prairie, preached the first
Methodist sermon in Lafayette. In 1826, Mr. Vredenburg was appointed to the Crawfordsville Circuit, and occasionally preached in Lafayette, which was then an out-
post on that work, but without any regularly organized
society among the Methodists. In 1827, Rev. Henry
Buell rode the Crawfordsville Circuit. In 1827–28, Eli
P. Farmer succeeded Mr. Buell. In 1828–29, Stephen
R. Beggs, with John Strange as presiding elder, was appointed to the Crawfordsville Circuit, and formed a good
class in Lafayette; twenty in all, only five of whom
were males; but up to this date no permanent or formal
organization had been made, and no permanent place of
public worship had been provided. Ministers preached
wherever they could, sometimes in a private house,
then in Eli Huntsinger's wheelwright-shop, which was a
small log-cabin on the corner of Mississippi, now South
and Ferry Streets; sometimes in an unfinished public
building; then again in the log-tavern, on what is called

now Second Street, near Ferry (still standing, and owned
by H. Taylor) ; and sometimes in the open air. Pastors
and people realized that they were indeed "pilgrims
and strangers, without any certain dwelling-place;" but
Lafayette has, thus far, proved to them and theirs a
"continuing city," and their descendants to-day may
justly claim, with Saul of Tarsus, that they are citizens
"of no mean city." (Acts xxi, 39.) At that date (1828)
all the buildings in Lafayette of every kind, great and
small, public and private, numbered just seventeen!
Allow five persons to each building—a large estimate—
will give a population of eighty-five souls. Here we
may mention the names of the Heaths, Fords, Samples,
Taylors, Vanattas, Harringtons, Millers, Tuttles, Pykes,
Wellses, and others, who settled in Lafayette from 1828
to 1830, and later families, who have been identified
with Methodism from the first, and are exerting a controlling influence upon its future destiny.

When Mr. Beggs was appointed to Crawfordsville
Circuit, the following were the principal preaching-places,
and in the order named : Crawfordsville, Fort Wayne,
Logansport, Delphi, Lafayette, Attica, Portland, Coving-
ton, and back to Crawfordsville again. The subordinate
and intermediate preaching-places, however, outnum-
bered the principal ones, so that the minister had to
preach from five to seven times each week. The following year the "Logansport Mission" was formed, embracing Logansport, Delphi, and Lafayette; and Mr.
Beggs was again appointed, but did not fill out the year.
(See "Early History of the West and North-west:" Rev.
S. R. Beggs. Pages 81–83.)

The next preacher was James Armstrong, with
Strange still as presiding elder. In September, 1830,
Mr. Armstrong preached in an unfinished store-room on

Main Street, built by John Taylor, Esq., on the lot
where the Galt House now stands, and then and there
made the first formal and thorough organization of Methodism in Lafayette.   An official board was appointed,
trustees elected, and the initiatory steps taken toward
procuring a lot and building a church.   A lot was purchased on the corner of Main and Sixth Streets, where
the "old bank building" now stands. and early the
following season a frame church was erected.   In that
church, while it was yet in an unfinished state, in June,
1831, the first regularly conducted quarterly-meeting
was held, John Strange, the presiding elder, being
present, and preaching with power.   That meeting was
a great event for Lafayette Methodism.   It had been
published throughout the country by the "circuit-rider,"
on his previous "round;" and people of all denominations, and some of no denomination, came, some from a
distance of fifteen and twenty miles, to see each other,
to hear the Word of life, and to worship the God of
their fathers.   Some came to see the city, and some to
see the "new church;" and many came to hear the presiding elder, whose fame as a pulpit orator filled the
land, and drew together great crowds whenever he
preached.   A large congregation—considering the time
and place—assembled; the women and children filled
the house, mainly, while the men stood listening without, or reclined under the shade of the adjacent trees.
The weather was exceedingly warm; but as the house
had neither doors nor windows as yet, it was well ven-
tilated!

All the services were largely attended, and of special
interest to the new settlement, embracing city and
country.   Quarterly conference attended to the tempo-
ralities of the Church.   On Sabbath morning the love-

14

feast was held, and at 11 o'clock A. M., Strange delivered one of his inimitable and overpowering sermons; and in the afternoon there was another sermon, at the close of which the sacraments of baptism and the Lord's-supper were administered. During this last service an incident occurred which we deem worthy of record; the material points of which are thus given by Sanford Cox, Esq., in his "Recollections of the Early Settlement of the Wabash Valley," pages 81, 82.

Armstrong, who was also an eloquent and popular preacher, and beloved by all who knew him, had preached his celebrated "Fish Sermon" with happy effect; and Strange, who was a man of surpassing personal beauty, piety, eloquence, and solemnity combined, conducted the services of the Eucharist. While the latter was addressing the communicants, bowed and in tears at the altar, and in the most tender and touching language, telling them of Christ as "the Lamb of God which taketh away the sins of the world," a group of thoughtless and giddy youngsters were gathered about the door, whose looks and actions denoted a spirit of levity wholly incompatible with the solemnity of the scene transpiring before them. Mr. Strange for a while seemed to take no notice of them, but continued to address the communicants in the most gentle, loving, and pathetic terms, when, suddenly starting up, as if awaking from a reverie, with flashing eye, in sterner tones, with corresponding gesture, and with a ringing emphasis, he said: "Did I say Christ was the *Lamb* of God? He *is*, to the humble, contrite, trusting believer; but to *you* sinners"— pointing back, with his long, bony finger, toward the irreverent young men at the door—" to *you*, sirs, *arouse* him, and he is '*the Lion of the tribe of Judah*,' TERRIBLE IN HIS JUSTICE; and by the slightest movement of his

omnific power, could dash you *deeper into damnation* in a
MOMENT than a sunbeam could fly IN A MILLION OF AGES!"
This immediate and unpremeditated passing from the
tender and pathetic to the stern and terrifying, was as
penetrating and overpowering in its influence as it was
sudden and unexpected in its transition. It thrilled and
startled the people like a beam of lightning from a sun-lit
sky. Its effect upon the young men at whom it was
aimed was wonderful. Hushed into profound silence
and fear, they stood pale and motionless, for the nonce.
One of them afterward said that, for the time, he felt
his hair instantly stand on end, and felt as if flying with
the speed of light toward the deep, doleful regions, so
eloquently and fearfully alluded to in the impromptu
and brilliant flash of rhetoric, which equals the most
sublime flights of Bridane, Bascom, or Simpson.

We will add that the young man who was the master-
spirit of the above group of irreverent lookers-on so eloquently rebuked, and who felt that he was "flying"
through space to Pandemonium swifter than Milton's
"Archangel ruined" *fell to his doom*, still lives in Lafayette, a worthy and exemplary member of a sister Church.
And whenever we see him passing about, with his now
whitened locks standing *a la* Jackson, we secretly won-
der whether it is really *natural* for his hair to stand out
like the quills of the "fretful porcupine," or whether it
was caused by the electric shock of Strange's potent eloquence on that sultry Sabbath evening in June, 1831,
making it "instantly stand on end."

Strange and Armstrong were followed on the circuit
by Samuel C. Cooper and Samuel Brenton, and these
last by Boyd Phelps and Wesley Woods. The latter
died soon after he entered upon the circuit, and was succeeded by S. R. Ball. In 1833, "Lafayette Circuit" was

formed, and Richard Hargrave and Nehemiah Griffith were appointed the preachers, and James Thompson presiding elder. William M. Clark and William Watson were the next preachers. At conference, in the Fall of 1835, Lafayette was made a station, and Dr. H. S. Talbot was stationed preacher for two years. He was succeeded by the following ministers, some of whom served two years, namely: Lorenzo B. Smith, J. A. Brouse, H. B. Beers, Amasa Johnson, J. M. Stallard, and Samuel Brenton.

This brings us down to 1844–45, which marks a new era in Lafayette Methodism, when it had built for itself a fine brick church and parsonage, on the corner of Fifth and Ferry Streets, where the society worships at the present time.

In 1849, the nucleus of a new Church was formed, under the labors of W. F. Wheeler, City Missionary, and in 1850, one hundred and forty members were set off from the old society, and a second charge, now the Ninth-street Methodist Episcopal Church, was formed, with T. S. Webb as pastor; J. L. Smith, D. D., Presiding Elder. It is now a strong, intelligent, growing Church; Rev. J. C. Reed, D. D., is at present pastor.

April 4, 1852, the German Methodist Episcopal Church was organized, under the Rev. C. Keller. At about the same time, the Colored Methodist Church was organized by Rev. Mr. Dunlap. This Church is very feeble in numbers and financial strength, though they have a very good property, embracing church, parsonage, and a brick school-house. There are not more than about one hundred colored people, all told, in Lafayette.

What is now the Sixth-ward (Oakland Hill) Methodist Episcopal Church began its history as a class, organized by Dr. Charles Nailor in 1859. In 1860, it became

Richard Hargrave

the head of the Lafayette Circuit. In 1866, it was made a mission appointment, Rev. A. Potter as supply, and Rev. S. Godfrey, Presiding Elder. In 1868, a nice brick church, sixty-five by forty feet, was built; and in 1869, Rev. F. Taylor was made pastor; Rev. I. W. Joyce, Presiding Elder. This Church is properly a branch of the Ninth-street Methodist Episcopal Church; Rev. P. S. Cook is now pastor.

In 1866, Rev. G. M. Boyd was appointed pastor of the " Old Fifth-street" Church, and under his labors, the long-talked-of enterprise of a new, more costly, and more commodious house of worship for the parent society was initiated. Two young men of the Church (John W. Heath, Esq., and Hon. Henry Taylor) bought a lot on the corner of Sixth and North Streets, for $7,000, and donated it to the Church for their new site. A subscription was circulated with encouraging success, and a good degree of interest awakened in the new enterprise. In the Fall of 1868, Rev. N. L. Brakeman was appointed pastor; Rev. William Graham, D. D., Presiding Elder; and in the following Spring the work of erecting the new building was commenced. When completed and furnished, it will have cost $70,000 or $75,000, will seat one thousand people, and will be one among the finest churches in the state, and *the* finest in the conference. The society has changed its corporate name, and is now known as Trinity Methodist Episcopal Church. It was inclosed in January, 1870, and will be ready for occupation, it is thought, by December, 1871.

In 1869, the society formed in Chauncey, a suburb of Lafayette, on the western bank of the Wabash, had become so strong as to determine to build a house of worship for itself. The enterprise was promptly entered upon, vigorously prosecuted, and early in 1870, their

house was dedicated.　The old Fifth-street Church (now
Trinity), notwithstanding its own heavy enterprise, then
in progress, set off thirty-six of its own members to the
Chauncey Church, gave of its sympathy and means to
aid the young and rising society, and bade it Godspeed
on its way.　In the Fall of 1870, Chauncey became a
station, and Rev. W. C. Davisson was appointed pastor.
Chauncey is the seat of the "Purdue Agricultural College," and is destined to become a place of no little importance.　Our church there is a Gothic frame structure,
and cost something over three thousand dollars.　Considering its style, character, and accommodations, it is a
marvel of cheapness.

The following table will give a bird's-eye view of the
present strength of Methodism in Lafayette:

NAME OF CHURCH.	Number of Members..	No. in the Sab.Schools.	Value of property...	When or-ganized.....
Trinity Methodist Episcopal Church.........	289	325	$80,000	1828–30
Ninth-street Methodist Episcopal Church....	235	241	20,000	1849
German Methodist Episcopal Church..........	109	120	7,000	1852
African Methodist Episcopal Church..........	25	35	3,000	1853
Sixth Ward Methodist Episcopal Church......	105	130	7,500	1859
Chauncey Methodist Episcopal Church........	70	100	3,500	1869
Total.......................................	833	951	$121,000	

In so condensed and rapid a sketch of the rise and
progress of Methodism in Lafayette as we have been
obliged to make, it is impossible to bring forward the
names of ministers (elders and pastors), and members,
male and female, whose lives and labors have left their
impress for good upon family, society, Church, and State.
God knows them, whether living or dead; their record
is on high, and their reward is sure.

The above table indicates but in part what Lafayette

Methodism *is*. No statistics (except those kept by the recording angel above) can show what Lafayette Methodism has *done* for God and humanity in the last forty-six or fifty years. Count the men and women who, during these years, it has put into the ministry, the week-day and the Sabbath-schools, as preachers and teachers, and the souls converted, or made wiser and better, through their labors; count the souls it has led to the Cross, and then given to other denominations from its altars and its fellowship, and the good they have done, and are doing; count the large number transferred by letter to other Churches, scattered through half the states in the Union, from New York to California; count the sainted ones from the ranks of infancy, childhood, youth, middle life, and age, whom it has given to the shining hosts of heaven—a much larger number, they, than we are aware, till we stop and think, and count their graves—and take into account all the secret, silent, unseen, and unknown influences which have gone out from all these, for good of which none but God can truly know, but which, like Nature's hidden powers, are the most potent, after all; combine, in imagination, all that has been accomplished for good by the living and the dead in these five different channels indicated, of human thought and feeling, influence and agency,—and then you only approximate the true reckoning, as it shall appear in the last day.

SOUTH BEND.

JOHN BROWNFIELD, Esq., of South Bend, has furnished the principal facts in the following sketch of Methodism in that locality. In a note, under date of February, 1871, he says:

"South Bend was laid out in 1830. I visited this

county in 1833. I heard brothers Robinson and Beswick preach in Niles. Their mission extended from Fort Wayne to Lake Michigan, embracing Goshen, South Bend, Laporte, and Michigan City, in Indiana; also, Niles and St. Joseph, in Michigan. I settled here in 1834. There were then about forty Methodists, and a population of one hundred and seventy-five. In 1836, our number increased considerably; the new-comers being chiefly from Ohio, and among them Albert and L. W. Monson, and Obadiah Hackey, father of Rev. J. C. Hackey. The population was then about five hundred. I am sorry to say that Methodism, for the last five or six years, has not kept pace with the population. The United Brethren, who were early on the ground, and, in 1836, built a church, have now no organization at all in our town. Presbyterians, Baptists, Campbellites, and Catholics have come in, in considerable numbers. Our present population is about eight thousand. The first and second charges embrace about four hundred members, or one in twenty of our entire population."

On the 24th of January, 1831, Rev. N. B. Griffith, and Benjamin Ross and family, arrived at South Bend, and found Samuel Martin and wife, and Benjamin Potter and wife, members of the Methodist Episcopal Church. Griffith came as a missionary. There was a deep snow on the ground, and the weather was intensely cold; and as the few families in the village were sheltered in cabins and half-faced shanties, no room could be had large enough to accommodate the people for preaching, and Mr. Griffith left to bring his family to this new field of labor. On the evening of the 30th of January, the Methodist families of the village assembled at the house of Benjamin Ross, and held a prayer-meeting, which was the first Methodist worship, if not the first Protestant worship, held in South Bend. Some time in March following, Rev. L. B. Gurley, who was a missionary from the North Ohio Conference, visited South Bend, but found the field pre-empted by Griffith.

Early in April, Griffith returned, and on the evening of the 6th of April collected the people in the bar-room in a small tavern kept by Benjamin Coquillard, a Roman Catholic, and preached to the people, and organized the first class in South Bend, consisting of Samuel Martin and wife, Benjamin Potter and wife, Benjamin Ross and wife, Rebecca Stull, and Simeon Mason; of which class Martin and Ross were jointly appointed leaders. In June, 1831, Wm. Stanfield and wife came to South Bend, and were added to the little class by certificate; and Stanfield was soon after appointed leader. About the same time, Samuel Newman and wife were also added to the class by letter.

The first report we have of this mission is in the General Minutes for 1832, Illinois Conference, Crawfordsville District, N. B. Griffith; members reported, one hundred and eighty. In 1833, it is called St. Joseph and South Bend Mission, with R. S. Robinson and G. M. Beswick as missionaries. The mission was included in the Mission District, James Armstrong, Superintendent; and they reported for the year three hundred and twenty-three members. 1834, it was called South Bend Circuit. It was still included in Armstrong's district. Boyd Phelps was in charge of the circuit, assisted by T. P. M'Cool; members reported at the end of the year, five hundred and eleven. At this time all Protestant worship in South Bend was held in a small log school-house, which stood on the site of the new brick school-house on St. Joseph Street, in the Second Ward. 1835, South Bend Circuit is in Laporte

District, of which R. Hargrave was presiding elder; R. Ball and T. P. M'Cool were the circuit-preachers. They reported, at the end of the year, six hundred and nine members. During this Conference year a house of worship was built for the Methodist congregation, but was not taken off the builder's hands, because it had been so badly built.

In the Summer of 1835, the second story of a house still standing on the south-east corner of Pearl and St. Joseph Streets, was fitted up for a school-house, and the Methodists held their meetings there; and in it they were blessed with a good revival, in which a number were converted and added to the Church; and there, in November, 1835, the first Methodist Sunday-school was organized, by the adoption of a constitution and the election of officers. This school had, however, previously met for a few months in the kitchen of John Brownfield, without any formal organization.

The first Board of Church Trustees was elected February 6, 1835, and consisted of Samuel Martin, Johnson Howill, John Rush, E. W. Sweet, and John Brownfield. At a meeting of the trustees, March 5th, they resolved to build a frame church, thirty-five by forty-five feet, with a fourteen feet ceiling. In June, a lot was purchased, and on the 6th of July the contract for building and plastering was let. But in February following it was discovered that the church was built on the wrong lot, which caused considerable trouble; but finally an exchange was effected, and the building permitted to stand; and early in the Fall of 1836 it was finished and occupied. In 1835–36, J. Wolf was appointed to the circuit, but remained only a part of the year. In 1836–37, South Bend and Mishawaka were united, and R. S. Robinson was the preacher, and was reappointed the next year. He was succeeded by James S. Harrison. Owing to an extraordinary emigration to Wisconsin, the membership was reduced this year to 145, but came up during the year to 195. In 1839, South Bend was made a station, under the pastoral charge of David Stiver, who reported, at the end of the year, 276 members. In 1850–51, a brick church, forty-eight by seventy-two feet, was built on the corner of Main and Jefferson Streets, and was dedicated by Rev. Dr. Berry and John L. Smith, on the 17th day of August, 1851, the basement having been previously occupied for several months.

When the state was divided into four conferences, in 1852, South Bend was included in the North-west Indiana Conference.

In 1853–54, the trustees of the Church in South Bend built Portage Chapel, or, the Church at Zeigler's, as the record has it. In 1868–69, the second charge in South Bend was organized. It is due to the ladies of South Bend to say, that, as early as 1846, when the Church was weak, and greatly embarrassed by unpaid debts, the "Methodist Ladies' Sewing Society" came to the relief of the Church trustees, by proposing to donate to them all the funds of their Society, *provided* the brethren would add thirty-three per cent to the amount of their donation; and the surplus, after the payment of their debts, should go toward the purchase of a parsonage. This generous act wiped out all the debts against the Church, and secured a parsonage.

Since that time, the "Ladies' Mite Society" has paid several hundred dollars for furnishing the parsonage; several hundred dollars toward building the present parsonage; three hundred dollars toward the church-organ; and five hundred dollars toward the new church edifice; besides assuming several hundred dollars more toward.

furnishing the church. In addition to this, the " College Aid Society," composed of Ladies of the Methodist Episcopal Church, paid six hundred dollars for furnishing " Heck Hall" as a Centenary offering. The enterprise of the Methodist ladies of South Bend is worthy of all praise. In 1868, the present church edifice was enlarged, remodeled, and modernized. The lecture-room was finished and occupied December 25, 1869, and the upper room finished in the Summer of 1871. The worshipers are called together by an excellent bell, which cost the congregation $2,500, and the church, independent of the lot on which it stands, is worth $25,000.

METHODIST EPISCOPAL CHURCH IN ANDERSON, INDIANA.

BY REV. W. H. GOODE, D. D.

THE Church in this place was small in its beginnings, and, like the town itself, had a long period of struggle before it reached any permanent prosperity. It has *no early history* to relate. For many years it was a feeble appointment upon a large circuit. With the settlement of the country, and growth of the Church, the circuits were narrowed down by repeated divisions, until in 1857, the town of Anderson was made a station. About that time, a career of growth and prosperity came upon the town, which has steadily continued, till it has become the largest and most flourishing place within the same range of the state capital. With this, the Church has kept an even pace in numbers and aggressive vigor. The good men, few in number, that fought through the early struggle, have passed to their reward ; and now a strong and devoted body of working Christian men are at the laboring oar.

At an early day, a rude structure for worship was put up on the outskirts of the village, as was the wont of that day, but never finished, the old court-house being the standing resort. In 1851, a comfortable frame church was erected, which has been occupied till this date (1871). An elegant and commodious church edifice is now approaching completion, inferior to none in the North Indiana Conference, and to few in the state. There is a comfortable parsonage, with ample grounds; all the Church property is eligibly situated, the ministry is well sustained, the social influences are good, and the entire aspect is inviting. The numerical relation of our Church membership to the present population is about one to twelve. The increased accommodations offered by the new and spacious church may be expected greatly to enlarge the influence and the membership.

PERU.

METHODISM was introduced into Peru about 1830, by Ancil Beach and Amasa Johnson. The first society was organized by Miles Huffaker, in 1834. Among the members of the first class are the names of Colonel William Reyburn and wife, George S. Fennimore and wife, Mrs. M'Gregor, and Mrs. M'Gwin. The first church was built in 1835. There are now (1871) two charges in Peru. Main-street Church is a two-story brick building, and was erected in 1850. The Church was divided, in 1854, on the pew and organ question. The second charge, the old Third-street—now called St. Paul's—have just erected themselves a neat Gothic house of worship. The population of Peru is a little over 3,700, of whom 350 are Methodists, being one in every ten and one-half of the population.

METHODISM IN TERRE HAUTE.

THE first mention of Terre Haute in the Minutes of the Conference, is in connection with the appointments made at the session of the Illinois Conference, at Vincennes, in the Fall of 1830. Terre Haute is mentioned in the Wabash District, of which George Locke was presiding elder, and Edwin Ray is appointed to Terre Haute as a supernumerary. In 1831, Terre Haute is coupled with Carlisle, and Enoch G. Wood and William Taylor were the preachers. In 1832, Terre Haute Circuit had Anthony F. Thompson and John Richey. In the Fall of 1833, Richard Hargrave and William Watson were appointed to the circuit; and in 1834, J. White and David Stiver were appointed to the circuit. At the session of the Indiana Conference, in October, 1835, held in Lafayette, Terre Haute was made a station, and S. L. Robinson was appointed in charge of it. It was then in Vincennes District, of which Aaron Wood was the presiding elder. Down to 1833, the district was called Wabash, and for the years 1828, 1829, 1830, and 1831, George Locke—father of Rev. John W. Locke, D. D.,—was the presiding elder, and during a portion of that time his family resided in Terre Haute. Mrs. Locke taught school and supported the family, while her husband traveled that large frontier district. Mrs. Locke conducted a boarding-school for young ladies, in Terre Haute, the first of the kind that was ever taught in that town, and probably the first in the state. Terre Haute was favored with a certain sort of cultured society from the beginning. Its proximity to Fort Harrison, a military post of considerable importance in that day, favored it with the society of the officers of the regular army, who were educated men. The religious element in the community was not strong, and their social amusements, as might be expected, partook of a gay and worldly type. A ball had been determined on, but in order to get the requisite number of young ladies, it was thought best by the managers to ticket those attending Mrs. Locke's boarding-school. Accordingly, one of their number was deputized to visit the school, inform Mrs. Locke of their purposes, and present the young ladies with tickets. Mr. Jones—for such we will call him—in pursuance of his mission, called on Mrs. Locke one afternoon, informed her of his errand, and requested to see the young ladies. Mrs. Locke thanked him for his kindness, and told him she would invite the young ladies into the parlor presently, when he could lay his message before them. Meanwhile, she engaged him in conversation so entertainingly, that the time ran rapidly by, and when she invited the young ladies into the parlor she informed Mr. Jones that tea was ready; and urged him so kindly and persistently to accompany the young ladies to the tea-table, that, although reluctant to do so, he could not decline. When seated at the table, Mrs. Locke said, "Mr. Jones, will you please ask a blessing?" Mr. Jones very politely, but with considerable embarrassment, begged to be excused. Mrs. Locke, as her custom was, then attended to that duty, and then entered into immediate conversation with Mr. Jones, endeavoring to make him feel as much at ease as was possible under the circumstances. She then said, "Mr. Jones, if I am not mistaken, you were once a professor of religion, and a member of the Methodist Church." He admitted that such was the fact. Said Mrs. Locke, "I would be glad if you would state, for the information of the young ladies, whether or not, when you were a member of the Church, attending to your Church duties, and in the enjoyment of religion, you were not a happier man than you are now, while depending on the pleasures of the world for enjoyment." He responded: "I have often thought that I was not only happier when in the enjoyment of religion than I am now, but that I was happier even as a penitent seeking salvation, than I am now; and I assure you there is no comparison between the enjoyment I had as a Christian, and what I now experience as a man of the world. My heart is now often sad and desolate, even amid scenes of gayety and mirth." She kindly exhorted him to come back to Christ, and regain his first love. Repairing to the parlor, at the close of supper, Mrs. Locke said, "It is our custom to have prayers immediately after tea," and handing Mr. Jones a Bible, requested him to read a chapter, and lead them in prayer, which he declined; when Mrs. Locke read a lesson, and engaged fervently in prayer, not forgetting to pray for Mr. Jones, that he might be reclaimed from his backslidings, and also for the young ladies, that they might not be led into temptation. When Mr. Jones withdrew, Mrs. Locke kindly invited him to call on them again; but he never found it convenient to accept the invitation. And he said to the managers, if any of them thought there was any fun in ticketing Mrs. Locke's young ladies to a ball, they were welcome to try it; as for himself, he should not undertake that task again.

The following sketch of Methodism in Terre Haute, from 1836 to 1848, is from the pen of Colonel Thomas Dowling:

"FIRST CHURCH ORGANIZATION.

"On the 29th day of February, 1836, John Jackson, Sylvester S. Sibley, Thos. Dowling, and James B. M'Call were severally elected trustees of the Methodist Episcopal Church of the town of Terre Haute, and were regularly, according to law, qualified as such. Their first meeting was held March 1, 1836. John Jackson was chosen President, James B. M'Call, Secretary, and

S. S. Sibley, Treasurer. The first business considered was the propriety of erecting a house of worship, as none then existed.

"On motion of Mr. Dowling,

"*Resolved*, That this Board, relying upon the liberality and good feelings of the people of Vigo County, will proceed to raise, by subscription, funds for the purpose of building a place of public worship for the use of the Methodist Episcopal Church of Terre Haute.

"On motion of Jas. B. M'Call, Thos. Dowling was appointed to draft rules for the government of this Board.

"This Board of Trustees at once proceeded to raise a fund to pay for the proposed church edifice, and the little brick on the corner of the present site of Asbury went up during the year.

"Terre Haute station was organized in 1836. The Rev. Aaron Wood was the first presiding elder, and Rev. Smith L. Robinson stationed minister. In 1837, John Miller was elder, and John A. Brouse preacher-in-charge. The elder continued in charge of the district till 1839, when Rev. E. R. Ames (now bishop) was appointed, with Ebenezer Patrick in the station, and continued till 1841. This year the Rev. John S. Bayless was sent to the Terre Haute Station.

"It will occur to the reader that the station started off in good time, with Aaron Wood, John Miller, and Edward R. Ames as its first three presiding elders. Perhaps the Indiana Conference did not hold three ministers of equal ability in those days. Two of them yet survive, as beacon-lights of Methodism, we hope not soon to go out forever. John A. Brouse, who was universally popular with the Church and people, yet lives. Brothers Robinson, Patrick, and Bayless have gone to their reward.

"The Methodist Church in Terre Haute had a feeble

15

footing in this small place till about the year 1841. The little brick church, which stood facing the south, on the present site of Asbury, was of small dimensions, and would not accommodate more than one hundred and fifty persons. In the year above named, this little edifice gave way to the present fine building, which was completed and occupied the following Winter. The Rev. John S. Bayless was the pastor in charge of the station while the building was in the course of erection, and I well remember how he complained about the tardiness with which the promised subscriptions were paid. As it was the first church building erected of any kind— the small church on the corner excepted—there did not seem to be a very feeling sense of obligation on the part of those who signed the paper pledging pecuniary aid. The principal business men came forward promptly and placed their dollars in the hands of the Building Committee; but another class, whose generosity far exceeded their ability, fell lamentably in the rear. Brother Bayless was, however, a first-class collector, full of energy and force, and did a wonderful amount of hard begging. This greatly helped to keep the treasury of the Building Committee from becoming entirely empty, and prevented a collapse of the enterprise for the year. The church was finally finished, with a debt of between three and four thousand dollars hanging over it, which was subsequently paid by the exertions of a few active members of the Church. Jabez S. Carter, who is yet living, was one of the most prominent in this act of justice to the creditors of Asbury. I think the debt was finally discharged in 1844–45, during the pastorate of the Rev. S. T. Gillett, who felt, as all Christian ministers should feel, that a Church debt is neither a moral nor a temporal blessing. Besides not looking well, it is a positive evil, which good men should not encourage.

"There are tides in the affairs of men and Churches, which, taken at the flood-tide, lead on to fortune and success. The erection of a new edifice, or the advent of a particular minister, very often gives a new and healthy impetus to the growth of a religious sentiment in community. From the location of a town two miles south of Fort Harrison, on the Wabash River (now Terre Haute, or *Land High*), in .1818, up to the year 1835, there was no church edifice of any kind within its borders. If there were any Church members, the fact has escaped my recollection. No doubt there were some in the neighborhood and in the county, and perhaps many such among the settlers in their *old* home in the states from whence they emigrated; but having no religious 'organizations' here, they drifted along as nonconformists, without any of the restraints of Church government. This was then a frontier town, older than Indianapolis, or Lafayette, or Springfield, Illinois. Above the site of the town, on the Wabash River, stood a military post (Fort Harrison), located as early as 1809, where one or more companies of United States troops were kept to protect the emigrants that sought homes in the West. When Terre Haute was located, in 1818, Indiana had just been admitted into the Union, and the country between this place and Vincennes was an almost unbroken wilderness. A 'settlement,' here and there, was the only evidence of civilization, and they were but few and far between. When Terre Haute was laid out, and lots sold, it attracted considerable attention, and emigrants sought it as an abiding-place. The beauty of its location was the theme of many a tongue and pen, and has so continued to the present day. Perhaps no town in Indiana presents a more beautiful and inviting landscape, or enjoys a higher reputation for unquestioned natural comforts. Such a place would necessarily invite and secure a good class of settlers. And hither they came from every portion and section of the country. New England, the Middle States, Pennsylvania, New York, Maryland, Virginia, Kentucky, the Carolinas, and even England, Canada, and Ireland, sent out their quotas to settle this modern El Dorado. The soldiers at the fort, and their accomplished officers of the regular army, were in the neighborhood for many years before the town was laid off. The new emigrants, principally young and unmarried, with these officers, formed at once a little society of their own, which it was difficult to excel in any of the older towns of the West. They were, as a general thing, young men of education and refinement, who had brought from their old homes those ideas of propriety which forbid the indulgence of the grosser vices. . If it were proper in such a paper as this, I could mention names which, in the subsequent history of Indiana, were connected with high official and social positions. We have, to-day, many of the descendants of these early settlers living in Terre Haute, scores of them the prosperous business men of our young city.

"This was the primitive population among whom the itinerant ministry of the Methodist Church had to inaugurate and build up its religious influence, as a branch of the Church of God. It was far from being hostile to the growth of good morals, or the spread of religion itself. While this can be truly said, there was a sentiment of quiet soberness about all manifestations of a religious nature, which many ministers mistook for a careless or hostile character. Nothing could be more unjust to the original inhabitants of Terre Haute, as subsequent events have abundantly proved. The facility with which Churches were organized and temples erected, when the proper agencies were employed, proved, beyond all doubt, that the right sentiment always existed, and only required an incentive to effort and action. When proper and rightful organization was effected; when a Church sanctuary was proposed and provided, the people flocked by hundreds to worship Almighty God, and Terre Haute became one of the favored locations for plain, practical Methodism.

"The greatest occasion for the manifestation of this interest in Church affairs was after the completion of 'ASBURY.' That was the 'tide' on which success was secured. The membership manifested their zeal and earnestness in the cause of religion, by securing a house dedicated to the worship of God, and *all* our people aided in the work. When the membership of a Church are earnest and practical workers, there is sure to be an outside influence which tells happily on all their surroundings. This was pre-eminently the case in Terre Haute. We had, in those days, say from 1841 onward, many excellent stationed ministers, aided by presiding elders of acknowledged ability. The venerable Allen Wiley had charge of the district in 1841. All the old membership remember this devoted man, and how earnestly he labored in the cause of his Master. In 1842–43, the district was favored by the appointment of George M. Beswick as presiding elder, with the Rev. Joseph Marsee as preacher-in-charge. Both these brethren were what is rightfully called *workers*. Brother Marsee was an especial favorite with all classes of our citizens. In 1844, Mr. Beswick was again the presiding elder, and the Rev. Samuel T. Gillet the preacher-in-charge. This last appointed was received with great favor by the congregation, and more especially by those who yet stood *outside* of the Church organization. The new minister was a gentleman of most agreeable and winning manners, and pronounced 'the right man in the right place.'. There was no question of his entire acceptability from the start; and he grew in favor with our citizens, in and out of the Church. His public discourses were of that order which stamped him as a scholar, and all awarded him the character of a true Christian minister. He was continued for two years, to the satisfaction of the Church and its congregation, and all regretted the *rule* which forbade his service for a longer period.

"At the Conference, in 1845, that body sent to us the Rev. W. H. Goode as presiding elder, and the Rev. Amasa Johnson as stationed minister. The Church and people had long known Mr. Goode, by reputation, and his transfer to the district was a matter of general rejoicing. Perhaps, in the whole range of the Conference members, no man could have been more heartily indorsed; and their judgment of the man, in advance, was entirely justified by his services to the district. He left his ministerial work, after four years of faithful service, greatly beloved by all. The Rev. A. Johnson was a *new* man, about and of whom the citizens in the Church and out of it knew nothing. He entered on his work, it may be truly said, without any prejudices for or against him. But he was not long here before the sterling qualities of his character became known. He was a very remarkable person. To the plainest of manners he united the quaintest of speech and expression. He was never undignified or frivolous, but always pointed and entertaining. As a preacher, but few could have been more successful. There was a *directness* in all that he uttered which went home to the heart and the understanding.

In the private circle he never forgot that he was a minister, and yet no man was more popular with our people. Brother Johnson remained in the station two years, and carried with him the love and affection of the Church over which he watched.

"The Conference of 1847 sent to the Terre Haute Station the Rev. John L. Smith, one of the oldest and best-known ministers in that body. Every one had a knowledge of him, either personally or by repute. To receive him kindly, and without dissent, was accepted as a matter of course. He was among the strongest and ablest in the long list of veterans which graced the Church a quarter of a century ago. Unlike his predecessor, every one knew and recognized John L. Smith as the peer of any individual in the Conference; and, by common consent, the appointment was considered one eminently 'fit to be made.' His ability as a preacher and his popularity as a citizen were the gifts which gave him a passport to any circle in Terre Haute. In looking back over the quarter of a century which has elapsed since brother Smith's advent to the principal Church here, the writer has not known one who so completely filled the character of an early Methodist minister. Strong in argument, forcible in manner and language, and often eloquent, his congregations and people increased to a noticeable degree. He will not soon be forgotten by our older citizens, among whom he labored for two years.

"The above narrative carries the history of Methodism in Terre Haute up to the Summer of 1848, and the further history must find another pen. The writer has aimed only to give a review of the elders and preachers who were workers on the district and on the station. It is proper to digress here and go back a few years, to notice the agencies by which the Methodist

Church has attained a strong and sure foot-hold in this young city.

"The establishment of Asbury College at Greencastle has greatly aided Methodism in this city, and especially at Asbury Church. The head of that College for many years, President (now Bishop) Simpson, was a great favorite in Terre Haute, and the writer of this flatters himself and his neighbors in the belief that Terre Haute was always a great favorite with the bishop. Be that as it may, the President of Asbury College manifested a strong interest in the people domiciled here. Very many times he left his quiet home at Greencastle to spend a Sabbath day in Terre Haute, and, on more than one occasion, prolonged his visit for many days, preaching in Asbury Church night after night. To say that the house was full, would but feebly express the crowds which attended on his ministrations. The church was jammed nightly, and even standing-room was not allowed to hundreds who sought admission. This was in 1842, 1843, and 1844. At our camp-meetings in Honey Creek, Otter Creek, and Raccoon, the kind and amiable Matthew Simpson was never absent. On these occasions he addressed thousands, and the amount of good which was done, while its fruits were visible in the changed lives of hundreds in this neighborhood, can only be known on the great day 'for which all other days were made.' These were years of unexampled prosperity to the cause of Methodism and the religion of the Savior. The commanding eloquence and the earnest prayers of that good and great man produced a wonderful impression in the community; hundreds of the best-known and most prominent of our citizens were in constant attendance at the then new church. The matter and manner of these sermons were new in this place, and it is quite unnecessary for me to define them. That style of preaching belongs to himself alone. I would remark, however, that in no town in Indiana could President Simpson address a people better prepared to appreciate his wonderful gifts. It was in those years that Methodism got the start of all the other denominations in this place; and when I say that Asbury College aided Asbury Church in her career of usefulness, it is simply acknowledging a fact patent to every old inhabitant of Terre Haute. Like all excitements, it begat a spirit of rivalry in the Churches, and, in that way, revivals became numerous."

Terre Haute has now two churches, Asbury and Centenary, and one good parsonage, worth on the aggregate $43,000. There are in these charges over six hundred communicants, and more than one thousand one hundred children in their Sabbath-schools; and the prospect for Methodism in Terre Haute in the future is brighter than at any former period. The greatest obstacle to the progress of Methodism in Terre Haute has always been a disposition on the part of those who have assumed to be the leaders in the more wealthy and fashionable circles of society to conform to the questionable amusements of the world; and because the discipline of Methodism is less pliant in that respect than that of some other Churches, a persistent effort has been made to produce the impression that Methodists were less intelligent and less cultivated than the members of some other Churches. But the experiment of letting the Church down to the world can at best only result in temporary success, and is sure to be followed with more lasting evils. An earnest and Scriptural piety is the best guarantee of the Church's permanent prosperity. And while it is the glory of the Church to lift up the lowly, to hunt for the outcasts, and to preach the Gospel to the poor, Methodism is too thoroughly the patron of education, and her communicants average so well in the general class of good society, that the day of her reproach on the score of ignorance is gone by. Her mission is to all classes of society, and right well has she thus far fulfilled it.

METHODISM IN MADISON.

METHODISM was early introduced into the city of Madison. A class was formed among the early settlers, and regular circuit-preaching established. Among the early Methodist families was the family of old Mr. M'Intyre, who for many years was one of the prominent and wealthy men of the city. Rev. Gamaliel Taylor, who came out from Baltimore, was also among the early Methodists. He was a zealous and efficient local preacher, and a prominent citizen of the state, and was for some time United States Marshal for the District of Indiana. His oldest son, John H. Taylor, Esq., was for a number of years clerk of the Circuit Court for the county of Jefferson, of which the city of Madison is the seat of justice. He was for many years recording steward. Father Taylor always dressed in a round-breasted coat and white neck-handkerchief. He was remarkably neat in person, commanding in appearance, active in his movements, and earnest and consistent in his piety. The family of Robinsons were also Baltimore Methodists, and settled in Madison in an early day. Several families of Richeys settled in and near Madison in an early day, some of whom still remain, and are prominent in the Church. David Wilson was among the early Methodists in Madison; and, at a little later date, John Pugh, John Woodburn, and William Thomas are found among the active

Methodists of the place. The Radical controversy of 1828 rent the Church in two in Madison, and produced great bitterness for a number of years; but finally the waning fortunes of Radicalism left the field to the old Church.

For a number of years Madison was the most prominent and prosperous town in the state. The first railroad in the state had its river terminus at Madison, and after it was opened, the Madison and Indianapolis Railroad enjoyed a monopoly of the carrying trade and travel for a number of years. All of the goods shipped to the interior passed through Madison; and the travel from a great part of the state, for Cincinnati and points further east, also went through that place. But after the railroad system of the state became developed, Madison was left at one side; her commerce declined; and, although a beautiful and healthy city, she has not been able to compete with her more eligibly situated rivals. In their Church extension movements the Methodists of Madison have not been fortunate. Wesley Chapel was centrally and eligibly located, being in the heart of the city, and on one of its principal streets. When Third-street—since called Roberts Chapel—was organized, instead of building in one end of the city, where it could have had a legitimate field of its own, those having the enterprise in charge determined to build as near Wesley Chapel as they could; and, as was to have been anticipated, they became rivals and antagonists, when they should have been mutual helpers in promoting the salvation of the people. St. John's, in the upper part of the city, was well located at the time it was built; but when a change of circumstances made it desirable to reduce the number of charges in the city, the location of the churches has been found to be an impediment in the way.

The charges now are: Wesley, members, 150; Trinity, 224; North Madison, which includes some country appointments, and numbers 314 members. The Church property is valued at $16,400. The Sabbath-school children number 645.

METHODISM IN VINCENNES.

METHODIST preaching was established at Fort St. Vincent at an early day. Tradition says that General Harrison held the candle for Rev. William Winans to read his text, at a night service in the fort. The early settlers, being French traders and Roman Catholics, and Vincennes continuing to be the head-quarters of the Romish Church in Indiana, being the residence of the Bishop for Indiana, has drawn to it a large Catholic population, and made it relatively an unfruitful field for Protestantism. But through the liberality of Mr. Bonner, Dr. Hitt, and a few large-hearted Methodists, a good Methodist church was built at an early day, and Vincennes was among the early and desirable stations in Indiana Conference.

Vincennes has one church, valued at $10,000, one parsonage, valued at $2,500, a membership of 271, and 275 children in Sabbath-school.

HISTORY OF METHODISM AT FORT WAYNE.

BY order of General Wayne, a fort was erected on the banks of the beautiful Maumee, in the year 1794, where the city of Fort Wayne now stands. From that time until about the year 1827 or 1828, there were but few persons there save military men, Indian traders, and Miami Indians. Occasionally a Methodist preacher, traveling through the country, preached the word of life to the soldiers, trappers, and traders living there. The first

Methodists who became permanent citizens were Rev. James Holman and his wife, in the year 1831. He was a local preacher, and, without command of conference or bishop, commenced, immediately after his arrival, to hold prayer and class meetings, and fearlessly to declare the whole counsel of God. Frequently his congregations did not number more than eight or ten persons. He first preached in private rooms and shops. As soon as there was a school-house built, it became the church for all— Protestants and Catholics. The first regular pastor was Rev. N. B. Griffith, who was appointed to Fort Wayne Mission in the Fall of 1831. This Mission was organized by the Illinois Conference, and was in the Madison District, Rev. Allen Wiley, Presiding Elder. The first class regularly organized, under the supervision of the pastor, Rev. Mr. Griffith, consisted of Rev. James Holman, class-leader; Mrs. Holman, Robert Breckenridge, Hannah Breckenridge, and Desdemona M'Carty. Before the close of this Conference year Mr. Griffith obtained permission and preached in the Masonic Hall—a small brick house which stood near the canal basin. Richard S. Robinson was Mr. Griffith's successor. He was appointed to Fort Wayne Mission in the Fall of 1832. Allen Wiley was presiding elder, and the mission was still in the Madison District. During this Conference year there were added to the society, James Hamilton, Eliza Hamilton, Cynthia Edsall, and Mary Alderman. At the close of this year the Church consisted of nine members. In the year 1833, this mission was set off from the Illinois Conference by the organization of the Indiana Conference. Boyd Phelps was the pastor, and James Armstrong presiding elder. In 1834 and 1835, Freeman Farnsworth was the pastor, and Richard Hargrave was presiding elder, on Laporte District, in which

Fort Wayne was now included. In 1835 and 1836, J. S. Harrison was pastor, and preached in the court-house. In the Conference year of 1836 and 1837, Stephen R. Ball was pastor. This year the mission was in Center-ville District, and David Stiver was the presiding elder. The preaching-place was changed from the court-house to M'Junkins's school-house. In the Conference year of 1837 and 1838, Stephen R. Ball was continued as pastor; Richard Hargrave was presiding elder. In 1838 and 1839, James T. Robe was pastor. The charge was now a circuit, and was connected with the Logansport Dis-trict, George M. Beswick, Presiding Elder. In the Con-ference year of 1839 and 1840, Rev. Jacob Colclazer was pastor. During this year the first Methodist Sab-bath-school was organized at Fort Wayne. Stephen R. Ball was superintendent; teachers, Eliza Hamilton, Char-lotte Breckenridge, Hannah Johns, Theodore Hoagland, Oliver Fairfield, and John M. Miller. The school was organized with about thirty-eight scholars. A collection was taken for Sunday-school books, amounting to twenty-five dollars and sixty-two cents. Two of the above-named teachers are still living in Fort Wayne—Eliza Hamilton, a member of Berry-street Church, and John M. Miller, a member of Wayne-street Church, both noted for their liberality and zeal.

The growth of Methodism in this city has been grad-ual but permanent and progressive. The following is the present status: Three churches, worth $36,000; two par-sonages, worth $13,000; and a membership of between six and seven hundred.

FORT WAYNE COLLEGE.

FORT WAYNE COLLEGE, under its present organization, is the result of a consolidation of the Fort Wayne Female

College and the Fort Wayne Collegiate Institute, on the
10th of October, 1855. The first of these was intended
exclusively for the education of females; the latter, for
males only. The present institution educates both. The
Fort Wayne Female College originated with the North
Indiana Conference at its third session, held in Laporte,
in 1846. The Conference, at that session, resolved to
found such an institution, located it at Fort Wayne, and
appointed therefor a temporary Board of Trustees. On
the 18th day of January, 1847, the General Assembly
of the State of Indiana passed an act incorporating the
Board of Trustees thus appointed by the Conference,
and giving to Fort Wayne Female College all the legal
rights and privileges usually belonging to such institutions; this act of legal corporation to take effect on
the 19th day of June, 1847; at which time the Board
met, and organized by the appointment of the proper
officers. The Collegiate Institute had been organized
by the friends of the Female College in May, 1853;
and, though having a separate act of incorporation, was
a little more than an adjunct of the College. It was,
therefore, thought best by the friends of both institutions to unite them under one management, and form
a single institution, for both males and females. This
was effected, as before stated, on the 10th of October,
1855; since which the joint institution has been known
as Fort Wayne College. For several years it was
seriously embarrassed with debt; but, through the exertions of Rev. R. D. Robinson, as financial agent, while
acting as President of the College, it was relieved of its
burdens, and entered upon a career of greater prosperity.
Since the Centenary Year, 1866, financially, the institution has been more prosperous than formerly, and the
buildings and grounds have been greatly improved. The

grounds and buildings are estimated at sixty thousand dollars. The following have served as Presidents of the College: A. C. Heustis, A. M., 1847; Rev. G. M. Round, A. M., 1848; Rev. C. Nutt, D. D., 1849; A. C. Heustis, 1850 and 1851; Rev. Samuel T. Gillet, D. D., 1852; Rev. Samuel Brenton, A. M., 1853 and 1854; Rev. R. D. Robinson, A. M., 1855 and 1866, inclusive; Rev. F. M. Heminway, A. M., 1868; Rev. J. B. Robinson, A. M., 1869 and 1870.

METHODISM IN EVANSVILLE.

CIRCUIT-PREACHING was established in Evansville when it was a small village; and, although the society was not large in numbers, they early asked to be made a station, that they might have regular Sabbath preaching. Two local preachers by the name of Wheeler, and another by the name of Parrott, aided much in introducing Methodism into that part of the state. Few portions of the state are richer in interesting local Methodist history than Evansville and its vicinity; but the author has been disappointed in securing the accurate data that will enable him to furnish a reliable history of the introduction and progress of the Church in that locality; and hence this brief extract. The present charges are Trinity, Ingle-street, Trinity City Mission, and Evansville Circuit, with an aggregate membership of 1,145, with a Church property valued at $108,500. They have 1,250 children in Sabbath-school.

CHAPTER XIII.

Social Achievements of Methodism—Hon. Amos Lane—Hon. Henry Blasdell—Hon. John H. Thompson—Rev. Samuel Brenton—Hon. James Whitcomb—Hon. Joseph A. Wright—Hon. Elisha Embree—Hon. R. W. Thompson—Hon. Henry S. Lane—Hon. A. C. Downey—Hon. Will Cumback—Mrs. Larrabee—Mrs. Locke—Mrs. Julia Dumont—Father Stockwell—Hon. W. C. De Pauw—John C. Moore—Indiana Missionaries—Elect Ladies—Eveline Thomas—Lydia Hawes.

WHILE the mission of Methodism has been emphatically to the common people, and while its leaders have never sought the patronage of the State, nor courted the special favor of those in power, it has, nevertheless, contributed its share toward molding the institutions of the State, developing and applying its educational resources, shaping its legislation, educating the public conscience, and furnishing a respectable share of our leading public men. Several of the members of the Convention that framed the first Constitution for the State were Methodists; among whom was Rev. Hugh Cull, of Wayne County, who lived to be over a hundred years of age; and Dennis Pennington, from Harrison County, who also served a number of years in the State Legislature. William Hendricks, who was secretary of the Convention, who was the third Governor of the State, and for some time a representative in Congress, was, in his later years, a member of the Methodist Church.

Hon. Amos Lane, a leading lawyer of Lawrenceburg, and who represented his district several terms in Congress, became a member of the Church late in life. He

16

had been a regular attendant upon the ministry of the Church all through life, and his house was always a welcome home to the itinerant. His wife, who was a lady of superior endowments and liberal education, was a consistent, earnest Methodist, and carried the savor of true piety into all the circles in which she moved.

Hon. Henry Blasdell, the worthy and popular Governor of Nevada, himself an active Methodist, is the son of worthy Methodist parents in Dearborn County.

Hon. John H. Thompson, who united with the Church in his boyhood, was in public office in Indiana during the most of a long life. He was commissioned a justice of the peace by Governor Harrison before the State Government was organized. He was a member of the State Legislature for several terms, and served twelve years as president judge of a judicial circuit. He was Lieutenant-Governor for one term, and was Receiver of Public Moneys' for several years. He was continually in important offices for a period of thirty years. He never shrank from a frank profession of his faith on all suitable occasions. He was gathered to his rest in the ninetieth year of his age.

Rev. Samuel Brenton, the son of a worthy local preacher, himself an itinerant preacher until impaired health compelled him to desist, was for some time President of Fort Wayne College, and for three terms a representative of that district in Congress, where his ability as a statesman was manifest and acknowledged.

Hon. James Whitcomb, twice Governor of the State, and United States Senator at the time of his death, was a Methodist, and a superior Sunday-school teacher. He possessed superior talents, and was a gentleman of culture, and his administration as a governor left an impression on the State for good that will never be wiped out.

Hon. Joseph A. Wright, twice Governor of the State, twice United States Minister to the Court of Berlin, and for some time United States Senator by appointment, was from early manhood a Methodist, a liberal-minded and efficient Christian worker.

Hon. Elisha Embree, for some time circuit judge in the southern end of the State, and for one term a representative of his district in Congress, carried with him, on the bench and into the halls of national legislation, the influence of a noble Christian character.

Hon. R. W. Thompson, a gentleman of rare talents as an orator, ripe in scholarship, profound as a jurist and statesman, served for many years in Congress, and filled other important trusts confided to him by the National Government, has, through a series of years, been identified with the Church, sharing her privileges, and cheerfully doing her work.

Hon. Henry S. Lane, the gifted orator and distinguished statesman, a representative in the National Congress for several terms, Governor of the State, and United States Senator, is an earnest Church worker, and has given much time to the educational interests of Methodism in Indiana.

Hon. A. C. Downey, a distinguished jurist, and one of the Supreme Judges of the State, has been a faithful Church member from his boyhood, and is an earnest defender of Christian morality, and a consistent exemplifier of Christian graces.

Hon. Will Cumback served one term as a representative in Congress, and one term as State Senator, and was elected Lieutenant-Governor of the State. Served as United States Paymaster in the army, during the Rebellion, and has filled sundry offices, from the State and National Government, and always maintained a true

Christian character. He is an earnest Sabbath-school worker, and a bold advocate of Christian morality.

Methodism has furnished two of the most popular and efficient Presidents of the State University that that institution has ever had—Dr. Daily and Dr. Nutt. She has furnished three of the Superintendents of Public Instruction for the State; to wit, W. C. Larrabee, who served two terms; G. W. Hoss, who served two terms; and Miles J. Fletcher, who was killed by a railroad disaster, during the War, early in his term of service. Methodism is well represented in all the professions. She has furnished a liberal share of writers and educators, considering the age of our State. Few schools have done more to advance female education than the seminary founded at Greencastle by Mrs. Larrabee, and conducted by her for a number of years. Mrs. Locke, the wife of Rev. George Locke, and mother of Rev. John W. Locke, D. D., was among the early educators in Indiana. She taught school and supported the family, while her husband traveled and preached the Gospel to the poor. Mrs. Julia Dumont, of Vevay, was in the front rank of gifted writers and poets, in the early history of the State. Father Stockwell, of Lafayette, Hon. W. C. De Pauw, of New Albany, and the late John C. Moore, founder and patron of Moore's Hill College, each, by their generous contributions to the cause of education, rank in the list of public benefactors. These are some of the contributions of Methodism to the front ranks of cultivated society in Indiana.

Methodism in Indiana has contributed to the number of Christian workers in heathen lands. Two of the missionaries now laboring in South America, Rev. H. G. Jackson, Superintendent of the Missions, and Rev. Thomas B. Wood, son of Dr. Aaron Wood, are both from

Indiana. Rev. W. S. Turner, from Indiana, was the first Methodist preacher ever stationed in the Sandwich Islands. Joseph R. Downey and wife, who went as missionaries to India, in 1859, have, by their labors and their death in that mission field, established a bond of sympathy between that vast empire and Christian hearts in Indiana, that will never be broken until Christ shall receive the "heathen for his inheritance, and the uttermost parts of the earth for his possession."

But the glory of the Church is seen, not so much in the prominence of a gifted or privileged few, nor in the liberality of her wealthy men, although these are elements of power, and may be instruments of good, as in the thousands that have been reclaimed from sin, and are walking in the light of Christian purity and love, and in the tens of thousands who, converted in their youth, have been guided in the paths of knowledge and usefulness and honor, through the Church's instrumentality.

In nearly every community there have been "elect ladies" who by their intelligent piety, and ardent yet unostentatious Christian zeal, have contributed much to the Church's influence. Eveline Thomas, in the city of Madison, although a lady of comparatively delicate constitution, and retiring disposition, was, nevertheless, in that community, for the space of some twenty years, a recognized Christian power. The depth of her Christian experience, the strength of her faith, and the cheerfulness of her piety, combined with Christian activity in the sphere of her labor, gave her a prominence that she never sought, and a power of which she was all unconscious. Lydia Hawes, of Indianapolis, whose singing is almost national in its reputation, not so much from its artistic culture as from the rich tones of her voice, especially when under strong religious emotion, and the melting pathos with which she gives utterance to the grand truths of theology, and the great and precious privileges of Christian experience as embodied in the hymnology of the Church,—her labors have been wonderfully blessed through a period of more than thirty years. Few ministers equal her in efficiency, in times of religious revivals. She is remarkably successful in leading penitents to Christ; and the fervor of her prayers, the inspiration of her singing, and the narration of her rich Christian experience, often make a profounder impression than the most searching appeals from the pulpit.

CHAPTER XIV.

The Fathers—Rev. A. Wood, D. D.—Rev. Joseph Tarkington—Rev. Enoch Wood, D. D.—Rev. John Schrader—Rev. John Miller—Rev. Amasa Johnson—Rev. Asa Beck—Rev. James Scott—Rev. Elijah Whitten—Rev. Henry S. Talbott—Rev. Richard Hargrave—Rev. Robert Burns—Rev. John W. Sullivan—Rev. David Stiver—Rev. James T. Robe—Rev. Charles Bonner—Rev. John Kearns—Rev. John C. Smith—Rev. John A. Brouse—Rev. James Havens—Rev. Calvin W. Ruter—Rev. Allen Wiley—Rev. Augustus Eddy.

THE FATHERS.

PROMINENT among the fallen heroes of Indiana Methodism who toiled, suffered, and died to lay the foundations of the Church, in the early settlement of our state, are the names of John Strange, Allen Wiley, Calvin W. Ruter, James Armstrong, James Havens, N. B. Griffith, James L. Thompson, James Jones, William Shanks, William Cravens, Edwin Ray, Amasa Johnson, and George M. Beswick. These, with many of their associates, many of them their peers in ability, and equally useful in their day, though not so widely known, all died in the faith. But some of the Fathers are yet with us, whose heroic deeds and self-sacrificing piety the Church will garner up and cherish as a precious legacy.

REV. A. WOOD, D. D.

BROTHER WOOD was licensed to preach, August 24, 1822, by John Strange, then presiding elder of Lebanon District, Ohio Conference, by a vote of the Quarterly Conference of Mad-river Circuit, and the same Fall was admitted on trial into the Ohio Conference, and appointed as junior preacher on London Circuit, with George W. Maley as preacher-in-charge. He traveled 2,260 miles during the year, and preached 233 times.

Brother Wood's parents were eminently pious. He was saved in his youth from every form of immorality, and early obtained a knowledge of his personal acceptance with God, through faith in Jesus Christ, and united with the Church. He was born in Virginia, October 15, 1802, and was brought by his parents to the state of Ohio when but three years of age. He had aptness for learning, and secured a good English education, including a knowledge of English grammar. He formed in youth a taste for reading, and a habit of study, which have characterized him all through life. In the Summer of 1820 he began to lead prayer-meetings, and occasionally exhort; and in December, 1820, he was licensed to exhort by R. W. Finley; and during that Winter he took his first lesson in itinerancy, traveling a part of the way around the circuit with A. S. M'Lane. During 1821, Mr. Wood spent most of his time in school, working on the farm out of school hours, and in the Winter of 1821–22 he taught school.

September 10, 1823, the Ohio Conference closed its session in Urbana. At this session young Wood was appointed to Connersville Circuit, in the eastern border of Indiana. On the 12th of September he left his father's house for his new circuit; this was on Friday, and he rode to Father Mosser's, who resided twelve miles from Dayton. On Saturday he rode to Centerville, Indiana, which he reached late in the evening, having traveled sixty miles during the day. He spent the Sabbath in Centerville, and preached in the court-house; and on Monday, October 15, 1823, arrived at Connersville, the head-quarters of his new circuit. During this year he traveled 2,250 miles, preached 288 times, did not miss a single appointment during the year, and received forty dollars for his support.

In September, 1824, the Ohio Conference met at Zanesville, at which Mr. Wood was received into full connection, and ordained deacon by Bishop Roberts. At this Conference he was appointed to Madison Circuit as junior preacher, with Allen Wiley in charge.

Beginning with 1822, Dr. Wood traveled the following circuits: 1822, London Circuit, in Ohio; 1823, Connersville, in Indiana; 1824, Madison; 1825, Vincennes; 1826, Bloomington; 1827 and 1828, Mt. Carmel, in Illinois; 1829, Corydon, Indiana; 1830, Vincennes; 1831, Mt. Carmel, Illinois,—when he located, and remained in the local ranks until 1834, when he was appointed presiding elder on Vincennes District, having been readmitted into the Conference. In 1836 and 1837, he was agent for Indiana Asbury University. In 1837, he was stationed in New Albany. In 1838, he was appointed presiding elder on Laporte District, where he remained four years. In 1842, he traveled Laporte Circuit. In 1844 and 1845, he was agent for Indiana Asbury University. From 1846 to 1851, he was agent for the American Bible Society; in 1852 and 1853, stationed in Terre Haute; 1854, Greencastle District, where he remained four years; 1858 and 1859, stationed in Indianapolis. From 1860 to 1862, he was agent for Asbury University; 1863, stationed in Perrysville, and returned the second year; but during the year was put in charge of Indianapolis District, where he remained until Conference, when he was stationed in Ninth Street, Lafayette; 1866 and 1867, stationed in Michigan City. In 1868, he was appointed Moral Instructor in the Northern Indiana State-prison, at Michigan City, which position he still holds. No other man in Indiana has had so large and varied an experience as Dr. Wood. He has enjoyed a personal acquaintance with the leading men of all parties in every county in the state. In his early ministry his circuits, many of them, embraced several counties apiece; and when presiding elder his districts included large portions of the state. And in his work as Bible agent, and agent for Indiana Asbury University, he was brought in contact with the people in every part of the state. He has had a healthy mind in a healthy body all through life. He enjoys an excellent flow of spirits, and has been a genial companion for intelligent people from his youth. His sermons are delivered extempore, except on special occasions. He is the author of several printed discourses. His oration on the occasion of the erection of the monument to Bishop Roberts, in the college campus at Greencastle, was a written performance, and reflected credit upon its author. As a preacher, he is fluent and perspicuous, and the matter of his sermons is evangelical and practical. He has represented his Conference in several sessions of the General Conference, and has always enjoyed the unlimited confidence of his brethren. He has been a faithful friend and patron of education, giving both time and means to the advancement of our literary institutions. His pulpit labors have been strengthened and enforced by the cheerfulness of his piety and the purity of his life.

REV. JOSEPH TARKINGTON.

THE following sketch of the life and times of Rev. Joseph Tarkington, one of the fathers of Indiana Methodism, will be none the less interesting because written in the first person:

"I was born near Nashville, Tennessee, October 30,

1800. My early religious training was in accordance with Episcopal usage, my parents having been reared in that order of faith. The first impressions on my mind in regard to the instability of earthly hopes and expectations, were made at the time of the severe earthquake which visited Tennessee and the Mississippi country in 1811. The incidents connected with this 'stirring time' are fresh in my memory to-day. Sixty years 'are as a few days' in this connection.

" On a pleasant Sabbath evening, the children, having retired early, were called down-stairs, with the announcement that the house was falling down; and in great fear and trepidation we sat up the entire night, my father going out frequently to ascertain whether evil-disposed persons might not have shaken the house, by some means, in order to terrify the family. The dusty old prayer-book was brought forth from its place, its pages scanned eagerly to find something pertaining to earthquakes; but as we could find nothing, we felt that the interests of a large and flourishing family were in jeopardy for lack of the much needed prayer. After a night of watching and fear, it was agreed that we should say nothing about our fears or their cause, lest we be ridiculed by our neighbors. But with the morning came the neighbors, with startling accounts of this strange visitation; and while they yet talked of this night of terrors, a sound like loud, distant thunder startled them. Rushing out of the house, they found the earth trembling violently and the trees vibrating hither and thither. 'Surely,' thought they, 'the end has come;' and the promises made to God by the terrified people were not few nor far between. But it was soon found that the earth was still in its orbit, and revolved as usual, and many forgot the solemn promises made to the Lord in the day of his power; but many others, as a result of this convulsion of nature, chose the better part—lived and died faithful followers of Him who holds the storms in his hands. But while I remember with satisfaction the salutary effect of this 'shaking' on the lives and conduct of many of my friends and acquaintances, I could not conscientiously recommend earthquakes as a usual means of grace.

"At the close of the war of 1812, my father moved to the territory of Indiana, and settled on White River, at the block-house built by General Harrison, now Edwardsport, Knox County. This was then a wild country, and, the war having just ended, the fear and dread of Indians still gave the pioneer and his children much uneasiness. On one occasion a band of Indians, on their way to Vincennes, came up to our cabin suddenly, and the children, in alarm, scattered in every direction. The Indians, comprehending the situation of the little palefaces, gave a hearty laugh, and resumed their journey, the squaws bringing up the rear, in regular 'Indian file,' each riding her pony, 'not sidewise, but otherwise.'

"Our family being sick much of the time at this place, it was deemed expedient to find another location. So, after the necessary examination, my father bought a piece of land in Monroe County, west of Bloomington; and to this place we moved in the Winter of 1816. In our new home we found it quite an undertaking to keep the family supplied with provisions. We could not send some of the smaller children to the corner grocery for needed supplies, but the older boys had to go regularly seventy-five miles to Shakertown for corn, which they got ground into meal when that was possible; but when that could not be done, they took the corn home on their horses, and it was afterward pounded in home-made wooden mortars. If my memory does not deceive me, the bread and mush made of this pounded corn tasted a little better than any eaten before or since that time.

"It would be hard to forget some of the scenes of this frontier life. One, in particular, made an impression on my mind never to be eradicated. On one occasion, as I was returning with a load of corn, accompanied by an older brother, we met a neighbor who was traveling on a similar errand, who informed us that our little brother George had died at home two days before, and that in all probability we should see his face no more. With grief-stricken and heavy hearts we hastened on, and arrived at home in time for the burial. Our father had made a coffin by splitting a piece of timber, scooping out a trough from the lower, and a corresponding excavation from the upper piece, and then fastened them together with wooden pins. Thus prepared, the remains of our little brother were placed therein, and, with the assistance of our neighbors—two or three persons, all told— the coffin and its contents were lowered to its final resting. This was the first burial on Indian Creek, Monroe County.

"Soon after we settled in Monroe County, and while the country was comparatively a wilderness, Methodist preachers would have appointments to preach wherever they could have hearers. The first meeting to which the children of the Tarkington family had access was just eight miles distant. We were all anxious to go; so the larger children of the neighborhood, boys and girls, walked this little distance barefooted, with shoes in hand, until near the house, where a halt was called for putting on shoes before going into meeting. The good, broad, substantial shoes of that day, were not made of glove-kid and paper-lined, but were made to last from season to season, and to descend from child to child, as they grew to fit them. The preacher was the Rev. Morgan, and his text was Songs of Solomon ii, 3 : 'As the apple-tree among the trees of the wood, so is my beloved among the sons. I sat down under his shadow with great delight, and his fruit was sweet to my taste.' It had been a long time since any of his hearers had seen or tasted an apple; hence, his descriptions and comparisons were the more striking and vivid to their minds. He contrasted the wicked as the tree of the woods, very knotty, and exceedingly crooked—with the righteous as the healthy apple-tree, very smooth and comely, and abounding in much good fruit. His description of the large, ripe, luscious apples, caused many of the young people, as well as old, to yearn after the good apples they had enjoyed in the years gone by. One of the results of that memorable sermon was that the writer had to make a pilgrimage seventy miles, to Knox County, in quest of young apple-trees; and the pilgrimage resulted favorably, for I carried home on horseback twenty-four trees; and some of these same trees still stand in the old orchard at Stanford, where, near by, may be found the graves of my parents and brothers, who there sleep in Jesus.

"It was not very long, however, before there was a change for the better in reference to preaching. Rev. Daniel Anderson, a very good preacher, was sent as missionary to the new settlements in this part of the country. His work extended over much territory, and he preached in the cabins or in the open air, as circumstances dictated. He held a camp-meeting during this year near Eel River; and I remember well, while plowing in the field, that the families of Freeland, Rollins,

and others, went past, with their bread, venison, and
bedding packed on their horses, *en route* to camp-meeting. Mr. Benjamin Freeland had four children converted to God at this meeting, and, with true missionary
zeal, one of them stopped on their return, and exhorted
me to turn to the Lord and seek the new peace in which
he now rejoiced; and as he talked with an earnestness
irresistible, I promised to attend the approaching camp-
meeting near Bloomington, and endeavor to seek the
Lord; and I kept my promise faithfully. I went to the
meeting intending to avail myself of all its privileges
and benefits; and on Sabbath evening, under the preaching of John Schrader, I was caused to cry for mercy,
and about 11 o'clock I found joy and peace in believing
on Jesus Christ. This was August 27th, 1820.

"It will not be deemed surprising to many readers
of these lines when I say that the events of that blessed
camp-meeting, and the experience of that Sunday night,
will never be forgotten by the one so much benefited
thereby. It had been my desire that the Lord would
bless me in private, and in a peculiar manner, and my
prayers had been directed to this end; but before the
blessing came, I was willing to receive it in any manner,
and on any terms. I left this camp-meeting, however,
without connecting myself with the Church, not having
made up my mind fully with which branch of God's
people I expected to make my future home. Subsequently, however, at a class-meeting led by my old
friend, D. Rollins, I gave my name to Rev. David Cham-
berlain, as a probationer in the Methodist Episcopal
Church. My parents were present, and saw with deep
emotion the step I was taking. From this time forth
the great concern in my mind was that father and
mother, brothers and sister, should find the new hope, in

which I was so happy. It was not long before I was found leading in prayer at our class-meetings, and occasionally exhorting my young friends to accept the overtures of mercy, and travel with me to the heavenly country. In my public efforts in prayer and exhortation, I found great difficulty on account of my limited education; but feeling that there was something for me to do for the Heavenly Father, I commenced the study of English Grammar under the direction of my class-leader; and as I was in earnest, with a direct object in view, I made rapid progress. I was soon appointed class-leader by the new preacher, John Cord, and was much encouraged in my new position during the year by a gracious revival of religion in our neighborhood. The next year (1822) Rev. James Armstrong was sent to the Bloomington Circuit, and, being a great favorite with my parents, he preached frequently at our house; and it was during this year that I received license to exhort at his hands. During the year 1824, at a local conference—a feature that existed only four years in our Church—I was licensed to preach the Gospel; and when Armstrong handed me the paper announcing the fact, he stated that there was immediate use for me, that one of the preachers on Booneville Circuit had failed on account of ill-health, and that I must depart for my field of labor immediately. Excuses of every kind proved unavailing, and as it seemed to be the will of the Lord, I consented to go.

"When it became known in the neighborhood that I expected to go away, the members of my old class requested me to try to preach them a farewell sermon. Accordingly, a meeting was held at my father's house, the neighbors were all there, and I talked as well as I could, urging them to hold fast to the faith, that we might all meet in heaven, etc. At the close of the sermon I opened the doors of the church, and two or three came forward. A slight pause ensuing, my father and mother, hand in hand, presented themselves as candidates for membership in the Church. O, the joy of that hour! The long-prayed-for event had happened! To God be all the glory!

"The next morning found me on my way to my new field of labor, accompanied by the presiding elder, James Armstrong. It required about three weeks to get round to Booneville, and during this time we attended nine quarterly-meetings. By the time we arrived at our destination, I began to know, to some extent, at least, what itinerancy meant. We found the Rev. O. Fisher at his post. The quarterly-meeting was held in the court-house in Rockport, and on Sunday night, after the sermon by Fisher, I tried to exhort in the fear of the Master. Many came forward for the prayers of the Church, and conversions were numerous. It was a season of power, the victory on the Lord's side. The next morning Fisher, myself, and others went into the country, to brother Barnett's, for breakfast. When taking leave of the family, and invoking the blessings of God to rest upon them, brother Fisher got to singing and shouting, and forgot that I was holding his horse, and patiently waiting for him outside. After waiting a long time, I hitched the horses and went into the house, and prevailed on him to resume our travels. After traveling some distance, he again commenced singing, then shouting; then he jumped off his horse, and singing and shouting was the order of the day. His horse, used to such things, waited by the way-side; men and women passing, stopped to see what was the matter; and the feeling seeming to be contagious, the triumphant shout of victory, mingled

17

with the penitent cry for mercy, made the woods reverberate, and God was greatly glorified.. This brother Fisher, my first colleague, was one of the most holy men I ever knew.

"At the close of the Conference year, we started to Conference at Charlestown, stopping on our way at a camp-meeting on Paoli Circuit. Here we met Richard Hargrave, who was also on his way to his first conference. At this meeting we saw, for the first time, that celebrated preacher, Rev. William Cravens, noted for his peculiarities. The old man, discovering that George Randle, one of the young preachers, was dressed in what was considered a fashionable coat, said to Armstrong, in the hearing of all, 'Where did you get this young fogmaroony?' Armstrong replied, 'In the Wabash country.' 'Well,' said Cravens, 'I'm afraid you'll never Methodize him.' Armstrong made no reply, but Randle, greatly incensed, made some snappish rejoinder, and utterly refused to preach at this camp-meeting, on account of this occurrence. Many were the apologies and excuses given for this speech of Father Cravens, but it was not arranged satisfactorily until the good old man got a new coat for Randle, cut in the most approved Methodistic style. These men, Cravens and Randle, were both singular men, but there was a vein of goodness and frankness about the former that made him friends wherever he traveled.

"On one occasion, Cravens preached a sermon at a camp-meeting near Bloomington, in which he censured severely a recent Indiana Legislature, which had divorced almost all the numerous applicants who applied to it for that purpose. At the dinner hour, Dr. Maxwell, who had been a member of the said Legislature, endeavoring to justify its action in this respect, instanced many supposable cases, in addition to the case given in the New Testament, wherein it would be cruelty to refuse divorces. Not attempting to answer the arguments in detail, Cravens straightened himself up, and said, 'Is n't it wonderful Christ did not think of that?' This good-natured sally ended the discussion.

"We arrived in due time at the seat of the Conference. We junior preachers had to remain in the country adjacent until the commencement of the Conference. This Conference consisted of about twenty preachers, Bishops M'Kendree and Roberts presiding, the sessions held in an up-stairs room in the house of James Sharpe. I was received on trial, and appointed to Patoka Circuit, James Garner, Preacher-in-charge. Garner left his family at Charlestown, and was only able to visit them twice during the entire year. This might seem neglectful, yet how could he do better, when his entire receipts were twenty-eight dollars, my own fourteen dollars, while Holliday, the presiding elder, who lived in Greene County, Illinois, got little or nothing. Verily, the man who preached for money alone, in that day, was a little liable to disappointment. The outfit of the itinerant, at that day, in addition to horse, saddle, and bridle, was a pair of saddle-bags, Bible, hymn-book, thread and needles for repairs, and a package of tallow candles. I always carried candles to read by, and many cabins were thus lit up that had not seen the light of candles hitherto. The year on Patoka Circuit concluded with a good camp-meeting, at which Revs. Aaron Wood and Richard Hargrave, from neighboring circuits, were present, and labored faithfully and efficiently in the service of the Master. And now, while I remember these two young men, and reflect that they are yet on the watch-towers, strong men for duty, preaching the same Gospel as of old, and that I have been spared through the lapse of forty-five years to witness the achievements of these heroes, I thank God and take courage.

"At the Conference in Vincennes, in 1830, I was appointed to Vevay Circuit. It was during this year that the wonderful camp-meeting on Crooked Creek, above Madison, was held. The good results of this meeting were felt in that part of the country for many years thereafter. About one hundred and forty persons were converted to God, and the power manifested in the conviction and conversion of these persons was a marvel in the eyes of the stanchest believers. Fear and trembling seized sinners as soon as they came within the sacred influence, and a yielding to God seemed inevitable.

" In the Fall of this year I was married by Allen Wiley, the presiding elder, to Maria Slawson, who has traveled the path of life by my side ever since. It was customary among those in high life, in that day (and we were of that respected class), to enjoy wedding tours, in order that the young couple might begin life under as favorable auspices as possible; consequently, we took our wedding-tour. We did not go to Niagara and to the White Mountains, nor to Lake Superior or to California, but we went to *Conference*. We were married in Switzerland County, spent our first Sabbath at the noted camp-meeting on Crooked Creek. At its close, we resumed our travels, resting the first night near Columbus, taking a late breakfast at this place. Next morning we started west to Bloomington, via Brown County. Shortly after we started, it commenced raining, and continued all day long. To my suggestion that we had better stop at some house until the rain ceased, my spirited young bride answered, that she could stand the rain if I could. So we rode along all day, single-file along the trail, until night overtook us. Arriving near the old salt-works, on Salt Creek, we found three little cabins, one-half mile apart. Stopping at the first one, we were told they could not accommodate us; going on to the second, we found all the family sick; and when we got to the third one, the woman informed us that she had nothing at all to eat; that her husband was then gone to the settlements for food, and that she could do nothing for us. In this extremity, we returned to the first cabin and asked the woman if we could not come in out of the rain. In answer, she said we must first go over to the salt-works and ask her husband. Leaving my bride waiting in the dark and rain, I made my way as best I could to the works, and after our situation was fully stated, the husband agreed that we might stay with them, but as he had no place for our horses it would be necessary to build a pen for their accommodation. He soon arranged a torch, by the light of which we built a high fence around the horses, cut a few stalks of green corn from his little garden-patch, and then we went into the house, carrying our saddles with us, and we were heartily thankful we had a roof over us. We were soon warm and comfortable; and, after holding family prayer, in which we remembered at a Throne of Grace the kind family who were entertaining the benighted strangers, we retired, occupying the only bed in the cabin. The bedstead was constructed by driving two pins into the wall, with boards laid across them, and then the straw bed. It was the best they could do, and we were content. My bride had in her pocket a biscuit brought from home, and the great question was, which should eat it. We finally compromised by dividing it. In the morning we found the horses all right, and we were soon on our way. When we arrived at Bloomington, where we had expected to have broken our fast, we concluded to wait until we got to Stanford, where our relatives were glad to receive us; and at two o'clock in the afternoon we sat down to our first meal since breakfast the preceding day. And now, as I write of the experience of that trip, my young bride knitting at my side, her hair much lighter now than then, gives it as her opinion that, while love is essentially necessary and very sustaining under ordinary circumstances, yet, for long bridal trips on horseback, she advises the newly married pair to depend mostly on a diet more substantial.

"In the above sketches of my early life I have not written much of my own success in preaching the Gospel. I am glad, however, to remember many pleasant seasons I have enjoyed while trying to do my duty to God in pointing sinners to the Savior; and I am expecting to enjoy the reunion of many friends in the better country, in the blest 'by and by.' I have seen the Church in its infancy, have witnessed its privations and discouragements, as also its successes and achievements. I bless the Lord, that while I can boast of knowing the simplicity and earnestness of the former times, I have delighted in the glory and grandeur of the latter days; and my strong faith is, that if our Church is only true to herself, the golden day of her power and usefulness is yet in the future. So mote it be."

REV. ENOCH G. WOOD, D. D.

ENOCH G. WOOD entered the traveling ministry in the Illinois Conference in 1827, at its session in Mount Carmel, Illinois, and his first appointment was to Charlestown Circuit, Indiana, as junior preacher, with George Locke and C. W. Ruter; the latter being on the supernumerary list. Brother Wood has been on the effective list of itinerants ever since. In youth he drew the

W. WELLSTOOD SC.

REV. E. G. WOOD, D.D.

Gospel sword, threw away the scabbard, and has maintained his position in the front of the army of invasion for *forty-four years*, and still claims to be a young man. He is young in heart, young in enterprise, and young in mental vigor, although mature in years and in experience; and having spent the whole of his ministerial life in Indiana, and half of it in the presiding eldership, he deserves to be ranked among the fathers of the Conference. Dr. Wood is an able preacher. His style is argumentative, and his sermons instructive. He lights the sanctuary with "beaten oil." He does not sacrifice to God that which cost him nothing. His sermons give evidence of close thought and careful preparation; and yet he uses the pen sparingly, if at all, in his pulpit preparations. Most of his sermons would do to go to the press just as delivered, and yet it is doubtful if he ever wrote a sermon in full. He has been a practical and earnest friend of education, giving much attention to the building up of the literary institutions under the care of the Church. Few men have given themselves as unreservedly to the work of the ministry as Dr. Wood, and prosecuted that work with equal zeal and singleness of purpose for so many years. Dr. Wood has ever enjoyed the full confidence of his brethren. He has been four times elected to represent his Conference in sessions of the General Conference.

REV. JOHN SCHRADER.

JOHN SCHRADER is now the oldest minister in Indiana. He entered the itinerancy in the Tennessee Conference in 1813, and has traveled large circuits in Indiana, Illinois, Missouri, and Arkansas. He preached the first sermon in New Albany, organized the first class, and administered the sacrament of the Lord's-supper to them.

for the first time. That was in the Spring of 1818. He had been removed in the middle of the year, and placed on Silver-creek Circuit to supply the place of John Cord, who had to leave the circuit in consequence of having his house consumed by fire; and, as the circuit was not able to make up his loss, and meet the pressing demands of his family, Mr. Cord had to leave the circuit, and devote his attention for a season to secular pursuits.

In taking charge of the circuit, he organized a few new preaching-places, one of which was New Albany. A few members had organized themselves into a class. To these Mr. Schrader preached in a tavern kept by a Mrs. Ruff, and administered the sacrament of the Lord's-supper; doubtless the first time that the ordinance was ever administered in that city. Upon the organization of the Missouri Conference in 1816, Mr. Schrader was included within its bounds. Upon the organization of the Illinois Conference, he fell within its bounds; and upon the organization of the Indiana Conference, he was included within its territory. His name has been long on the superanuated list in the Indiana Conference, but the vine which he helped to plant in this virgin soil has sent out its branches, and overshadowed the land. He has seen "the wilderness blossom as the rose;" has lived to see "a little one become a thousand, and a small one a strong nation."

REV. JOHN MILLER.

JOHN MILLER was received on trial in the Missouri Conference in the Fall of 1823, when that Conference included the settled portions of the country, from the western border of the Ohio Conference to the then province of Texas. His first appointment was to Sangamon Circuit, in Illinois, in Illinois District, with Samuel H.

Thompson as presiding elder. His second appointment was to Indianapolis Circuit, in 1824; the Missouri Conference having been divided, and the work in Indiana and Illinois included in the Illinois Conference. Indianapolis was included in Madison District, and John Strange was the presiding elder. His third appointment was Paoli. His fourth appointment was Illinois Circuit. His fifth appointment was Vincennes Circuit. His sixth appointment was Washington Circuit. In ·1829, he was appointed to Mount Carmel Circuit, and, in 1830, was reappointed to the same charge. In 1831, he was appointed to Corydon Circuit. At the organization of the Indiana Conference, in 1832, he was included in the Indiana work, and was appointed to Charlestown Circuit; and henceforward his name is connected with the work in Indiana. Brother Miller has traveled our largest circuits, filled some of the best stations in his Conference. He has been a presiding elder, and a delegate to the General Conference, and has been ever true and faithful in all the relations he has sustained. For the last few years he has been on the superanuated list. His ministerial record is remarkably faultless. A man of large heart, warm sympathies, true friendships, unaffected modesty, and genuine piety, he was greatly loved by the people whom he served. In the days of his vigor he had a musical voice, which he knew well how to manage, for he was a charming singer.

REV. AMASA JOHNSON.

AMASA JOHNSON was received on trial into the traveling ministry at the first session of the Indiana Conference, in 1832, and was identified with the work of the ministry in Indiana till the close of his life. Of him Hon. R. W. Thompson said, in his discourse before the

Indiana State Methodist Convention, on the "Fallen Heroes of Methodism:" "Having been received into the Church by Amasa Johnson, I should do injustice to my own feelings if I did not avail myself of this occasion to bear testimony to his self-sacrificing devotion, his unquestioned purity, and wonderful native abilities. Few men have entered the ministry with less education; and yet his great sagacity, extraordinary memory, and fine fund of common sense, enabled him to overcome his early disadvantages; so that he at last became one of the most effective and convincing preachers I ever heard. He made no attempt at oratory in its highest sense; but, as he drew all his illustrations from familiar things, he never failed to reach both the judgment and the heart. If beauty is the greatest when unadorned, then his eloquence was of no inferior kind; for it wore none of that clothing which a cultivated imagination gives; it was direct, impressive, and irresistible—the true eloquence of Nature. He had a keen and just sense of responsibility to God, and followed after truth for its own sake. Such men as he deserve far more of the world's respect than they generally receive, because the world loves show and ornament; but those to whom his ability and sterling worth are best known, will remember him, as I do, with sincere admiration for his memory."

REV. ASA BECK.

Asa Beck was admitted on trial in the Illinois Conference in 1828, and traveled successively Columbus, Fall-creek, Wayne, Connersville, and Franklin Circuits. At the organization of the Indiana Conference he was included in the work in Indiana. He has traveled many of the largest circuits in the Conference, and was for many years an efficient preacher; and his labors were blessed to the conversion of many souls to God. Father Beck has been for a number of years on the retired list.

REV. JAMES SCOTT.

THE name of James Scott first appears in connection with the work in Indiana in 1826, when he traveled Madison Circuit; and from thenceforward for many years he is found among the active and laborious itinerants who preached the Gospel and planted Churches in the new settlements throughout Indiana. He possessed a keen, analytical mind, and in his early ministry was fond of debate. Several champions of Universalism had reason to remember the clearness of his logic, and the keenness of his satire, as well as his thorough familiarity with the Bible. Age and growing infirmities compelled him to superannuate a number of years since.

REV. ELIJAH WHITTEN.

ELIJAH WHITTEN was admitted on trial in the Indiana Conference at its first session in 1832. He had embraced religion a few years previous to this date, in Cincinnati, in the great revival in that city, under the ministry of Rev. Dr. Wilson. Whitten soon found that Calvinism was opposed to his clearest convictions of truth, and that the doctrines, usages, and general spirit of Methodism better accorded with his convictions and tastes; and he accordingly united with the Methodist Church, entered the itinerant ministry, and devoted himself with unusual energy to the work of the ministry, until failing health compelled him to superannuate. In the days of his vigor, few men could present the doctrines of Christianity in a clearer or more forcible light than he.

REV. HENRY S. TALBOTT.

HENRY S. TALBOTT was admitted on trial in the Illinois Conference in the Fall of 1830. In the division of the Conference, he fell in the Indiana Conference, and is still identified with the itinerancy in the Indiana Conference. He resigned the practice of medicine for the work of the ministry. He was a man of considerable culture, and an excellent preacher. He filled a number of responsible appointments, including that of presiding elder and delegate to the General Conference, and deserves to be ranked among the fathers of Indiana Methodism.

REV. RICHARD HARGRAVE.

RICHARD HARGRAVE entered the traveling connection in the Fall of 1824, and has been identified with the work of the Methodist ministry in Indiana ever since. In the days of his vigor he was the prince of preachers. With a dignified and impressive personal presence, a clear, full voice, a distinct and ready utterance, and a thorough familiarity with Bible themes and Bible doctrines, and a heart in full sympathy with his work as a Christian minister, his sermons were listened to with interest, although of unusual length. His sermons were no brief essays on distinct topics, as is quite too much the style of the pulpit now, but they were elaborate discussions of the grand doctrines of revelation. For nearly fifty years he has occupied a prominent place among the pulpit orators of the land. He has given to the public an excellent volume of sermons. Age and growing infirmities have compelled him to superannuate, although his heart is in full sympathy with the itinerant work.

REV. ROBERT BURNS.

ROBERT BURNS entered the traveling ministry in the Illinois Conference in the Fall of 1826, and was a zealous, laborious, and successful traveling preacher. He was gifted in exhortation. His appeals to the consciences and understandings of his hearers were searching and powerful. He continued effective until age and physical infirmities compelled him to locate.

REV. JOHN W. SULLIVAN.

JOHN W. SULLIVAN entered the traveling connection on trial, in the Indiana Conference, at its session in Madison, in the Fall of 1833, and has been connected with the itinerancy in Indiana ever since. He has been eminently useful, having had numerous revivals under his ministry. In his earlier ministry he was an excellent singer, and often powerful in exhortation. He was an excellent manager of revival meetings, and a good pastor. He has filled a number of important charges in his Conference with great acceptability. For several years past he has been Moral Instructor to the Southern Indiana State-prison at Jeffersonville.

REV. DAVID STIVER.

DAVID STIVER was admitted on trial in the Indiana Conference in 1832, and labored efficiently for a number of years, and was appointed presiding elder on Centerville District in 1838. Owing to unfortunate domestic troubles, he desisted from the active work of the ministry for a number of years, but maintaining his Christian and ministerial standing as a local preacher. But yielding to his convictions of duty, and the judgment of his brethren, he re-entered the Conference, and continued to labor until age and failing health compelled him to superannuate.

REV. JAMES T. ROBE.

JAMES T. ROBE entered the traveling connection in the Illinois Conference in 1831, but on the organization of the Indiana Conference the ensuing year, he fell within its bounds, where he labored faithfully for a number of years, and finally located in the state of Michigan, where he has continued as a local preacher, rich in Christian experience, and ripening for the heavenly garner.

REV. CHARLES BONNER.

CHARLES BONNER was admitted on trial in the Illinois Conference in the Fall of 1828, and appointed to Fallcreek Circuit, in the vicinity of Indianapolis. His subsequent fields of labor were in Indiana; and, upon the division of the Illinois Conference, and constituting the Indiana Conference, he was included in the bounds of the latter, where he continued to labor efficiently for a number of years, when he located, entered into secular business, was unfortunate in trading, went to California, and met a sad death by being pierced through the body by the prongs of a pitchfork, as he was getting off from a load of hay. Charles Bonner was a good man, and, while in the work of the ministry, an efficient preacher. He was a remarkably industrious man, but that industry was directed more to manual labor, in improving parsonage and church property, cultivating his garden, and chopping his own wood, than in intellectual labor for the better prosecution of his work as a minister. The Church is always the loser when her ministers have to give their attention to manual labor or secular pursuits; and no man can be eminent as a minister, or long sustain a respectable position in the ministry, who gives his time and strength to outside duties. Charles Bonner was a true friend and an admirable colleague, in the days of the old-fashioned circuits with two preachers, when the circuits had from twenty-four to thirty appointments to be filled by each preacher once in four weeks. He gathered many into the Church, and his memory is cherished by his co-laborers in the ministry.

REV. JOHN KEARNS.

JOHN KEARNS joined the Illinois Conference in 1827, and labored some twenty odd years in Indiana, filling a number of important stations, and serving for some time as presiding elder. He finally transferred to Minnesota, for a change of climate, where he continues an efficient minister of the Gospel.

REV. JOHN C. SMITH.

JOHN C. SMITH was admitted on trial into the traveling connection, in the Illinois Conference, at its session in Vincennes, in the Fall of 1830, and appointed to Rushville Circuit with Amos Sparks. His next appointment was Lawrenceburg Circuit, where he remained two years; and in the organization of the Indiana Conference he was included within its bounds, and early took high rank as a gifted and zealous minister. For a number of years he was recognized at the head of the young men of his age in the ministry in Indiana. No young man had entered the ministry in Indiana, at that day, whose educational advantages were superior to those of brother Smith. His style of preaching was popular, and through his labors multitudes were gathered into the Church. One of the most extensive revivals of religion ever enjoyed by the Church in Indianapolis, was under his ministry while pastor of Wesley Chapel, on the corner of Meridian and Circle Streets, in 1836 and 1837. Some years since, impaired health induced him to retire from the active work of the ministry.

REV. JOHN A. BROUSE.

JOHN A. BROUSE was admitted on trial in the Indiana Conference in the Fall of 1833. He traveled several large circuits, filled some important stations, was presiding elder for several terms, and once a delegate to the General Conference, and one year an agent for Asbury University. The financial demands upon him necessary to the support and education of a large family, induced him to retire from the active work of the ministry, and give his attention to secular pursuits.

REV. JAMES HAVENS.

FEW names are more familiar in Methodist circles in Indiana than that of James Havens. He entered the traveling connection in the old Ohio Conference in 1821. He came to Indiana a few years later, and settled in Rush County, two miles west of Rushville, where he raised a large family, and where the family continued to reside until the children were all grown. Notwithstanding his family was located, Mr. Havens was emphatically an itinerant, traveling large circuits and districts, and often absent from home for weeks at a time. Mr. Havens's early education was defective, and he could barely read when he joined the Conference; but he had an energy that no obstacles could break down, a perseverance that never abated until its end was reached, and an ability for both mental and physical exertion that enabled him to accomplish what to most men would have been impossible. He arose to a front rank in the ministry, and made an impression upon general society that has been abiding. His knowledge of human nature was wonderful, and he read the character of those with whom he came in contact by a sort of intuition, and he rarely ever made a mistake. His reproofs were scathing; and, in the early settlement of Indiana, he was for many years emphatically a terror to evil-doers. The stories of his encounters with the rowdies and roughs that were wont to disturb the early camp-meetings, and his uniform victories over them, would constitute a volume of thrilling interest. And, although fearless as a lion in the presence of danger, he was, nevertheless, a man of the tenderest sympathies and warmest friendships. The results of his labors are seen in the social order and the general respect for religion which every-where prevail throughout our state, as well as in the multitudes that were converted to God through his ministry. The fathers labored, and we are entered into their labors. Mr. Havens secured a good general education, and was well read in theology and Church history. He was a delegate to several sessions of the General Conference. His sermons were well prepared, though never written. When asked why he did not use the pen in preparing for the pulpit, his reply was: "Do n't you think the devil can read writing? I do n't intend that he shall either forestall me or flank me." During a large part of his ministry he filled the office of presiding elder, and exerted a commanding influence, both among preachers and people.

REV. CALVIN W. RUTER.

Calvin W. Ruter was admitted on trial into the traveling connection in the old Ohio Conference in 1818. His ministerial labors were spent in Indiana. Upon the organization of the Missouri Conference he was a member of that body, as also of the Illinois Conference while it included the work in Indiana. During his long ministry he was several times placed either on the supernumerary or superannuated list, but, with returning health, was always found in the active itinerant ranks. He was for many years secretary of his Conference. He was an early and zealous friend of learning, and was one of the founders of Indiana Asbury University. He was a superior preacher, and one of the honored fathers of Indiana Methodism.

REV. ALLEN WILEY.

ALLEN WILEY entered the ministry in 1818, in the old Ohio Conference, but Indiana was the theater of his ministerial labors; and from 1818, down to 1848, the time of his death, he was closely identified with the interests of the Church in Indiana; and he, perhaps more than any other one man, molded the character of Indiana Methodism. He looked more to the future than most of his associates, and he organized and planned and worked for the future. His literary attainments were remarkable for the times in which he lived. He was a good Latin and Greek scholar, and every-where recognized as a profound theologian. As a minister, his sermons, while presiding elder, made a profound impression. They were usually lengthy; seldom, on the Sabbath, less than an hour and a half in length, but always listened to with interest. He was one of the projectors of Indiana Asbury University, and early saw the necessity for denominational schools. He was a remarkable student, and retained his habits of study to the close of life.

REV. AUGUSTUS EDDY.

AUGUSTUS EDDY was licensed to preach in 1821, near Xenia, Ohio. He was admitted on trial in the old Ohio Conference, at its session in Zanesville in 1824; and here commenced that grand itinerant career which continued to the close of life, without a blot upon his character. His first appointment was to the old Miami Circuit. He continued to travel large circuits until 1831, when he was appointed presiding elder of the Scioto District, where he was continued two years. He then traveled two years on the Columbus District. In 1835, he was stationed in Cincinnati, western charge, with Christie and Hamline as co-laborers. In 1836, he was transferred to Indiana Conference, and stationed in Indianapolis. His next appointment was Indianapolis District; then Whitewater District. He was next stationed at Wesley Chapel, Madison; then presiding elder of Madison District; and from Madison District he was appointed in charge of Lawrenceburg District. In 1848, he was transferred to the Ohio Conference, and stationed at Chillicothe. He was successively stationed at Hamilton and Xenia, and was then appointed presiding elder on West Cincinnati District. In 1855, he was transferred to North Indiana Conference, and stationed in Richmond. His next appointment was Indianapolis District, where he remained four years. He was then stationed at Kokomo, but a vacancy occurring on the Richmond District, he was appointed in charge of it, and served until the middle of the ensuing August, when he was appointed post-chaplain in the United States Army at Indianapolis, which position he continued to fill for about four years. He was then returned to the Richmond District, where he labored for three

years. He was then appointed presiding elder on Anderson District, where he continued to labor until smit-
ten down with disease. He closed his active work at
Greenfield, where he held his last quarterly-meeting,
January 15 and 16, 1870. His disease was malignant
erysipelas, which terminated fatally on the 9th of February, 1870. He was permitted to die at home, sur-
rounded by his children and friends, in full possession
of his mental faculties, and in the triumphs of Christian
faith. Mr. Eddy was an instructive and entertaining
preacher; his social qualities were fine; he was happy
at home, and delighted in the society of his friends. He
was three times elected to a seat in the General Conference. His life was grand and heroic. In the vigor of
early manhood he buckled on the Gospel armor, and he
never laid it off. His manly voice was a trumpet-blast
that gave no uncertain sound; and when his Captain
called he was at the post of duty, ready to obey the
summons. The workman is removed, but his work
remains.

CHAPTER XV.

Methodist Educators—Rev. W. H. Goode, D. D.—Rev. Cyrus Nutt, D. D.—Rev. W. C. Larrabee, LL. D.—Dr. Tefft—Rev. T. H. Lynch, D. D.—Rev. John Wheeler, D. D.—Rev. T. A. Goodwin, A. M.—Rev. Philander Wiley, A. M.—Dr. Benson—Rev. William M. Daily, D. D.—George W. Hoss, A. M.—B. T. Hoyt, A. M.—Prof. Joseph Tingley, Ph. D.—Prof. S. A. Lattimore—Rev. Daniel Curry, D. D.—Dr. Nadal—Dr. Bragdon—Rev. B. F. Rawlins, D. D.—Albin Fellows, A. M.—J. P. Rouse, A. M.—Rev. B. W. Smith, A. M.—Rev. W. R. Goodwin, A. M.—Rev. O. H. Smith, A. M.—William H. De Motte, A. M.—Rev. Thomas Harrison, A. M.—Rev. J. P. D. John, A. M.—Rev. John W. Locke, D. D.—J. M. Olcott, A. M.—Rev. J. H. Martin, A. M.—Rev. L. W. Berry, D. D.—Rev. Thomas Bowman, D. D.—Rev. Erastus Rowley, D. D.—Rev. G. W. Rice—Rev. A Gurney—Rev. R. D. Utter.

METHODIST EDUCATORS.

REV. WILLIAM H. GOODE, D. D.,

HAS the honor of being the pioneer Methodist educator in Indiana, so far as an official appointment by the Church is concerned. In May, 1837, while traveling Lexington Circuit, within the bounds of the New Albany District, he was elected Principal of the New Albany Seminary, upon the resignation of Philander Ruter, A. M. Rev. C. W. Ruter, Presiding Elder of New Albany District, who was also chairman of the Board of Trustees of the Seminary, released Mr. Goode from his circuit, and he took immediate charge of the Seminary. At the ensuing Conference, which convened in New Albany in the Fall of the same year, Mr. Goode was appointed to the charge of the Seminary, and at the same time laboring jointly in the pulpit with the pastor of New Albany Station.

Mr. Goode rendered efficient service both as a teacher and an administrator, while he remained in the institution, but feeling himself called to the pastoral work, before the next session of the Conference, he resigned the charge of the Seminary, and George Harrison, A. M., was elected in his place.

About the commencement of the year 1854, while pastor of Richmond Station, Mr. Goode was elected to the presidency of the branch of Whitewater College located in that place. He consented to this, simply for the purpose of winding up the affairs of the department, and saving the institution from embarrassment. His services were not only financially valuable, but also of service to both teachers and scholars. Having wound up the affairs of the College in accordance with his designs, his presidency expired with the expiration of the College.

INDIAN WORK IN THE SOUTH-WEST.

MARCH 15, 1843, at Mr. Goode's residence in South Bend, being then in charge of the district embracing all the north end of Indiana, he received, under the hands of Bishops Soule and Morris, an appointment to the superintendency of the Fort Coffee Academy, an institution about to be established among the Choctaw Indians, in the tract of country to which they had been removed, lying west of the state of Arkansas, and still known as the "Indian Territory." This institution had been provided for by an act of the General Council of the Choctaw Nation, appropriating from their annuity fund six thousand dollars a year, for a term of twenty years. This act had received the sanction of the proper department at Washington. By concurrence of the Council and the Government authorities the entire control and management of the institution were committed to the Missionary Society of the Methodist Episcopal Church, the society adding one thousand dollars per annum to the endowment. Male and female departments were separately provided for. The organization of the institution, with the entire control of its funds, was placed in Mr. Goode's hands, subject always to open inspection of his books and accounts by the authorities of the Choctaw Nation, and to annual examination by a committee of the Conference. With this, also, he had a missionary charge among the Indians.

Rev. H. C. Benson was transferred from Indiana Conference to take the place of principal teacher. Rev. John Page, of Arkansas Conference, an educated Choctaw, was Mr. Goode's assistant in labors among the natives. Other assistance was obtained as needed, from sources outside of the Conference. On receiving his appointment, Mr. Goode went immediately to the Indian country. The site fixed for the male department was that of "Old Fort Coffee," vacated by the United States Government some four years previous, and then held by an Indian claim. It was a beautiful and commanding site, upon a high bluff of the Arkansas River, thirty miles above the state line. He took possession of the premises, bought out the Indian claim, remodeled some of the fort buildings, removed others and rebuilt in their places, and enlarged the farm-lands attached. Rev. H. C. Benson came on in a few months, and in the Autumn of that year the male department was opened. It was a manual-labor institution. The pupils selected by the General Council were boarded, clothed, and instructed in labor as well as in literary studies. The work prospered under Mr. Goode's hands, and among its first students were those that have risen to places of prominence and usefulness among their people. As soon as the state of the finances would permit, buildings were placed under contract for the female department at New Hope, five miles distant from Fort Coffee, which were completed and occupied after Mr. Goode's return to Indiana. Mr. Goode had been transferred to Arkansas Conference, of which the Indian work was then an appendage. In 1844, he aided in the formation of the Indian Mission Conference at Tah-le-qua, in Cherokee Nation, serving as its first secretary. His connection with that work and with the South terminated with the Louisville Convention in 1845. Having been elected to that Convention, he declined a seat, but attended its sessions as a spectator till separation was determined upon. At this point he resigned his work, and received a transfer back to North Indiana Conference, with an appointment to Peru District, then just vacated by the death of Rev. B. Westlake. And so terminated Mr. Goode's work in the South. The institution passed into the hands of the Methodist Episcopal Church South, and lingered on till near the expiration of the twenty years' term, when it expired in the confusion of the Rebellion.

KANSAS AND NEBRASKA WORK.

Mr. Goode was appointed, in 1854, to the superintendency of missions in Kansas and Nebraska, which were designed mainly for the white settlers, but embraced labors among the Wyandots, Delawares, Shawnees, Kickapoos, and other Indian tribes resident in the country. No strictly literary work was under his control at that time. The Church South had possession of our formerly flourishing institutions among the Shawnees, which had been built by Mr. Goode's labors. His labors among the Indians were interesting, and in a good degree successful. He entered the field single-handed and alone. Transferred to Missouri Conference; stayed long enough to lay the foundation of three annual conferences, and to see about one hundred ministers at work. He organized Kansas and Nebraska Conference in 1855, holding its first session in a cloth tent at Lawrence; formed Nebraska Conference in 1860; Colorado, in 1864. While there, served four years as a member of the General Mission Committee. Few men have made a more valuable or a more enduring impression upon the interests of the Church than Dr. Goode.

REV. CYRUS NUTT, D. D.

THE first meeting of the trustees of Indiana Asbury University was held in March, 1837; at which time Mr. Nutt was elected preceptor of the Preparatory Department, and arrangements were made to have that department opened at an early day. It required seven or eight days at that time to make the trip from Meadville, where Mr. Nutt then resided, to Greencastle, by the most speedy mode of travel, which was by stage and steam-boat. Mr. Nutt left Meadville about the 7th of May, and traveled by stage to Pittsburg, and thence by steam-boat to Cincinnati, and thence by stage to Greencastle, where he arrived on the sixteenth of the same month—having walked, however, from Putnamville to Greencastle, as there was no public conveyance from the outside world to Greencastle at that day. Mr. Nutt was born in Trumbull County, Ohio, September 4, 1814. His early educational opportunities were necessarily limited in so new a country. His parents were educated people, and he was taught reading, writing, arithmetic, geography, and grammar, at home, during such leisure hours as could be redeemed from manual labor. He, however, attended the country school in his neighborhood, when in session, which was about three months in the year. Such was young Nutt's desire for a liberal education that he improved every opportunity for the acquisition of learning; and when, at the age of eighteen, his father proposed to deed him a piece of land, in consideration of his faithful labors on the farm, he told him he would rather have a good education than any property. His father at first spoke discouragingly, but finally agreed to give him his time, and let him get an education by working his own way. He went immediately to an academy to prepare himself for college; and in four years from that time he graduated at Alleghany College, Meadville, Pennsylvania, having supported himself by teaching during the Winters, and at the same time keeping up his college studies. He graduated in 1836, and was immediately appointed preceptor of the Preparatory Department in the same institution; which position he filled for six months, when he was elected to the charge of the Preparatory Department of Indiana Asbury University, which had just been chartered by the Legislature of Indiana. Mr. Nutt was converted at a camp-meeting when in his twentieth year. He was appointed to the charge of a class of young men, as class-leader, while in college. He was licensed to exhort, and then to preach; and he preached his first sermon not long after his arrival in Greencastle.

He entered upon his duties at Greencastle on the 5th of June, 1837, commencing the Preparatory Department in a small one-story brick building, with only two rooms; the larger of which was occupied by the town school. The smaller room was then the only place accessible; and there Dr. Nutt began the literary

Very truly yours

Cyrus Nutt

instruction of this since renowned University of the West. At the meeting of the Board of Trustees in September of the same year, Mr. Nutt was elected Professor of Languages. In 1841, he was elected Professor of Greek and Greek Literature and Hebrew, which he held until the Fall of 1843, when he resigned and took pastoral work in Indiana Conference, and was appointed to Bloomington Station. He had been admitted into the Conference at its session in Rockville in 1838, and ordained deacon by Bishop Soule at Indianapolis in 1840, and elder by Bishop Morris at the Conference in Centerville in 1842. He remained in charge of Bloomington Station two years, and the year following was stationed at Salem. His ministry was eminently successful in each of these charges. In the Fall of 1848, he returned to the University; having been elected to the Chair of Greek Language and Literature, made vacant by the resignation of Professor B. F. Tefft, who took charge of the *Ladies' Repository*, at Cincinnati. In 1849, Dr. Nutt was elected President of Fort Wayne Female College, which he accepted and held for one year, when he resigned and accepted the Presidency of Whitewater College, which had been tendered him by the trustees of that institution, the climate of Northern Indiana not agreeing with Mrs. Nutt, who was a native of Kentucky. He entered upon the duties of the Presidency of the Whitewater College at Centerville, Indiana, in the Fall of 1850. The school flourished under his administration, and the number of students increased from one hundred and forty to more than three hundred. During the whole of this time he held the position either of trustee or Conference Visitor to Indiana Asbury University, and took a lively interest in all the affairs of the Church He remained five years at the head of

Whitewater College, when he resigned to again enter upon the active work of the ministry; and at the session of the North Indiana Conference in Goshen, in 1855, he was appointed presiding elder on Richmond District, where he remained two years; during which an almost constant revival was in progress nearly all over his district.

In the Fall of 1857, he was elected to the Chair of Mathematics in Indiana Asbury University. He was elected Vice-President of the Faculty. Hon. David M'Donald, who had been elected to the Presidency of the University, having declined to accept, the charge of the administration of the University devolved upon Dr. Nutt for nearly two years, during one of the most critical and important periods in its history, until Rev. Thomas Bowman, D. D., took charge of the institution, in the Spring of 1859.

The University was conducted with great skill and success by Dr. Nutt and his associates, and fully recovered from the disaster that had unfortunately overtaken it in 1856–57. In 1859, he received the degree of Doctor of Divinity from his *Alma Mater*, Alleghany College, and from which he had received, in due course, the degree of A. M. in 1839. In 1860, he was a delegate to the General Conference, from North Indiana Conference, leading his delegation, and served in that memorable session as a member of the Committee on the Episcopacy, and also on the Committees on Education, Judiciary, and Lay Delegation, and proved himself an industrious and useful delegate. In 1860, Dr. Nutt was elected President of the Indiana State University at Bloomington, which position he still holds (1871); and under his prudent and skillful management the State University has greatly prospered. The annual income has increased from six thousand five hundred dollars to twenty-five thousand dollars. The Faculty numbers thirteen, and the students have increased from about one hundred to more than three hundred, all of whom are in the regular College Classes and the Law Department, the Preparatory Department having been abolished in 1867. Four thousand five hundred volumes have been added to the library, and the philosophical and chemical apparatus has been greatly enlarged.

The State University has prospered beyond precedent since Dr. Nutt has been at the head of its affairs. Dr. Nutt was elected President of Iowa State University in 1842, but declined to accept. He was a member of the State Convention in 1854, which organized the State Teachers' Association, and established the *Indiana School Journal*. Both as a minister of the Gospel and as an educator, Dr. Nutt has been eminently successful, and will leave upon the generation that comes after him an abiding impression for good.

REV. W. C. LARRABEE, LL. D.

PROFESSOR LARRABEE was a pioneer teacher in the Methodist Church. An academy at New Market, New Hampshire, afterward transferred to Wilbraham, Massachusetts, and the institution in New York City under the charge of Dr. Bangs, were the most prominent Methodist schools in operation when he began to teach. Augusta College, in Kentucky, and a few academies, were just beginning to get under way. Besides those engaged in these schools, the other early teachers in the Methodist Church were his contemporaries, or came after him. When he commenced, the great system of education which the Church has built in America was only dreamed of. The workmen were laying the foundations, all unconscious of the magnitude of the fabric which was to be built thereon. When his work is measured, it will be found to have been second in importance to that of few, if any, educators of his generation.

Mr. Larrabee was born at Cape Elizabeth, in Maine, a few miles from the city of Portland, December 23, 1802. His early opportunities for acquiring an education were limited. The story of his heroic struggles to acquire an education is instructive, but can not be here related. Acting upon the advice of judicious friends, he resolved to acquire a liberal education. He entered the Sophomore Class in Bowdoin College at the commencement of 1825. He taught during vacation. During two terms of his Junior, and also his Senior Year, he labored as assistant in the Maine Wesleyan Seminary, at Kent's Hill. He graduated in 1828, second in a class of twenty. Immediately after graduation he was, upon the recommendation of Professor Upham, called to the charge of a newly established academy at Alfred. Here he spent two years happily and prosperously. When the Wesleyan University at Middletown was opened, he was appointed tutor, and the actual teacher of the school, under the direction of Dr. Fisk, who was not yet ready to take personal charge of the institution. There were five or six Freshmen, and some twenty Preparatory, in his class. This was the beginning of the Wesleyan University. The following year, Mr. Larrabee was elected Principal of the Oneida Conference Seminary at Cazenovia, New York.

In 1835, Professor Caldwell having resigned the Principalship of the Maine Wesleyan Seminary, to accept a professorship in Dickinson College, Mr. Larrabee accepted the charge of that institution, and while engaged in that institution, he assisted Dr. Jackson in the first geological survey of the state. Mr. Larrabee was a delegate to the General Conference of 1840, which met in the city of Baltimore. Here he met Dr. Simpson, then President of Indiana Asbury University, E. R. Ames, and other Indiana delegates, who, among other things, were looking for a professor for the new university in Indiana. The result of this acquaintance was, that at the ensuing meeting of the Board of Trustees he was elected Professor of Mathematics and Natural Science in Indiana Asbury University. He accepted the position, and removed to Indiana in 1841. Dr. Simpson retired from the University in 1848, having been elected editor of the *Western Christian Advocate*, at Cincinnati. Rev. E. R. Ames was elected to the Presidency of the University, but declined; and for one year the duties of the Presidency devolved on Professor Larrabee, in addition to the regular duties of his Chair.

While professor in Asbury University, Mr. Larrabee visited West Point Military Academy as a member of the Examining Committee.

In 1852, Mr. Larrabee was elected editor of the *Ladies' Repository*. He declined accepting the position, having been nominated for Superintendent of Public Instruction for the State of Indiana; but he discharged the duties of editor of the *Repository* for six months. Professor Larrabee was elected Superintendent of Public Instruction, and was the first the State ever had. Here, as in many other departments, his work was that of a pioneer. He entered upon the duties of his office, November, 1852. The few public schools that were in the state were poorly organized. They had to be reduced to system, and in accomplishing this, Mr. Larrabee had to encounter a large amount of popular prejudice. But he was enthusiastic in his work, and felt that he had a mission to fulfill in the department of education, and was glad of an opportunity of shaping the educational policy of the State. He had taken a deep interest in the debates on common schools, in the Constitutional Convention. He had watched the progress of the School Law of 1852 through the Legislature, and had aided in shaping it. He believed if the law were carried out according to its intent, that it would give the state an educational system equal to the most advanced States in the Union. He personally visited most of the counties in the state, made explanations, and answered objections. He worked diligently and conscientiously; but the measure and value of his success can not be easily determined, for the decisions of the Supreme Court, and acts of succeeding Legislatures, in accordance with them, and to satisfy local prejudices, overthrew, for the time being, the most marked features of the law, and the ones to the development of which he had directed his chief efforts.

In 1854, Mr. Larrabee was defeated for a re-election, owing to intense political excitement, and the defeat of the State ticket on which his name was placed. In 1856, he was elected to a second term. The school system was still staggering under the blows of the Supreme Court, and consequent modifications of the School Law, and the results so fondly anticipated and earnestly labored for by Professor Larrabee were not realized. He retired from office in January, 1859, and, notwithstanding he failed to see the fruit of his labors as a general suerintendent, as he desired, the results of his labors are yet seen; and the system of public schools inaugurated by him are now the pride and glory of the State.

Professor Larrabee commenced preaching in 1821, and became a member of the Conference in 1832. He was an instructive and entertaining preacher; but his great life-work, and that for which he will be chiefly remembered, is that of an educator. At the time of Professor Larrabee's death, there were more men in prominent positions who had received their education in whole or in part from him than from any other educator in the Methodist Church. Professor Larrabee contributed to the literature, as well as to the scholarship of the Church. His "Scientific Evidences of Natural and Revealed Religion," composed chiefly of such of his college lectures as bore on that subject, was published during his connection with Asbury University. Also, "Wesley and his Coadjutors," and "Asbury and his Coadjutors." He also published a volume, consisting chiefly of articles that had been contributed to the *Ladies' Repository*, with the title of "Rosa Bower." Professor Larrabee died on the morning of the 4th of May, 1859, after a confinement to his bed of about six weeks. Mrs. Larrabee had died the January preceding.

Professor Larrabee was a remarkably kind-hearted and generous man. He was a ripe scholar, and "apt to teach." Few men equaled him in the duties of the recitation-room. His memory will remain fragrant while any of his pupils live. Hon. R. W. Thompson said of him, in his sketches of the "Fallen Heroes of Methodism:" "Larrabee had a mind well stored with classic literature, and, though not eloquent in the popular sense, was not deficient in those high qualities of mind without which oratory can not exist. His style was easy and graceful, showing at once the extent of his erudition. While his mind had a mathematical tendency, yet much that he said and wrote bore the impress of a refined fancy, and left the most lasting and valuable impressions."

REV. B. F. TEFFT, D. D.

DR. TEFFT graduated at the Wesleyan University, in Middletown, Connecticut, in 1836. He taught in the Maine Wesleyan Seminary four years; from whence he was called to the Principalship of the Providence Conference Academy, where he remained but one year, when he entered the pastoral work, and was stationed in the city of Boston. Dr. Tefft came to Indiana in 1843, having been elected Professor of Greek Language and Literature in Indiana Asbury University; which position he filled for three years, when he entered upon the editorship of the *Ladies' Repository*, at Cincinnati, which position he occupied for six years. He was then elected to the Presidency of Genesee College, New York. His next official position was that of United States Consul to Stòckholm and Sweden, and then United States Minister to the same country; and for several years Dr. Tefft has spent most of his time in Europe. Although he remained but a few years in Indiana, yet he made an abiding impression in favor of sound and sanctified learning, and deserves a prominent place among the Methodist educators of the State. His scholarship was thorough, and his abilities, whether as a teacher, writer, lecturer, or preacher, were of a high order. He had the rare faculty of inspiring young men with a love for learning; and many who now occupy prominent positions in different parts of the world, owe much of their success in life to the inspiration and instruction which they received from Dr. Tefft.

REV. THOMAS H. LYNCH, D. D.

THE name of Thomas H. Lynch, D. D., occupies a worthy place among educators in the Church, he having

devoted several of the best years of his life to the work
of teaching, and given his means and personal influence,
through a series of years, to the development and sustaining of our institutions of learning. Mr. Lynch is a
native of Ohio. He was born in Waynesville, Warren
County, Ohio, January 23, 1808. His parents emigrated from South Carolina to Ohio in the year 1805.
They left the South because of their inveterate hostility
to the institution of slavery. His father died when the
subject of this notice was only six years of age. His
mother was a woman of refined culture, and deeply
pious. She gave to her children a Christian education;
all of whom made a profession of religion, and became
Church members in early life. It was the wish of his
mother, and also of his guardian, that Thomas should be
educated with a view to the profession of law as the
business of his life. At the age of fifteen years, in addition to the usual elementary branches of education, he
had accomplished the studies of algebra, trigonometry,
and surveying. In March, 1825, he engaged to teach
school for one year in the neighborhood of the Hon.
Jeremiah Morrow, then Governor of Ohio. His compen-
sation for teaching was at the rate of six dollars per
scholar for the whole year. One-half of this sum was to
be paid in cash, the rest in country produce. The most
of his pay, however, was received in wheat, for which
thirty-seven and a half cents a bushel was allowed. The
wheat was sold to Governor Morrow for *thirty-one and a
fourth cents* a bushel. Turning wheat into cash at this
rate was thought, by the friends of the young school-
teacher, to be a very fine financial operation. With the
means thus raised, young Mr. Lynch started to college. He entered the Miami University as a student in
May, 1826. While a student at the University he was

employed by Dr. Bishop, the President, to teach a class of Indians, just from the wilds of Arkansas. In the mean time, yielding to the convictions that had followed him from early years, Mr. Lynch had united with the Methodist Episcopal Church, under the ministry of the late Rev. Arthur W. Elliott, then in the vigor of his manhood, and in the power of his evangelical labors. This was on the 13th day of November, 1825. He remained in the University until September, 1827, when, having received an invitation from the trustees of Augusta College, Kentucky, through the Rev. Dr. Martin Ruter, its President, he entered that institution in the dual capacity of student and tutor. He pursued a full Collegiate Course of four years, classical and scientific, and graduated August 4, 1831. He received for his services as tutor two hundred dollars per year—a sum sufficient, at that time, to pay all his needed expenses. Augusta College was at this time the only successful Methodist College in the United States. Her students came from every section of the Union. Indiana sent many of her promising sons there to be educated, among whom was John W. Locke, now of the Indiana Asbury University. Among her graduates we may name Dr. Howard, President of the Ohio University, and Dr. R. S. Foster, of the Drew Theological Seminary, and Dr. Dandy, of Chicago. At the time of which we now write, the Faculty of Augusta College consisted of Rev. Martin Ruter, D. D., President; Rev. J. P. Durbin, Professor of Ancient Languages; Rev. J. S. Tomlinson, Professor of Mathematics; F. A. W. Davis, M. D., Professor of Chemistry and Natural Science; Rev. Arnold Treusdale, Principal of the Grammar School, and Thomas H. Lynch as Tutor. The College enjoyed great prosperity for many years. In the fierce contest between the North and the South upon the subject of slavery, this noble institution fell a victim between the fires of the adverse parties. The Legislature of Kentucky, in a fit of prejudice and passion, repealed its charter, and deprived it of its privileges. Thus this once prosperous and ardently cherished seat of learning lives only in history, and in the fond remembrance of its friends, its patrons, and of its widely scattered alumni.

After leaving college, Mr. Lynch studied law in the office of the late Hon. John Woods, of Hamilton, Ohio, a lawyer of eminent ability and large practice, and for several years an active member of Congress from his district. Mr. Lynch was admitted to practice law by the Supreme Court of Ohio, in December, 1832, and was soon after commissioned by Governor Lucas as Attorney for the State, which office he held for two years. While engaged in his chosen profession, he sought to quiet his convictions of duty in regard to the ministry by preaching on Sabbath-days. The effort was a vain one. He felt, "Woe is me if I preach not the Gospel of Christ!" Sickness came upon him; death seemed to stand at his door. He covenanted with God to spare his life, and he would " preach the unsearchable riches of Christ." God heard his prayer, and brought him up as from the gates of death. He closed up his law business, and offered himself to the Ohio Conference. Just at this time, Mr. Lynch was unexpectedly elected again as a member of the Faculty of Augusta College, where he labored in teaching and preaching until September, 1842, when he became a member of the Kentucky Annual Conference of the Methodist Episcopal Church, and was appointed to Transylvania University, in the Department of Ancient Languages. He held this position until 1846, when the Church South was fully organized. The University then passed from the control of the Methodist Episcopal Church to that of the Church South. It finally fell, as did Augusta College, a victim to the ravages of the slavery question. Rev. H. B. Bascom, D. D., was its President. He was the master-spirit of the Southern movement. He wrote in defense of slavery. He was chosen a bishop of the Church South. Here let the curtain drop; a sad chapter follows; let it not be written by human hands.

Under the advice of Bishops Morris and Hamline, Mr. Lynch remained in the Kentucky Conference (South) until the Summer of 1849, when, through the kindness of brethren of the Indiana Conference, he was invited to allow his name to be submitted to that body for recognition as a member among them. He had been opposed to the separation of the Southern Conference from the Methodist Episcopal Church, and his position was well known. Mr. Lynch often speaks of the pleasure it affords him to make kind mention of those who manifested an interest in his behalf at this time. He received letters from Rev. E. R. Ames, Rev. F. C. Holliday, Rev. S. T. Gillett, Rev. J. C. Smith, and Rev. L. W. Berry, most cordially inviting him to come to Indiana. The invitation was accepted. At the session of 1849, held at Rising Sun, Mr. Lynch was recognized, by a unanimous vote, as a member of the Indiana Conference, and he was appointed by Bishop Janes to St. John's, Madison. In 1850, he was elected President of the Indiana Female College which institution he conducted for several years, with marked success. He has been an active member of the South-eastern Indiana Conference from its organization. He has served seven years as presiding elder, and ten years in the pastorate as station preacher; and at the time of this writing is enjoying a prosperous and happy year as pastor of Grace Methodist Episcopal Church, Indianapolis. Nearly forty-six years ago, while but a youth, he united with the Methodist Episcopal Church. During almost the whole of this time he has been employed in the public and active service of the Church, in some department of its varied interests.

REV. JOHN WHEELER, D. D.

MR. WHEELER was one of the first graduates of Indiana Asbury University, having graduated in 1840. He was some time professor in the University, and was called from there to the Presidency of Baldwin University, at Berea, Ohio, and from there to the Presidency of the Iowa State University. Dr. Wheeler is an efficient teacher, and an able and prudent executive officer as a college president.

REV. THOMAS A. GOODWIN, A. M.

MR. GOODWIN graduated at Asbury University in 1840. He entered the ministry in Indiana Conference, and was an efficient minister for several years; but there being a great demand for teachers, Mr. Goodwin located, to take charge of an academy. He spent several years in teaching. Has been known extensively as the editor of the *Brookville American* and *Indiana American*. He has been a liberal contributor to the periodical literature of the Church, and is a model of industry and effectiveness as a local preacher.

REV. PHILANDER WILEY, A. M.

MR. WILEY was a graduate of Indiana Asbury University, of the class of 1843. He has been for some years Professor of Greek in the University, and has a high reputation for ripeness in scholarship, especially in the Greek language and literature, and of skill and thoroughness in teaching.

DR. BENSON.

Rev. Henry C. Benson graduated with honor in Indiana Asbury University, in 1842; was received into Indiana Conference at the ensuing session, and appointed to Mooresville Circuit, where he labored about half the year. In the Spring of 1843, transferred to Arkansas, to serve the Indian missions then appended to that Conference; joined William H. Goode at Fort Coffee, as principal teacher of the male department of the academy then just established among the Choctaws; labored successfully in that department, and also preached, as occasion would permit, among the Indians; assisted in the formation of the Indian Mission Conference, and acted as one of the secretaries at its first session; remained there until the Southern separation in 1845, when, with W. H. Goode, he transferred back to North Indiana Conference, and re-entered the pastoral work; had established a reputation which led to tempting inducements to remain in the South, but declined, from an unwillingness to come under the jurisdiction of the newly formed Southern Church; subsequently published an interesting volume, entitled, " Life among the Choctaw Indians."

After passing several years of successful pastoral labor in some of the prominent stations of the Conference, he was elected to the Chair of Greek Language and Literature in Asbury University, which he filled with acceptability for several successive years.

About 1851, he was transferred to California Conference, where he labored in the pastorate, presiding eldership, and other ministerial relations, till 1864, when he was elected to the editorship of the *Pacific Christian*

Advocate, and became a member of the Oregon Conference. In 1868, he was changed by election to the editorial chair of the *California Christian Advocate,* the duties of which he is now (1871) fulfilling at San Francisco. He is again a member of the California Conference, with a pleasant family residence at Santa Clara. He was a member of the General Conferences of 1864 and 1868; in the latter, was chairman of the Committee on Boundaries. He received the degree of D. D. from his *Alma Mater* in 1864. His life-record thus far has known no failure. Faithful, competent, energetic, in every relation still vigorous and active, he gives promise of extended years of usefulness to the Church.

REV. WILLIAM M. DAILY, D. D.

WHILE serving as stationed preacher in Bloomington, Mr. Daily graduated in the College Course to the degree of A. B., in the Indiana State University, in 1836. In 1839, while stationed in St. Louis, Missouri, he received the degree of A. M. from three different colleges; to wit, Indiana University, Augusta College, Kentucky, and M'Kendree College, Illinois; and, in the Fall of 1849, was elected Professor of Elocution in St. Charles College, Missouri. He returned to Indiana, and resumed the work of the ministry in Madison, in 1840.

While traveling Bloomington District as presiding elder, in 1851, he received the degree of Doctor of Divinity from his *Alma Mater,* his old preceptor, Rev. Philander Wiley, D. D., of the Protestant Episcopal Church, being President.

In 1853, he was elected President of Indiana University, to succeed his old preceptor, who had died. Dr. Daily entered on his duties as President and Professor of Mental and Moral Science and Belles-Lettres, in the

Fall of 1853. During Dr. Daily's Presidency, the old University building burned down, and the present new and beautiful buildings were erected. The endowment fund was lost by an adverse decision in the courts, and through his influence the whole amount was refunded by the State, and the institution again placed on a substantial basis.

In 1856, he received the degree of LL. D. from the University of Louisville, conferred by the Law Department, which was presided over by the ablest and best law scholars in the country. During Dr. Daily's Presidency of Indiana University, the institution came up from eighty students to over four hundred; and prior to his resignation he graduated the largest classes of any college in the state at that time. In 1859, he resigned the Presidency of the University, and retired to his home in Madison. At the breaking out of the Rebellion, he gave the whole of his influence to the support of the Government. At the close of the War he went South; and now (1871) is identified with the missionary work of the Church in that long-neglected land, and among a long-oppressed race. He is presiding elder in Louisiana Conference, with head-quarters at New Orleans.

GEORGE W. HOSS, A. M.

PROFESSOR HOSS graduated at Indiana Asbury University in 1850. His parents were comparatively poor, and he struggled hard to procure an education. He was a native of Ohio, but came to Indiana in 1836, and helped to open up a farm till the Fall of 1845, when he entered Asbury University as a student. Having to earn means for his own support, he was out of college two terms, and for three years he taught two hours each day in Mrs. Larrabee's Female Seminary, in addition to keeping up his college studies. Immediately on his graduation he was elected Principal of the Muncie Academy, at Muncie, in Delaware County, where he remained two years. In 1852, he was chosen Teacher of Mathematics in the Indiana Female College, in Indianapolis, under the Presidency of Rev. Thos. H. Lynch. In 1853, he was chosen First Literary Teacher in the Institute for the Blind, in Indianapolis. In 1855, he was elected President of Indiana Female College. He held this position one year, when he was elected Professor of Mathematics in the North-western Christian University, at Indianapolis. As the institution was under the control of another religious denomination, his election was a compliment to his scholarship and his popularity as a teacher. He continued in that position until March, 1865, when he resigned; having been, in the Fall of 1864, elected Superintendent of Public Instruction for the State of Indiana. On tendering his resignation, the students expressed their friendship and their appreciation of his services by presenting him a silver tea-service worth seventy-five dollars.

Mr. Hoss served with efficiency, and, in 1866, was re-elected. He was urged by many of the teachers and friends of education throughout the state to be a candidate for a third term; but he had determined, and had so declared, that he would not allow his name to be used in connection with the office for a third term. During his superintendency, he procured the passage of an extended bill of amendments to the School Law, among which was provision for establishing an excellent system of teachers' institutes, and providing for local taxation in towns and cities—versus a Supreme Court decision—thus supplementing the State revenue, and keeping the schools in the towns open ten months in the year. He

drafted the bill providing for the establishment of a
State Normal School, and secured its passage through
the Legislature with but slight modification. Mr. Hoss
also secured the passage of a Fund Bill, requiring county
,auditors to examine all school-fund records in their
office, and report to the Superintendent of Public Instruction—in which reports he and they should settle.
By this means he secured what had never been attempted, a reliable fund basis for over $3,000,000, held
by counties in settlement, and gained for the State
$24,500, which, as per former reports, had been lost.

In 1868, Professor Hoss was unanimously elected to
the Chair of English Literature and Practice of Teaching in the State University; and, being urged by the
Faculty and trustees of the University to enter immediately upon the duties of his professorship, he yielded
to their persuasions, and resigned the Superintendency
of Public Instruction, in October, 1869. His term of
office would have expired on the 15th of the ensuing
March.

In 1862, Professor Hoss became the principal owner
and publisher of the *Indiana School Journal*. When he
took the *School Journal* it was embarrassed with debt,
and had but three hundred and fifty subscribers. He
soon ran up the subscription list to eighteen hundred.

During 1862–63, while Professor Hoss was teaching
in the North-western Christian University, he also acted
as Superintendent of the City Schools in Indianapolis,
giving his afternoons to the public schools, and teaching
in the University in the forenoon.

Professor Hoss held a large number of teachers' institutes in different parts of the state. He has contributed largely, with his pen and tongue, to sound learning and Christian morality. He is an earnest advocate

of total abstinence from intoxicating drinks, and has written an excellent tract on " Temperance in the Public Schools." Professor Hoss's record as an educator is one of which the State and the Church are alike proud. He is a remarkably industrious man, and is as ardently devoted to the interest of Sabbath-schools as to the cause of general education.

BENJAMIN T. HOYT, A. M.

PROFESSOR HOYT was a native of New England. He graduated at the Wesleyan University at Middletown, Connecticut. After teaching for some time in the East, he came to Indiana in 1852, and for a few years had charge of an academy in Lawrenceburg, when he accepted the Presidency of the Indiana Female College in Indianapolis, which position he resigned to accept a professorship in Indiana Asbury University, where he remained until the time of his death, in 1866. Professor Hoyt was a superior educator; and whether in charge of a seminary, or in a professor's chair, he performed his duties thoroughly and efficiently. He was an active Sabbath-school worker, and a valuable Christian citizen. His educational career was a useful one, and his death, in the vigor of his manhood, and in the midst of his labors, was a source of deep regret among the Christian educators of the State.

PROFESSOR JOSEPH TINGLEY, PH. D.

PROFESSOR TINGLEY was born in Cadiz, Ohio, March 3, 1822, and received the most of his education in Alleghany College, at Meadville, Pennsylvania; but through the influence of Dr. Simpson, who was his cousin, and was then President of Asbury University, Mr. Tingley was induced to graduate at Asbury University, in 1846.

Two years after his graduation, Mr. Tingley was elected to the Chair of Natural Sciences, which he has filled until the present (1871). In 1860, he was elected Vice-President of the Faculty. In 1865, he received license to preach. Professor Tingley is an enthusiast in the department of Natural Science. He is "apt to teach," and has a readiness of illustration, and a mechanical genius that fits him admirably for his chosen position. Professor Tingley deservedly ranks high among literary men in the department of Natural Science. Thoroughness is a marked characteristic of all that he does; and, as a recognition of his attainments, the University in which he has been so long an efficient professor, conferred upon him, in 1871, the degree of Doctor of Philosophy. The many students that have recited to Professor Tingley, carry with them a grateful remembrance of his personal kindness, as well as of his professional ability.

PROFESSOR S. A. LATTIMORE.

Mr. Lattimore graduated at Asbury University in 1850. He was elected Professor of Greek Language and Literature in Asbury University in 1852. In 1861, he was elected Professor of Natural Sciences in Genesee College, New York, where he served for several years, and is now (1871) Professor of Chemistry in Rochester University. Professor Lattimore is noted for thoroughness and breadth of scholarship. He is a gentleman of cultivated manners and pleasant address. Quiet and unostentatious in his social bearing, he is recognized as an able professor and an influential promoter of true science. In the nine years he taught in Asbury University, he shared the confidence and esteem of the Faculty and the students, and gave promise of future eminence as a scholar and teacher.

REV. DANIEL CURRY, D. D.

DR. CURRY was personally identified with educational interests in Indiana from 1854 to 1857, having accepted the Presidency of Indiana Asbury University in 1854, and continued in the discharge of its duties until 1857, when he resigned and returned to New York.

Dr. Curry graduated at the Wesleyan University in Middletown, Connecticut, August, 1837. Immediately after his graduation, he took charge, as Principal, of the Troy Conference Academy, at West Poultney, Vermont, which position he filled until 1839, when he resigned, and accepted a professorship in the Georgia Female College, at Macon in that state, where he remained until 1846, when he resigned and went North. In 1841, Dr. Curry entered the itinerant ministry, and has for many years ranked high as an able and instructive divine. Dr. Curry had associated with him as professors, while at Greencastle, Dr. Nadal and Dr. Bragdon, both of them eminent as scholars and divines. Perhaps no college in the land had an abler Faculty than Indiana Asbury University, while Dr. Curry was at its head; but owing to a variety of causes, the administration of the college became involved and embarrassed, and Dr. Curry tendered his resignation. As a man of intellectual force, Dr. Curry has few superiors. He is an able and perspicuous writer. He tries to control men more by mere intellection than is found practicable. The reason that is clear to his mind is not always equally clear to all other minds; and men are largely governed by other influences than mere reason. Dr. Curry is a man of a warm and generous heart, and whose friendship is prized by a host of admiring friends. Dr. Bragdon was a graduate of Wesleyan University, and Dr. Nadal, of Dickinson College.

BENJAMIN F. RAWLINS, D. D.,

WAS some time President of Asbury Female College. He was a graduate of Indiana Asbury University, of the class of 1849. Dr. Rawlins is more extensively known as an able preacher, the ministry being his chosen profession. He is a frequent contributor to the periodical literature of the Church.

ALBION FELLOWS, A. M.,

GRADUATED at Asbury University in 1854. He filled, for some time, the Chair of Languages in Fort Wayne Female College.

JOHN P. ROUS, A. M.,

GRADUATED at Asbury University in 1855. He taught some time as Professor of Languages in Brookville College, as Principal of the Preparatory Department in Indiana Asbury University, and as Principal of Stockwell Academy.

BENJAMIN W. SMITH, A. M.,

ALSO a graduate of Asbury University, of the class of 1855, taught some time as Professor of Mathematics in Cornell College, and as President of Valparaiso Male and Female College.

W. R. GOODWIN, A. M.,

TAUGHT for some time as President of Brookville College, and Professor in Illinois Wesleyan University. He is more generally known throughout Indiana and Illinois as a popular and efficient preacher. He is also a frequent contributor to the Church papers. He graduated at Asbury University, in the class of 1856.

OLIVER H. SMITH, A. M.,

GRADUATED at Asbury in 1856, and spent several years in teaching, as Principal of Thorntown Academy, and President of Rockport Collegiate Institute. Mr. Smith is an able and efficient preacher.

WILLIAM H. DE MOTTE, A. M.,

TAUGHT for some time in the Indiana Institute for the Deaf and Dumb, and as President of Indiana Central Female College, and as President of Jacksonville Female College, Illinois. Mr. De Motte graduated at Indiana Asbury University in 1849.

REV. THOMAS HARRISON, A. M.,

A NATIVE of England, was educated in an academy in Yorkshire, England, and has spent twenty years in teaching. He was for several years President of Moore's Hill College; during which time he filled the Chair of Mental and Moral Philosophy and Natural Science. He is at present Professor in Brookville College. Previous to his coming to Indiana, he taught in the Ohio Conference High School, Springfield, Ohio; and in the Linden Hill Academy, New Carlisle, Ohio. He received the honorary degree of A. M. from the Ohio University, at Athens. Professor Harrison is an able preacher, and an instructive lecturer on moral and scientific subjects.

REV. J. P. D. JOHN, A. M.,

Is a native of Brookville, Indiana. Poor health brought his school-boy days to a close when he was but twelve years of age, with the exception of a few months; yet such was his desire for learning, and such his strength

20

of will, and his readiness to acquire knowledge, that he succeeded in obtaining a good education. He commenced teaching in his seventeenth year, and has continued ever since. He taught three years in the public schools of his native county, and eight years in Brookville College. During the first years of Professor John's connection with Brookville College, he was Professor of Mathematics, and during the past two years he has been President of the institution. Professor John received the honorary degree of Master of Arts from M'Kendree College, in Illinois, in 1867. And if his achievements hitherto are an earnest of his future, the Church has a good deal to expect from Professor John.

REV. JOHN W. LOCKE, D. D.

DR. LOCKE was the son of Rev. George Locke, one of the early pioneers of Indiana Methodism. He was born in Paris, Bourbon County, Kentucky, February 12, 1822. He made a profession of religion and united with the Church in his twelfth year. After the death of his father, in 1834, he assisted his mother in school until the organization of the New Albany Seminary, in 1837. Dr. Locke's mother had been accustomed to teach school in her husband's life-time, and the chief support of the family came from her earnings during the four years he was presiding elder on Wabash District; and, after the death of her husband, she had no other dependence. She met the responsibilities of her situation heroically, and literally raised her children in the school-room, and laid in their young minds the foundation of thorough mental discipline, and inspired them with the determination to become scholars.

Young Locke entered the New Albany Seminary in 1837, and prepared for college. Most of the time during his stay in the Seminary he assisted his mother in her school—teaching when his class-mates studied, studying when they played, and reciting when they recited. This overwork in his youth materially impaired his health during a number of the years of his early manhood.

In the Spring of 1839, he entered the Freshman Class in Augusta College, and graduated in 1842. He taught school in Portsmouth, Ohio, until the Fall of 1843. On the 15th of July, 1843, just nine years after the death of his father, he was licensed to preach, and recommended for admission into the Annual Conference. In the Fall of 1843, he was admitted into the Ohio Annual Conference. He was ordained a deacon by Bishop Hamline in 1845, and an elder by Bishop Janes in 1847. In 1850, he transferred to Indiana Conference, and was stationed in Vevay for two years; and then stationed in Rising Sun one year, when he was elected President of Brookville College in 1853, and remained in that position four years. In 1856, he was appointed presiding elder of Connersville District, which position he filled four years. In the Fall of 1860, he was elected Professor of Mathematics in Indiana Asbury University, which position he yet holds, and the duties of which he performs with marked ability.

Dr. Locke was a member of the General Conference of 1860, and also of 1868. He received the degree of Doctor of Divinity from Dickinson College in 1868. Dr. Locke was elected President of Baker University, in Kansas; but the climate not agreeing with him, he returned to Indiana after an absence of a few months, retaining his position as Professor of Mathematics in Indiana Asbury University. Dr. Locke is an able and popular preacher, and enjoys the pastoral work; but, yielding to what he deems an imperative call of duty, he continues in the work of education.

JOHN M. OLCOTT, A. M.

PROFESSOR OLCOTT graduated at Indiana Asbury University in the class of 1860. He taught four years as Principal of the High School in Lawrenceburg, some two years in Columbus, and was Superintendent of the Public Schools in Terre Haute for six years. He is ardently devoted to the cause of education, and is a contributor to the literary journals of the country. He is an advocate of the broadest and most thorough culture. He lacked but a few votes, in 1866, of being nominated on the Republican State ticket for Superintendent of Public Instruction for the State—a fact highly complimentary for one of his age.

REV. J. H. MARTIN, A. M.

REV. J. H. MARTIN is the present efficient President of Moore's Hill College. He received his education at Wood Vale Academy, Pennsylvania, and at the Ohio Wesleyan University. He entered upon the work of teaching in 1856, and has devoted fifteen years laboriously and successfully to that work. The first three years of his teaching life were spent in Middletown, Pennsylvania. In 1859, he came to Franklin, Indiana, and soon thereafter took charge of the Superintendency of the Union Schools of that city. In 1864, he accepted the Superintendency of the Public Schools in Edinburg, which position he filled for some two years, when he resigned to accept the Presidency of Brookville College, which position he resigned in 1869, and returned to Edinburg again to accept the Superintendency of the Public Schools of that place. His return to Edinburg was induced mainly by domestic affliction. In 1870, he was elected President of Moore's Hill College. While in Franklin and Edinburg, Professor Martin held the position of School Examiner for Johnson County. Professor Martin is ardently attached to the profession of teaching, and brings to the discharge of his duties a zeal, an ability and enthusiasm, that make him eminently successful.

REV. SAMUEL R. ADAMS, A. M.

Professor Adams was a graduate of the Wesleyan University, at Middletown, Connecticut. He chose the profession of teaching as his life-work. He came to Indiana in 1854, and had charge of an Academy at Wilmington for some time. On the opening of Moore's Hill College, in 1856, he was elected President of that institution, which position he retained until his death. When the Government called for troops to suppress the Rebellion, most of the students of sufficient age in the College under his care volunteered; and, actuated by patriotism toward his country, and by an affectionate regard for the young men under his care, President Adams also volunteered as a Union soldier, and accepted a commission as chaplain, which position he filled with such efficiency and zeal as prostrated him with sickness, and ended his life before the termination of the War. He met death at the post of duty, although that post was far from home and friends.

MILES J. FLETCHER, A. M.

Miles J. Fletcher was born in Indianapolis, in 1828, and was a son of Calvin Fletcher, Esq., who, although he had emigrated into the wilderness at an early day, had gained for himself a good general and classical education, and also brought with him from New England that love of educational advancement which is so characteristic of the sons of the Land of Steady Habits; so that, although young Fletcher's school privileges were limited to a few Winter months in the year, yet, with his other brothers, he had constantly the advantages of home instruction, which was of more value in building the noble characteristics of his nature than any training he could have received in academic halls.

In 1847, he entered Brown University, at Providence, Rhode Island; at which institution he graduated with honor in 1852, having interluded his years of student-life by a year of home-work. He was prominent in his class for his general knowledge. He cared but little for mathematics, although he acknowledged its importance, and he was never deep in love with the classics; but in historical information and logic, he stood head and shoulders above his fellows.

In the Spring of 1848, while spending a vacation in the village of Uxbridge, Massachusetts, influenced by a letter from a brother, he became a sincere and earnest inquirer for the path of life; and He who has said, "Seek and ye shall find," soon opened the "wicket-gate" to one who knocked and asked with his whole soul. Without a moment's delay, he identified himself with religion. He united with the Methodist Episcopal Church, the one in which he was trained from childhood; he took an active, yet modest, part in the college and class prayer-meetings, and, with new light and zeal, taught a class that had long been under his charge in Sabbath-school. In this connection it may be proper to give Professor Fletcher's testimony in regard to the aid given to a seeker of religion by previous Sabbath-school instruction. About the time of his conversion, a spirit of religious inquiry came upon many of the students in Brown University. Some, reared under the cold, rationalistic, semi-infidel influences that characterize certain portions of New England, were incarcerated, at their first awakening, in Doubting Castle, and only after long and severe struggling were enabled to break away. But Professor Fletcher remarked that all whose minds had been prepared by early Sabbath-school teachings, escaped all the gloom of doubt, and the temptations to skepticism.

Before his graduation he had determined on the career of a teacher. To him the preparation of the mind and heart for the world's broad field of battle was a high and holy calling. Immediately upon his graduation, he entered upon his duties as Professor of English Literature in Indiana Asbury University, at Greencastle. With characteristic zeal and energy he labored in his department. He had the faculty of rendering his branches entertaining to the students. He was the friend of his pupils—not holding them off by any false notions of professional dignity, but wooing them to companionship by the kindness of his manners. He visited them in sickness, closed their eyes in death, gave encouragement to them in their despondency, and employment to ameliorate their poverty. His life as a professor was intermitted by a year given to the assistance of his father, and a year spent at Cambridge Law School. The truth is, he was so efficient with his hands, head, and heart, that there was a constant temptation on the part of his friends to tax his time and strength.

In the Fall of 1860, he was elected Superintendent of Public Instruction for the State of Indiana. In this capacity his labors were incredible. He brought honest industry and system to bear so efficaciously that at the time of his melancholy death, the machinery of his office was in fine working order. All this was accomplished notwithstanding the heavy drain upon his time incident to the Rebellion. When the firing upon Sumter aroused the nation, he assisted, at the request of the Governor, in the drilling of raw recruits for the three months' service at Camp Morton. Immediately thereafter, by appointment, he visited the armories of New England, and purchased the first arms for our State. In August, 1861, he made an arduous and dangerous journey to Western Virginia, in search of his brother, Dr. William B. Fletcher, who was captured in July by the rebels— to whose pen we are indebted for the facts of this sketch. He visited Washington on the same fraternal mission. When the whereabouts of his brother was ascertained he spent many weeks in ameliorating his condition, and achieving his release, by exchange, from the loathsome warehouse prison at Richmond.

At home again, he resumed his system of county visitation and lecturing on education, until once more interrupted to hasten with the first boat that reached Pittsburg Landing after the bloody battle of Shiloh, to carry relief to the sick and wounded. Here he labored with such assiduity that he brought on an infirmity that would have gone with him through a long life. Professor Fletcher was killed on the 10th of May, 1862. He had left Indianapolis on the ten o'clock night-train for Terre Haute, in company with Governor Morton, Dr. Bobbs, Adjutant-General Noble, and several other citizens, on an expedition to our army at Corinth, to bring home such of our sick and wounded as were there able to travel, and provide hospital stores and accommodations for the others. At Terre Haute they took the connecting train for Evansville, which reached Sullivan, the scene of the catastrophe, about one o'clock. As the train was approaching that station it ran into a freight-car, which had been left either on the track or on a switch so close to the track that the passenger-cars jostled against it, or it had been run on the track after the retirement of the switchmen at that station. The noise and jar of the collision made Professor Fletcher put his head out of the window to see what the matter was, and something—probably the freight-car on the switch which the train was passing—struck him on the side of the head, crushing his skull, and killing him instantly. The loss of such a man at such a time, and in such a manner, produced a profound sensation.

Professor Fletcher had elements of popularity equaled by few. He was big-hearted and brave. He was tender and considerate to the poor and downtrodden He was frank and outspoken, and no one felt or feared that there was any dissimulation or concealment about him. He was the soul of honor, and the type of generosity, and, withal, had an inexhaustible flow of spirits, that gave a fascination and charm to his society, and made him popular, without an effort to be so. He was a prodigy of work; and he did his work so thoroughly and so well that his friends were always taxing him with extra labor. He was no politician; and perhaps no other office in the gift of the State would have seduced him from his professorship; but he felt that, in the capacity of Superintendent of Public Instruction, he could accomplish for the cause of education in the state at large, more than he could in any other position.

REV. L. W. BERRY, D. D.

DR. BERRY was elected President of Indiana Asbury University in 1849, as the successor of Dr. Simpson.

He entered upon the duties of his office in the Fall of the same year, which position he held for five years, when he resigned, and re-entered the active work of the ministry. In 1855, he was elected President of Iowa Wesleyan University, where he labored with efficiency. A number of leading Methodists, determining to found a university at Jefferson City, Missouri, and looking around for a suitable man to put at the head of their enterprise, selected Dr. Berry, who, upon the advice of his friends, accepted the position of President and financial agent. He had barely entered upon his work, when he was prostrated by a severe attack of sickness, that terminated his life in July, 1858. His disease was asthma, combined with erysipelas, which produced paralysis of the throat, tongue, and lips, depriving him almost wholly of the power of speech, and of the ability to swallow either nourishment or medicine. Dr. Berry received the honorary degree of D. D. while President of Indiana Asbury University.

While Dr. Berry's career as an educator was creditable, his reputation rests chiefly on his ability and efficiency as a preacher. Dr. Berry entered the Ohio Conference on trial in 1834, and traveled a part of the year as junior preacher on Oxford Circuit. At the end of the year he discontinued, and entered Oxford University as a student; and although he did not complete the College Course, he laid the foundation for a good education, and he retained the habit of close and systematic study all through his life.

He was admitted on trial in the Indiana Conference, in the Fall of 1838, and continued in the itinerancy till the close of life. His sermons were prepared with labor, and delivered with earnestness, and often with marked success.

Eng^d by H.B.Hall&Sons 62 Fulton St.N.Y.

Yours Truly
Thos. Bowman

REV. THOMAS BOWMAN, D. D.

DR. BOWMAN, the present popular President of Indiana Asbury University, was educated at Dickinson College, Carlisle, Pennsylvania. He entered the ministry in early life, and soon took high rank as a preacher. But his literary attainments and aptness to teach pointed him out as a successful educator, and the Church called him to the work of literary instruction. He came to Indiana in 1858, as the successor of Dr. Curry in the Presidency of Indiana Asbury University, which position he has filled with uniform acceptability and marked efficiency. His administrative ability is of a high order. He makes no display of authority, and secures obedience to discipline without seeming to demand it. As a preacher, his style is perspicuous and entertaining; his matter instructive and evangelical. He addresses alike the head and heart, and few preachers are equally popular with all classes of hearers. Perhaps no man in the Church is called upon oftener, or called farther, to dedicate churches than Dr. Bowman; and on such occasions he is proverbially successful in raising money, having opened the hearts of his hearers until he has free access to their pockets.

REV. ERASTUS ROWLEY, D. D.

DR. ROWLEY, who has for some years been President of De Pauw Female College at New Albany, is a gentleman of ripe scholarship and rare executive ability, and has rendered the cause of Christian education substantial service.

REV. D. HOLMES,

OF North-west Indiana Conference, gave several years to the work of education. He is both a ripe scholar and an able divine. He is more solid than showy, more profound than pretentious.

REV. G. W. RICE

HAS for some years had charge of the academy at Battle Ground, and is a successful educator.

REV. A. GURNEY

WAS for some years President of Valparaiso Male and Female College. The institution is now under the charge of Rev. R. D. Utter.

Indiana Methodism has given to the public a large corps of well educated and efficient teachers. The Church erred in multiplying denominational schools to so large an extent, but that evil is being corrected, and the Church is more wisely concentrating her efforts upon the endowment and liberal patronage of a few of her more central and prominent institutions.

CHAPTER XVI.

Methodist Educational Institutions—Early Funds controlled by Presbyterians—Effort to amend the Charter of the "State University"—
The Legislature memorialized—"Indiana Asbury University"
founded—First Meeting of the Board of Trustees—First Commencement—"New Albany Seminary"—"De Pauw College"—"Fort
Wayne College"—"Whitewater College"—"Brookville College"—
"Moore's Hill College"—Educational Record of Indiana—Names
of Institutions—Number of Teachers—Scholars—Value of School
Property.

EDUCATIONAL.

THE State funds for educational purposes in Indiana,
as in most of the Western States, were for many
years under the almost exclusive control of Presbyterians, who assumed to be the especial guardians and patrons of education. It is impossible, at this day, to comprehend the self-complacency with which their leading
men in the West assumed to be the only competent educators of the people, and the quiet unscrupulousness
with which they seized upon the trust-funds of the
States for school purposes, and made those schools as
strictly denominational as though the funds had been exclusively contributed by members of their own commun-
ion. A young man who, in either the Miami University
at Oxford, Ohio, or Lexington, Kentucky, or Bloomington, Indiana, would have questioned the correctness of
any of the dogmas of Calvinism, would have been an object of unmitigated ridicule and persecution. Such was
the spirit of exclusiveness with which State colleges were
managed, in the early settlement of the Western coun-

try, that for many years but few students, except those from Calvinistic families, were found in the State colleges. This tended to throw other denominations upon their own resources, and induced them not only to build up denominational schools, but caused them, in due course of time, to assert their rights in the management of the State institutions; and the result has been that, in those states as Ohio, Kentucky, Indiana, Illinois, and Iowa, where Presbyterian greed has been most conspicuous, they now occupy, in educational matters, a subordinate position. When, in 1834 and 1835, efforts were made in Indiana so to change the management of the State University, by amending its charter, that the trustees should be elected by the State Legislature, instead of being a self-perpetuating corporation, a storm of indignation was raised among those who controlled the State University; and it was made the occasion of heaping all sorts of opprobium on the head of the Methodist Church. The movement was said to be an effort on the part of the Methodists to get a Methodist professor in the State University; and it was tauntingly said, in the halls of the Legislature, that "there was not a Methodist in America with sufficient learning to fill a professor's chair, if it were tendered to him." Such taunts proved a wholesome stimulus to Methodist enterprise and independent Church action in the department of education, and the result is seen, in part, in the investment of more than half a million of dollars in property for school purposes; in the employment of more than fifty teachers in Methodist schools in Indiana; in the endowment of denominational colleges second to none; and in the chief control of the State University, from which we had been so long and persistently excluded. And all this accomplished, not by the seizure and appropriation of public funds, but by the willing contributions of our people, and by the moral force of the numbers and intelligence of our communicants.

At the first session of the Indiana Conference, held in New Albany, October, 1832, a committee, consisting of Revs. Allen Wiley, C. W. Ruter, and James Armstrong, was appointed to consider and report on the propriety of establishing a literary institution, under the patronage of the Conference. The committee reported, but no action was had, beyond providing for the collection of information, to be reported to the next Conference.

While the Conference felt that, on many accounts, it would be desirable to have an institution of learning under its own control, yet it was thought if we could get any thing like an equitable share of privileges in the State University at Bloomington, that that would meet the wants of our people for several years; and accordingly, at the Conference of 1834, it was resolved to memorialize the Legislature on that subject. A memorial from the Conference, and similar memorials from different parts of the state, numerously signed, were sent up to the Legislature. The memorialists did not ask that the University be put, either in whole or in part, under the control of the Church; they simply asked that the trustees of the University should be elected for a definite term of years, and the vacancies, as they occurred, should be filled by the Legislature, and not by the remaining members of the Board of Trustees.

The memorials were referred to an able committee of the Legislature, but from some cause the committee never reported. It was easier to strangle the report in the committee, than to justify a refusal of the reforms asked by the memorialists. Failing in their efforts to secure a reform in the manner of controlling the State University, the members of the Conference turned their thoughts earnestly toward the founding of a literary institution of high grade, under the control of the Church. At the session of the Conference of 1835, a plan was agreed upon for founding a university.

Subscriptions were taken up and proposals made from different parts of the state, with a view of securing the location of the university. Rockville, Putnamville, Greencastle, Lafayette, Madison, and Indianapolis were the principal competitors. Rockville presented a subscription of $20,000; Putnamville, about the same amount; Indianapolis and Madison, $10,000 each; and Greencastle, the sum of $25,000; and at the session of the Conference in Indianapolis, in 1836, the university was located at Greencastle. At the next session of the Legislature the institution secured a liberal charter, under the name of

INDIANA ASBURY UNIVERSITY.

THE first meeting of the Board of Trustees was held in 1837, when it was resolved to open the Preparatory Department, which in due time was done under the principalship of Rev. Cyrus Nutt, a graduate of Alleghany College. Rev. M. Simpson was elected President of the University in 1839; and the first regular Commencement was held in 1840, when President Simpson was duly inaugurated; the charge being delivered by Governor Wallace.

NEW ALBANY SEMINARY.

THIS institution came under the care of Indiana Conference in 1837. In May, 1837, William H. Goode, who was traveling Lexington Circuit, was elected Principal of New Albany Seminary, and, by the approval of his presiding elder, Rev. C. W. Ruter, who supplied his place on the circuit, entered immediately upon his duties as the successor of Philander Ruter, A. M. And at the ensuing session of the Conference, which was held in New Albany in the Fall of the same year, Mr. Goode was appointed in charge of the Seminary. Preferring the pastoral work, he resigned before the next session of the Conference, and was succeeded by George H. Harrison, A. M., who continued in charge of the Seminary for several years; and, although the Seminary was discontinued as a Conference institution, and ceased, it, nevertheless, accomplished great good in its day, and showed that the Methodist Church was then, as now, the real friend of Christian education.

That errors were committed in the early management of our denominational schools, is now apparent. The efforts of the Church were too much divided, and the schools did not rest on a sufficiently solid pecuniary basis. New Albany Seminary is worthily succeeded by

DE PAUW COLLEGE FOR YOUNG LADIES,

In the same city. The College is a credit to the city, and an honor to its noble founder and patron, whose name it bears. Other seminaries and colleges, local in their influence, but useful in their day, sprang up in different parts of the Conference, and flourished for a while; but as the system of public schools improved, and graded schools were established, the demand for Church seminaries was less, and the Church is wisely concentrating on a few of her more central and important institutions.

WHITEWATER COLLEGE,

At Centerville, with a branch at Richmond, flourished for some years, and had the efficient labors of Cyrus

Nutt, D. D., and of Wm. H. Barnes, A. M., and other efficient educators; but was finally discontinued as a Church school.

Similar schools sprang up in each of the conferences, and, after flourishing for a season, were discontinued; and, although their discontinuance was a source of mortification to their immediate friends, perhaps they each accomplished more good than they cost; and, while they expired, their fruit remained.

Fort Wayne College was founded in 1846; Brookville College in 1851, and Moore's Hill College in 1853.

THE educational record for Indiana (1870) stands as follows :

Indiana Asbury University: Professors, 7; students, 344; value of property, $101,000; active endowment, $105,000; total value of property, $206,000.

INDIANA CONFERENCE.

DE PAUW COLLEGE for Young Ladies: Teachers, 9; scholars, 137; value of property, $50,000. Rockport Collegiate Institute: Teachers, 4; students, 98; value of property, $30,000.

NORTH INDIANA CONFERENCE.

FORT WAYNE COLLEGE: Teachers, 10; students, 250; value of property, $50,000.

SOUTH-EASTERN INDIANA CONFERENCE.

BROOKVILLE COLLEGE: Teachers, 6; students, 150; value of property, $27,000. Moore's Hill College: Teachers, 9; students, 365; value of property and endowment, $53,520.

NORTH-WEST INDIANA CONFERENCE.

Stockwell Collegiate Institute: Teachers, 7; students, 150; value of property, $40,000. Valparaiso College: Value of property, $30,000. Battle-ground Institute: Value of property, $10,000. Danville Academy: Value of property, $20,000. Dayton Academy: Teachers, 2; students, 100; value of property, $5,000.

There are sixty professors and teachers employed in colleges and academies in Indiana under the care of the Church, and nearly two thousand students receiving collegiate and academic training in these institutions.

VALUE OF SCHOOL PROPERTY.

Indiana Asbury University	$206,000
Fort Wayne College	50,000
Brookville College	27,000
Moore's Hill College	53,520
De Pauw College for Young Ladies	50,000
Stockwell Collegiate Institute	40,000
Dayton Academy	5,000
Rockport Collegiate Institute	30,000
Valparaiso College	30,000
Battle-ground Institute	10,000
Indiana Central Female College	11,000
Danville Academy	20,000
Total	$532,520

The above exhibit is incomplete, owing to the impossibility of obtaining full information; but it serves to show that Methodists are doing a reasonable share toward the education of the youth of the State. Many of the most efficient teachers in our graded schools, and a number of the superintendents of the schools in our cities, are graduates of Methodist colleges.

CHAPTER XVII.

INDIANA BISHOPS.

BISHOP ROBERTS.

ROBERT RICHFORD ROBERTS, although not a native of Indiana, and never a member of an Indiana
Conference, is, nevertheless, claimed as an Indiana
bishop, because he was a citizen of Indiana during nearly
the whole term of his episcopate. His mortal remains
rest in Indiana, and his worldly substance was all devoted to the support of Christian education in Indiana.
Bishop Roberts was a native of Frederick, Maryland.
He was born August 2, 1778. He was converted in the
fourteenth year of his age, and licensed to preach, and
admitted on trial in the Baltimore Annual Conference, in
the Spring of 1802. He traveled consecutively Carlisle, Montgomery, Frederick, Pittsburg, and Wheeling

Circuits. While in charge of the latter circuit, in 1808, he attended the session of the General Conference in Baltimore, and took part in its deliberations, participating in the famous debates on the question of making the presiding eldership elective. At the close of the General Conference, Bishop Asbury stationed him in the city of Baltimore. In 1809, he was reappointed to Baltimore. In 1810, he was stationed at Fell's Point, and in 1811, at Alexandria. In 1812, he was stationed at Georgetown, District of Columbia, and during this year he made the acquaintance of President Madison and his estimable lady, by whom he was highly esteemed. He was accustomed to visit them, and was received with the freedom and cordiality of private friendship. In 1813 and 1814, he was stationed in Philadelphia. In 1815, he was presiding elder on Schuylkill District, which included the city of Philadelphia. In 1816, he was elected to the episcopacy. The following fact, doubtless, contributed to the election of Mr. Roberts: There being no bishop present at the session of the Philadelphia Conference, which was held just previous to that of the General Conference, Mr. Roberts, according to the provisions of the Discipline, was elected to preside, although the youngest presiding elder in the Conference. During the session of the Conference many of the delegates to the General Conference, from New England and New York, who were on their way to Baltimore, stopped to look in upon the Philadelphia Conference; and beholding the dignity, ease, and propriety with which he presided, were convinced that he was a suitable man for the episcopacy. His elevation to the episcopacy was unlooked for as well as unsolicited by him. In December, 1819, Bishop Roberts removed from Shenango, his old home in Pennsylvania, where he resided a short time after his election to the episcopacy, to Lawrence County, Indiana. This was in the third year of his episcopacy. The mildness of the climate, the fertility of the soil, and cheapness in living, appear to have been the motives by which he was actuated in coming to Indiana. Although his circuit was the continent, and his exposures and perils great, he was permitted to die at home, which solemn event occurred on the 26th of March, 1843.

Bishop Roberts was a man of fine physical appearance. He would attract attention in any company. He sat, stood, and moved with great dignity, in private and public, without any apparent effort, or any stiffness of manner. He was five feet ten inches in height, with a heavy, robust frame, tending, in later years, to corpulency. God had called him to a work which demanded great physical as well as mental and moral force, and he endowed him for his vocation. His manner was always easy, and is, perhaps, as well expressed by the terms simplicity and naturalness, as by any others. His piety was deep, ardent, and uniform. He loved the social means of grace, as the class and prayer meetings, where he seemed to forget all official position, and appeared in the simple light of true Christian character. His piety was cheerful and active. The field of his labor was a continent, and, like Paul, he pressed to regions beyond, that he might preach the Gospel where Christ had not been named, that he might not build on another man's foundation. As a preacher, his manner was earnest rather than impassioned. His thoughts came readily, and were always clothed in appropriate language. He was a natural orator. His voice was full, and its tones rich and melodious. He commenced with a pitch of voice that all could hear, and his delivery was quite uniform. It was a full current from the beginning, and flowed on evenly to the end; and one felt that, impressive as his effort was, there was with him a large amount of reserved power. His sermons were practical and experimental. His thoughts were in sympathy with real life, and, hence, there was a freshness about his sermons that was always refreshing.

In his address on "The Fallen Heroes of Indiana Methodism," delivered before the "Indiana State Methodist Convention" in Indianapolis, in October, 1870, Hon. R. W. Thompson said of Bishop Roberts:

"I knew Bishop Roberts well—most intimately, considering the disparity in our ages. I had many opportunities of studying his character as it was developed in his intercourse with the world; and, all things considered, I do not hesitate to say, that for all the highest excellencies, for a profound knowledge of mankind, and the motives and springs of human conduct; for a deep, true courage; for pure Christian charity; for all, indeed, that goes to raise man up to the true standard of nobility, he may be entitled to stand in the foremost rank among all the men I have ever known. In the domestic circle he was as playful, simple, and ingenuous as a little child, fond of anecdotes, and somewhat skilled in telling them. Those of you who knew him well, remember that sly humor that twinkled in his face, and lit it up with animation and life, when he was recounting some rich and racy scenes he had observed in frontier life. In recounting these he seemed to be a boy again. But even in his playful moods he was 'every inch a man,' such a one as we may not soon 'look upon his like again.'"

Nobody could look at the benignant expression on Bishop Roberts's face without seeing that he was full of kindness and benevolence; gentleness beamed from every feature. I once witnessed an exhibition of these characteristics that made so strong and lasting an impression on my mind that I can not now omit it.

There resided in Lawrenceport—to which place the bishop had removed—a gentleman who had once been a Methodist preacher, and was still a member of the Church, but actively engaged in business. For some cause, which I have forgotten, he was induced to speak in unkind and rather harsh terms of the bishop, being a hasty and impetuous man. The bishop heard of it; and one night, when I was at this gentleman's house, he surprised him by suddenly stepping in. After a kind salutation, and a brief conversation upon ordinary topics, during which my friend was greatly embarrassed, the venerable old man turned directly to him and said: "Brother ——, I am told that you have spoken unkindly of me, and have called over to say to you what I thought I could best say in the presence of another, which is that I do not feel offended, but mortified, not on my own account, but yours. I am old enough to be your father, and on that account you ought not to speak harshly of me. But more especially ought you not to do so when you consider that I have given you no occasion for it. I never did you an injury, or wished you any harm; on the contrary, I have always treated you with kindness. But I am too old to quarrel, and incapable, I trust, of resentment. I have, therefore, called without an invitation, not to speak unkindly to you in return, but to say that I willingly forgive you, and will pray that God will also do so; having only one request to make, which is that you will not say hard things about me any more, as you ought not to say them about any body." Instantly observing how completely his adversary was discomfited by this Christian, paternal lecture, and as if to relieve him from his humiliation, he said, "Now, brother, we will pray together;" and he put up such a prayer to the Throne of Grace—so gentle and kind and spiritual—that my friend expressed his sorrow in copious tears. On rising from his knees, the bishop bade us good-night, and retired without another word of reference to the difficulty. That was the end of it.

As to the bishop's preaching, Hon. Mr. Thompson bears the following testimony:

"The first sermon I ever heard preached in Indiana was by Bishop Roberts, nearly forty years ago. I had just then settled in the county where he resided; and when it was announced that he would preach at Bono, near his home, I went there to hear him. I have not yet forgotten the impression under which I went. Having been raised an Episcopalian, I had acquired certain ideas of a bishop, which filled my mind. I had frequently heard the venerable and most excellent Bishop Mead, of Virginia, and the hand of the more venerable, and not less excellent, Bishop White, of Pennsylvania, had rested upon my head in the ceremony of confirmation. To these distinguished men I attached a degree of honor and respect far above that which I was in the habit of feeling for ordinary individuals. And thus impressed, I frankly confess that I was prompted by some little curiosity to see what sort of a man a Methodist bishop of Indiana could be. The weather was pleasant, the congregation large for the times, and the preaching out of doors in a beautiful grove. At the beginning of the sermon I stood at the outside of the audience; from which point, for the first time, my eye rested upon the venerable form of the noble old man, than whom, among all the varied associations of three-score years, I have never known a nobler or better. His gray locks were thrown back so as to expose to full view his magnificent fore-

head and brow, which were stamped with the unmistakable marks of thought and intellectual power. My
whole attention was at once arrested, and I drank in
every word, as it fell from his lips, with the deepest and
most intense interest, edging myself along to get nearer,
as if drawn to him by a cord that was too strong to be
resisted or broken. His introduction was in soft, but
distinct tones, as though he were a father addressing
kindly admonitions to his children. It was most fitly
spoken in that almost conversational style for which he
was eminently distinguished, and which he universally
adopted at the commencement of his sermons. But as
he advanced, he grew and strengthened and warmed up
with his subject, and displayed such eloquence and
power and vigor of thought, as has not often been heard
in Canterbury, or York, or Cambridge, or St. Peter's.
His clear and musical voice was re-echoed by the silent
grove, and not one who was brought under its spell
remained unmoved by its pathos. He did not employ
tropes and figures by way of ornament to his discourse,
but, grappling his subject like a giant, he portrayed
the majesty, power, and love of God in breathing words
and burning thoughts, that sank into the hearts and
souls of his hearers. At one time his style was simple,
yet always terse, exact, and perspicuous. At others he
rose to the very highest summit of eloquence, and
descended again, with a natural ease and dignity that
far surpassed all the teachings of the schools. Dealing
for a moment with common events, so as to arrest the
attention and excite the earnestness of his hearers, he
would, without artistic action or display, carry them
with him, by a sort of magic influence, into the loftier
regions of thought and reason, exhibiting, as he progressed, no less familiarity with the classic imagery of

Milton than with the inspired and majestic thoughts of St. Paul."

On the 18th of January, 1844, the remains of Bishop Roberts were disinterred, and removed to Greencastle. On the following day they were, by order of the trustees of the University, reinterred in the college campus. The religious services were conducted by Rev. John Miller, which were followed by an appropriate address by Professor W. C. Larrabee. The preachers of the four Indiana conferences united in erecting a beautiful marble monument over his grave, at a cost of four hundred and twelve dollars. The monument was erected by J. W. Weir & Brother, of Indianapolis. The work having been completed according to contract, its erection was celebrated on the 18th of May, 1859, in the following order : A procession was formed at the " First Church," in Greencastle, under the direction of Professor Miles J. Fletcher, and marched to the college campus, where a platform and seats had been prepared. The music was led by an excellent choir. Appropriate portions of Scripture were read by F. C. Holliday. Prayer was offered by Professor Cyrus Nutt and W. C. Smith, and an appreciative and richly historical funeral address was delivered by Rev. Aaron Wood. The mortal remains of the bishop's wife, who survived him several years, sleep by his side, and through the liberality of J. S. M'Donald, Esq., of New Albany, a substantial iron fence incloses their last resting-place.

From the commencement of his ministry, and down to his election to the episcopacy, Mr. Roberts filled a class of prominent appointments, including the cities of Baltimore, Washington City, and Philadelphia. For twenty-seven years as a bishop he traveled over the settled portions of this country, when the facilities for traveling were far different from what they are now. He was a model Christian gentleman, alike at home in the parlors of the wealthy and in the cabins of the frontier settlers. His qualities of person, mind, and heart fitted him well for his position as a Methodist bishop, whose diocese was a continent. He was "given to hospitality," and he showed his appreciation of learning by making "Indiana Asbury University" his heir, so that what little means he had accumulated will continue to promote the interests of sanctified learning as the years roll by.

BISHOP SIMPSON.

REV. MATTHEW SIMPSON was elected to the episcopacy in 1852. Although his father died when he was young, yet, acting upon the advice of judicious friends, and prompted by a strong desire for learning, he succeeded in securing a collegiate education. He was converted in his youth, and, yielding to his convictions of duty, he entered the traveling ministry, in the Pittsburg Conference, in 1833. In 1839, he was elected President of Indiana Asbury University, which position he continued to occupy until 1848, when he was elected editor of the *Western Christian Advocate.* He filled this position until 1852, when he was elected bishop.

Dr. Simpson, as President of Indiana Asbury University, did the cause of Methodism in general, and Methodist education in particular, in Indiana, a very great service. Denominational education among us in Indiana, as has been noted elsewhere, was the result of an inveterate prejudice against Methodism. Dr. Simpson's attainments as a scholar, and his ability both as a platform speaker and a preacher, gave him great influence throughout the state as a representative man, and enabled him utterly to destroy many of the erroneous

REV. M. SIMPSON, D.D.,

impressions that designing men had made on the public mind. As President of the University, Dr. Simpson displayed great financial skill and executive ability. For some time the endowment was inadequate to meet the current expenses of the institution, on the most economical scale; but such was the popularity of the Faculty, under the leadership of Dr. Simpson, that the income from the endowment fund was cheerfully supplemented by contributions for current expenses, from nearly every pastoral charge in the state. His influence over the students was almost unbounded. They not only respected and admired him—they loved him; and when absent only a few days they would, on his return, make some public demonstration of joy. As editor of the *Western Christian Advocate*, he met the largest expectations of the Church. The Church was fortunate in selecting him as one of her bishops. He brought to the duties of the episcopal office the same tireless energy, comprehensive plans, and singleness of purpose, that had characterized him as President of the University and editor of the *Western Christian Advocate*. A prince of preachers, Bishop Simpson's fame is more than national. His visits through Europe, as the representative of American Methodism, enabled him to make a profound impression on the public mind, and his sermons were every-where regarded as models of pulpit eloquence, combining, in a larger degree than almost any other man, scholarly culture, logical accuracy, and impassioned delivery. The bishop retains his habits of study. His versatility of talent, and his ability and willingness to work, are equaled by few. American Methodism has thus far been pre-eminently fortunate in the selection of her bishops. The office and the times have called for remarkable men, and the Church has furnished them. Bishop Simpson rendered great service to the cause of the Union by his public lectures, his personal influence, and his wise counsels, during the War of the Rebellion. He contributed largely to the efficiency of the sanitary measures inaugurated by the "American Christian Commission" during the War. He is admired and beloved by the whole Protestant Church; for, without abating any of his devotion to his own Church, he cultivates the truest Christian charity among all Christian people.

EDWARD R. AMES.

EDWARD R. AMES was born in Amesville, Ohio, May 20, 1806, and spent his childhood and youth upon a farm, where he developed a remarkably vigorous physical and mental constitution. Mr. Ames descended from an old Puritan stock. William Ames, originally of Somersetshire, England, came to America with his family, and settled in Braintree, New Plymouth Colony, Massachusetts, in 1643. He died in 1654, leaving behind him one son and six daughters. From this son descended a numerous posterity. Several of his descendants figured conspicuously in the scenes and events of the American Revolution. Fisher Ames was one of the most fiery and effective orators of his day. Bishop Ames's parents removed from Massachusetts to the North-western Territory in 1798. Of course young Ames's literary opportunities were limited in so new a country. It so happened there was an excellent circulating library in the neighborhood, to which he had access; and the bishop has often remarked of that library, as Carlyle of his attendance at the English University, that it gave him a taste for reading. His father died in 1823. At the age of twenty, he left the farm and entered as a student in the Ohio State University at Athens, where he spent some three years, supporting himself chiefly by his own exertions. During his attendance at the University he experienced an evidence of sins forgiven. At the solicitations of Bishop Roberts, in 1828, he accompanied him to the seat of the Illinois Conference, which met that year in Madison, Indiana. There young Ames became acquainted with Rev. S. H. Thompson and John Dew, from Illinois; and, under their persuasions, he was induced to go to Illinois, and open a High-school in Lebanon, which was so successful as to become the germ of M'Kendree College. Mr. Ames remained in Lebanon until 1830, when he entered the itinerant ministry in the Illinois Conference. When Illinois Conference was divided, and Indiana Conference was constituted, Mr. Ames was included in the Indiana Conference. In 1840, he was chosen a delegate to the General Conference, which met in Baltimore, and by that body elected Corresponding Secretary of the Missionary Society for the South and West. In that capacity he had supervision of the Indian missions, and his duties required an immense amount of traveling. It was before the era of railroads. The office was one of great labor, but right nobly and efficiently were its duties performed. During his four years in this office, he traveled some twenty-five thousand miles. During one tour he passed over the entire frontier line, from Lake Superior on the north to Texas on the south—of course being compelled to camp out during most of the route, and for a part of the way so destitute of provisions that himself and fellow-travelers subsisted several days on maple-sugar and water. He gathered a vast amount of information that was made available, both by the Church and the Federal Government. He systematized the missionary work, took an inventory of the missionary property, and got valuable grants from the Government for educational purposes among the Indians. The General Conference of 1844 abolished the office, and Mr. Ames took his place among the ranks of efficient itinerants in Indiana Conference. In 1849, he was elected to the Presidency of Indiana Asbury University, but declined the position. In 1852, he was elected to the episcopal office on the same ballot with Levi Scott, M. Simpson, and Osmon C. Baker. He was the first of our bishops to visit the Pacific coast, and was prepared by his counsels and experience to aid the brethren in laying wisely the foundations of our Church in that wonderful land. Bishop Ames is a man of close observation, of breadth of thought and comprehensiveness of view. His plans are far-seeing and statesmanlike. Something above the medium size, and a little inclined to corpulency as age comes on, with an intellectual cast of countenance, and a dignified bearing, his personal presence as a presiding officer is much in his favor. He is eminently a business man. His plans are practical. Few men can secure a more rapid and intelligent dispatch of business by an annual conference than he. Intensely patriotic, he gave the whole weight of his personal and official influence in favor of the Government in suppressing the late Rebellion. He was the first of our bishops to enter the Southern territory and reconstruct the old Church in our reconquered territory.

As a preacher, he is eminently instructive. His manner is calm, dignified, and collected. He has that quietness of manner that indicates conscious strength. His sermons, though not written, are carefully thought through. His style is a model of terseness and perspicuity. His sentences are never involved or obscure. His hearer is never in doubt as to his meaning. Without any display of rhetoric, he talks up into the higher regions of thought and feeling. While his sermons are richer in thought, and equally pure in diction with those of his earlier days, perhaps his most popular sermons were preached while presiding elder of a Western district, when, at his camp-meetings, thronging thousands would hang on his words, and be moved by his impassioned eloquence, as the forest is swayed by the wind.

While the bishop is an ardent Methodist, he cultivates and disseminates the broadest and truest Christian catholicity; and, while laboring to build up his own Church, he enjoys the confidence and friendship of the Protestant clergy from one end of the continent to the other. While he is a positive man, and, when occasion calls for it, can assume the functions and prerogatives of his office with remarkable promptness, he has, nevertheless, a great deal of the *suaviter in modo,* and he seems to take it on more and more. Indeed, the gentler Christian graces shine out more and more conspicuously as age comes on.

22

CHAPTER XVIII.

(FROM 1870 TO 1872.

Fortieth Session of the Indiana Conference—Death of B. F. Torr and Thomas A. Whitted—Delegates to the General Conference of 1872—Congratulations between the Electoral Conference and the Annual Conference—Statistics and Contributions—South-eastern Indiana Conference—Lay and Clerical Delegates to the General Conference—Thomas Ray—John W. Dole—William T. Saunders—Members—Church Property—Contributions—Largest Churches—Sketch of Rev. S. T. Gillett, D. D.—Twentieth Session of the North-west Indiana Conference—Electoral Conference—Resolutions against a Change in our Church Economy—Delegates to the General Conference — Members — Contributions — Educational — Twenty-ninth Session of the North Indiana Conference—Members—Contributions—Electoral Conference—Delegates to the General Conference—Resolutions on Conference Boundary—Lay Delegation—Rev. Thomas Bowman, D. D., elected to the Episcopacy—Sketch of Bishop Bowman.

INDIANA CONFERENCE.

THE Indiana Conference held its fortieth session in the city of New Albany, beginning on Wednesday, September 13, 1871. Total number of preachers comprising the Conference, 122. Of these, 111 were full members, and 11 probationers; 104 in the active work of the ministry, 17 superannuated, and 1 supernumerary. Bishop Clark, to whose episcopal supervision the Conference had been assigned that year, having died, Bishop Scott presided. Rev. S. L. Binkley was elected principal secretary, and O. H. Smith, J. H. Clippinger, and R. B. Martin, assistant secretaries.

Two members had died during the year; namely, B. F. Torr and Thomas A. Whitted. Brother Torr was admitted into the Conference in 1860. He was for some time a student in Asbury University. He was a young man of decided ability and marked individuality of character. Faithful and fearless in the discharge of duty, he was firm in his adherence to what he believed to be right. His last appointment was to Roberts and M'Kendree Charge, New Albany. He died November 4, 1870.

Thomas A. Whitted was a native of North Carolina. He was licensed to preach by the Bedford Quarterly Conference, in 1844. He traveled for several years as a supply, under the direction of the presiding elder. In 1853, he was admitted on trial in the Indiana Conference. He was an earnest, faithful preacher, and met death triumphantly, March 31, 1870.

The increase in the membership within the bounds of the Conference, during the year, was 2,759; the total membership, including probationers, was 21,007; local preachers, 224; number of churches reported, 333¼, valued at $694,800—the two most costly churches in the Conference, and perhaps in the state, being Meridian-street Church, Indianapolis, and Trinity Church, in Evansville. There were 73 parsonages reported, valued at $74,500. The contributions of members for Church purposes were as follows:

For the support of the Ministry	$77,784 38
For the Superannuated Preachers	1,287 04
For Missions	8,992 41
For Church Extension	347 90
For Bible Society	1,570 15
For Sunday-school Union	204 85
Expenses of Sunday-schools	6,382 71
For Tract Cause	58 45
For the Freedmen's Aid Society	235 28
Total	$96,863 17

To which should be added the personal donation of $2,000, from that large-hearted and earnest Christian layman, W. C. De Pauw, Esq., of New Albany.

The provisional plan for the introduction of lay delegates into the General Conference, having received more than the requisite number of votes, both from the ministry and the laity, the delegates from the several charges within the bounds of the Conference met, pursuant to the provisions of said plan, on the second day of the Conference, September 15, 1871, and duly organized by calling Hon. R. W. Thompson to the chair, and appointing F. M. Thair and Hughes East, secretaries. Hon. R. W. Thompson and Washington C. De Pauw were elected delegates to the ensuing General Conference, to meet in Brooklyn, in May, 1872, and Asa Iglehart, Esq., and Colonel T. J. Smith were elected reserve delegates.

The Annual Conference adopted the following resolutions, which were formally presented to the Electoral Conference, by a committee appointed for that purpose:

" *Whereas*, the last General Conference, after careful deliberation, did, in its godly judgment, send forth to the Church a ' Plan of Lay Delegation,' for the godly consideration of the ministers and people of the Methodist Episcopal Church; and, *whereas*, the ministers have, by vote in the Annual Conferences, accepted of such plan, and the laity of the Church have also, by vote, expressed themselves; and, *whereas*, by the provision of this plan, the quarterly conferences in the bounds of this Annual Conference have elected delegates to the Electoral Conference, to meet in this city September 15th, to elect delegates to the General Conference of 1872; now, therefore,

" 1. *Resolved*, That the Indiana Conference acquiesce in this great movement, as thus far consummated, and prays for its peaceful and wise consummation at the approaching General Conference.

" 2. *Resolved*, That we welcome our brethren, the laity, to the councils of the Church, in the confident belief that their love for the Church, and their interest in her prosperity, and their practical skill, will only add strength to our Zion, and enable her more fully and rapidly to accomplish her great mission in 'spreading Scriptural holiness over the land.' In this more intimate relation, we do most devoutly implore God's blessing alike on them and us.

" 3. *Resolved*, That the following members of this Conference be a committee to bear our fraternal greetings to the Electoral Conference, on Friday, the 15th inst., namely: C. Nutt, John Kiger, Wm. Meginnis, W. V.

Daniel, John Schrader, H. S. Talbott, W. C. Smith, J. C. Smith, H. Hays, S. Ravenscroft, J. R. Williams, and G. W. Walker."

H. S. Talbott presented the resolutions, and, on behalf of the Annual Conference, congratulated the Electoral Conference, and bade them a God-speed in their work. Hon. R. W. Thompson responded on the part of the laymen, and the utmost cordiality and confidence were manifested by all. Thus harmoniously and peacefully was this radical change effected in the organic law of the Church.

The ministerial delegates to the General Conference of 1872 were, J. J. Hight, Wm. K. Hester, Cyrus Nutt, and John Kiger. W. F. Harned and B. F. Rawlins were elected reserve delegates.

SOUTH-EASTERN INDIANA CONFERENCE.

THE South-eastern Indiana Conference met in Wall-street Methodist Episcopal Church, in Jeffersonville, Ind., September 6, 1871. George L. Curtis was elected secretary, and E. L. Dolph, W. S. Mahan, and A. N. Marlatt, assistant secretaries, Bishop Scott presiding.

The Laymen's Electoral Conference held its session on the second day of the Conference. J. C. M'Intosh, Esq., was elected president, and J. H. Stewart secretary. E. K. Hosford and J. C. M'Intosh, Esq., were elected delegates to the ensuing General Conference, to be held in Brooklyn, N. Y., in May, 1872. J. H. V. Smith, Esq., of Indianapolis, and D. G. Phillips, Esq., of Madison, were elected reserve delegates.

The ministerial delegates, on behalf of the Annual Conference, were, Enoch G. Wood, Sampson Tincher, and F. A. Hester; and the reserve delegates were W. Terrell and F. C. Holliday.

Three members of the Conference had died during the year, namely: Thomas Ray, John W. Dole, and W. T. Saunders. Father Ray joined the Indiana Conference at its session in Madison, in 1833. He had been for a few years on the superannuated list at the time of his death. He was killed by the express train, on the railroad, at Inwood, the place of his residence, January 31, 1871. From some cause, he did not observe the approaching train, as he was crossing the track, until it was too late for him to escape, and he was instantly killed. He was a good man, and doubtless "the chariots of Israel and the horsemen thereof" were in waiting to convey him to his heavenly home.

Rev. John W. Dole entered the traveling connection in the Missouri Conference, in 1835. He maintained a good Christian and ministerial character till the day of his death. He came to Indiana in 1845, and was identified with the work in Indiana from that time till the close of his life. He had been for a few years on the superannuated list. He was a good man, and met death triumphantly.

Rev. W. T. Saunders was a young man of promise. He entered the ministry, in the South-eastern Indiana Conference, in the Fall of 1859. He died in Madison, July 29, 1871, in the thirty-fifth year of his age.

The number of members and probationers, reported this Conference, was 24,390. The ministerial force comprised one hundred and twenty-one traveling preachers, twenty-one of whom were either on the superannuated or supernumerary list.

Number of churches.. 290
Their probable value...............................$768,500
Number of parsonages... 45
Their probable value...............................$47,750

The Church collections were reported as follows:

For the support of the Ministry.........................$70,405 06
For the Superannuated Preachers, etc.................. 1,282 77
Amount collected for the Missionary Society......... 7,218 49
Amount collected for Church Extension................ 683 70
Amount collected for the Tract Society............... 256 71
Amount collected for the Bible Society............... 888 75
Amount collected for Sunday-school Union.......... 220 67
Amount collected for support of Sunday-schools.... 4,627 80

The most expensive churches in the Conference are, Roberts Park Church, Indianapolis, of which Rev. J. H. Bayliss is the present pastor, and the First Church, in Greensburg, of which Rev. S. T. Gillett, D. D., is pastor. Roberts Park Church, when completed, will be the most elegant, and perhaps the best-arranged, Protestant church in the state. It is located in the center of an acre lot, fronting on Delaware and Vermont Streets, with alleys on the other two sides of the lot. The building is of white limestone, from the Ellettsville quarries, carved and rubbed, and edges beveled, and is one hundred and twenty-one feet long and seventy wide. The lecture-room, class-rooms, and parlors are on the first floor. The lecture-room will accommodate about eight hundred persons, and the main audience-room will seat about thirteen hundred.

The First Church, in Greensburg, is also a two-story edifice. It is built of brick, capped and trimmed with limestone. Its arrangements for Sabbath-school, class, and prayer meetings are excellent. The church-tower is something over one hundred and seventy feet high.

Rev. S. T. Gillett, D. D., the present pastor of the First Church, in Greensburg, Indiana, is a native of the state of New York, and came to Indiana with his father's family, in 1818. They landed at Old Fort Harrison, near where the city of Terre Haute now stands. They ascended the Wabash in a family flat-boat, which was propelled by hand-power all the way from the Ohio. His father died in ten days after their landing, from sickness brought on by imprudently leaving the boat without his coat, to greet the Indians lining the bank, many of whom remained in the country to receive their annuity, according to treaty stipulations. Sickness prevailing extensively on the prairies, the widow, with her children, took refuge in the healthy wooded country near the present city of Rockville, in what is now Park County. Although the lands had been sold by the Indians to the General Government, yet many of the Indians remained. Among these, a mission school was formed, by Elder M'Coy, of the Baptist Church, and here young Gillett received a portion of his early education. In 1819, he removed to Madison, Indiana, and became a member of the family of his half-brother, Colonel N. B. Palmer, and while there, pursued a classical course, preparatory to the study of medicine. As a life among the sick was uncongenial, he made application, through Hon. Wm. Hendricks, United States Senator from Indiana, for an appointment in the Government service, and received that of midshipman, dated December 1, 1826. In March following he was ordered to active duty at New York, and was attached to the steam-frigate *Fulton*, which, afterward, was blown up, with the loss of a large portion of her crew. His first cruise at sea was in the United States steamer *Lexington*, stationed in the Mediterranean, where his vessel remained three years and four months, giving the officers superior facilities for visiting its classic shores, more especially Italy, Asia Minor, and the Grecian Archipelago. His vessel returning in 1830, he was detailed, and permitted to visit his Western home, after an absence of nearly four years. The change from boyhood to manhood was such that an elder brother found it difficult to recognize him; yet his mother, with true parental instinct, clasped her son to her heart at first sight, and wept tears of joy over one who had been a subject of prayerful solicitude during the weary years of his absence.

At that time, the Naval Academy was not in existence as now organized, the Government furnishing instruction for the midshipmen at navy-yards and on board ships in commission. As an examination for promotion occurred annually, for those who had been five years in the service, three of them at sea, and as merit determined the place of each on the list, there was no small degree of anxiety on the part of the sixty composing the class of 1826, as to their success in the ordeal through which they were to pass. This induced young Gillett to press his studies while on shore, rather than indulge in the sailors' usual course of relaxation while on land. After some months of duty at the navy-yard in Pensacola, he was ordered to Baltimore, with some sixty others, for examination, among whom were Raphael Semmes, John A. Dahlgren, O. S. Glisson, S. C. Rowan, and C. S. Boggs, who were so prominent in naval affairs during the late Rebellion, and who, with the exception of Mr. Semmes, have been promoted to the Admiralty. The Examining Board was in session near two months, and, at its conclusion, placed the name of Samuel T. Gillett at the head of the list, giving Raphael Semmes, late Captain of the famous *Alabama*, the next number below him. Forty-two of the class passed, some failing, others fearing to come before the Board. Young Gillett's success was the more gratifying as the officers from the Eastern States affected to believe that those from the West could not compete with them.

In 1830 he was again ordered to sea, and was favored

with duty on board the *Delaware*, ship of the line. After landing His Excellency, Edward Livingston, Minister to France, at Cherbourg, the officers visited Paris, and other cities between that and the British Channel. The vessel then proceeded to the Mediterranean, and, during a stay of two years, he visited the south of France, west coast of Italy, Egypt, and Palestine. While witnessing an eruption of Mount Vesuvius, near Naples, he was placed in a perilous condition from a shower of molten lava, thrown from the crater in an oblique direction, falling in pieces of several pounds' weight around him and his companions. In Egypt he, with a company of officers, passed up the Nile to Cairo, and, being favored with horses and grooms from the pasha's stables, accompanied by Mr. Gliddon, United States Vice-Consul, visited the Pyramids, ruins of Memphis, Catacombs, and many other interesting localities in that semi-barbarous country, once the seat of literature and refinement as existing in ancient times. In Palestine, they were received by the Governor of Jerusalem, and provided with quarters in that most interesting of all cities to Bible students. Having peculiar facilities here, they visited the sacred localities of this city and the adjacent country, and then, rejoining the ship at Jaffa— the Joppa of Scripture—they passed up the coast, visiting Tyre, Sidon, and Beyroot, where the lamented Kingsley closed his eventful life. The *Delaware* then returned to Port Mahon, head-quarters of the squadron, and Mr. Gillett to the United States. We have given this brief review of his nautical life, as that and his extensive travels have had an important bearing on his usefulness as a minister.

On his return home, he was placed on "leave of absence," and entered the service of the State of Indiana as civil engineer in the preliminary survey and location of the Madison and Indianapolis Railroad. While thus engaged, the great crisis of his life occurred, wholly revolutionizing his views of duty and course of action. Reflecting on the insufficiency of worldly enjoyments—of which he had freely partaken—to satisfy the demands of the soul, he resolved to act on a remark dropped in his hearing by Mrs. Gillett, that "happiness was to be found in religion." Examining the Bible, to learn in what religion consists, he was fully awakened to a sense of his condition and danger as a sinner. After two weeks of penitence and prayer, the Savior came to his relief about noon, October 6, 1836, while at home reading the Methodist Discipline, his faith being aided by an illustration from sea-faring life. As a Church member, he resolved to live up to his whole duty; and to learn this, he commenced to read the Discipline through. While reading the Articles of Faith, he came to the second, when his attention was riveted to the statement of the two-fold nature of the Son of God—"very God and very man"—as exactly suited to human redemption. "If," said he to himself, "a soldier and sailor should be at variance, both parties would accept as mediator a marine, who, as soldier serving on shipboard, is both soldier and sailor. Now, Christ is very God and very man, and into his hands I commit my case." Immediate relief followed this act of trust, and the clear witness of the Spirit was realized in a few minutes, accompanied with joy unspeakable and full of glory. Such was his experience, as he has sometimes stated in the social meetings of the Church. Religious matters now appeared so important, that he resolved on a life henceforth to be devoted to human salvation, and immediately resigned his office of civil engineer, and commenced a course of theological study. On the third of March, 1837, he was confirmed by the United States Senate as lieutenant in the navy. Being passionately fond of the sea, he was, for a season, tempted to retain the commission so unexpectedly sent him, and, for the present, decline active ministerial life. The immediate result was a loss of religious enjoyment, and distaste for spiritual exercises. Being on a visit to his brother-in-law, Rev. W. H. Goode, D. D., at New Albany, he attended a camp-meeting near by, and, after a severe struggle over the sacrifice demanded, resolved to end the matter forthwith, resign his commission, and enter on the ministerial life. His religious peace returned, and, entering the altar at the camp-ground, he commenced, among the mourners, the future work of his life.

Soon after, in the Fall of 1837, in a letter to the Secretary of the Navy, he tendered his resignation, assigning the reasons impelling him to the sacrifice. The resignation was accepted, and the matter forever settled. He was duly licensed as a local preacher, and his recommendation from the Madison Quarterly Conference to the Indiana Annual Conference was presented by Rev. E. G. Wood, D. D., Presiding Elder, and he was received on trial at the session of 1837, in New Albany, and appointed to Lawrenceburg Circuit, James Jones and Silas Rawson, his colleagues. Their labors were successful, and extensive revivals followed. In 1838, he was reappointed to the same work, with Charles Bonner in charge. Lawrenceburg having been made a station, the circuit was called Wilmington. Extensive revivals crowned their labors in the twenty-two appointments, and seventeen hundred and ninety-nine members were returned to Conference. In 1839 and 1840, he was on Rising Sun Circuit, but was transferred to the charge of the Union Bethel, Louisville, Kentucky, by Bishop Soule, December, 1840. In 1841, he was sent to Lawrenceburg Station, but in May following was ordered to the navy-yard, New York, having been commissioned as chaplain in the navy, by Mr. Tyler. He remained there several months, but became satisfied he would be more useful in the regular work, resigned his commission, and was re-appointed to Lawrenceburg. In 1843 and 1844, he was in charge of Terre Haute Station, North Indiana Conference; in 1845, of Greencastle Station; and in 1846 and 1847, of Roberts Chapel, at Indianapolis. He was then four years on the Centerville District as presiding elder, and was delegate from the North Indiana Conference to the General Conference in 1852. At the close of this year, he was elected President of the Fort Wayne Female College, but declined the appointment, and was stationed at Asbury Chapel, Indianapolis, South-eastern Indiana Conference. While on the Centerville District, he was also elected President of Whitewater College, but served only until a successor could be obtained, preferring the regular work. In 1853, he was sent to the Connersville District, and remained three years. In 1856–57, he was in charge of Centenary Methodist Episcopal Church, New Albany, Indiana Conference. In 1858, he was on the Bloomington District. In 1859, he was placed in charge of Locust-street Church, Evansville, and remained two years. In 1861, he was placed on Evansville District. From Evansville District he was removed, in 1862, to Wesley Chapel, Indianapolis, and remained two years. In 1864 and 1865, he was on Bloomington Station, but was relieved, early in 1866, and placed in the Centenary agency, and raised, in connection with his colleague, Rev. Dr. Hight, over $30,000, in cash and subscriptions, for our literary and benevolent institutions. In the Fall of 1866, he was placed on the Indianapolis District, where he remained two years, when, on the division of the district by act of the General Conference in changing the boundary lines, he was again placed in charge of Asbury Station, Indianapolis, where he remained two years, and was removed, in the Fall of 1870, to the First Church, in Greensburg, where he is now laboring. Dr. Gillett's ministry has been abundantly blessed in the awakening and conversion of sinners, and in the sanctification of believers, as well as in promoting the educational and benevolent enterprises of the Church.

NORTH-WEST INDIANA CONFERENCE.

THE North-west Indiana Conference held its twentieth session in Crawfordsville, Indiana, beginning September 6, 1871, Bishop Ames presiding. J. C. Reed was elected secretary, and L. Taylor and J. L. Boyd assistants.

On the second day of the session the Laymen's Electoral Conference convened, pursuant to the provisional plan for lay delegation. Mark Jones was elected president; A. S. Morrow and Joseph Miller, vice-presidents; and W. C. Smith was chosen secretary, with R. S. Tennant as assistant secretary. Hon. H. S. Lane and John Brownfield, Esq., were elected delegates to the ensuing General Conference, to be held in Brooklyn, in May, 1872.

Congratulations were exchanged between the Laymen's Electoral Conference and the Annual Conference. The following preamble and resolutions, offered by Hon. Henry S. Lane, were adopted by the Electoral Conference :

"*Whereas*, the doctrines and economy of the Methodist Episcopal Church have been signally blessed, in the conversion and salvation of multiplied thousands during the last one hundred years; and, *whereas*, we are

unfalteringly opposed to all radical changes in that form of Church government which has so efficiently administered the Word of Life to millions
of anxious hearers; and, *whereas*, we hear with sincere regret that an effort
may be made, at the next General Conference, to introduce great, and we
fear dangerous, innovations in the government of our beloved Church;
therefore,

"*Resolved*, That we, the members of the Electoral Conference of the
North-west Indiana Conference of the Methodist Episcopal Church, in Conference assembled, declare that we are opposed to any change whatever in
our Church economy, looking to alteration in our plan of general superintendency.

"*Resolved*, That we believe a quadrennial election of bishops in our
Church would be fraught with great danger, and would imperil her peace,
prosperity, and success.

"*Resolved*, That, in the opinion of this Electoral Conference, the efficiency and almost unparalleled success of the Church, in the past, has been
largely attributable, under God, to the Christian zeal, energy, and efficiency
of our general superintendents; and that the life-tenure in that office is
essential to its Christian power and usefulness.

"*Resolved*, That a committee of three be appointed to bear our fraternal greetings to the bishop and members of the North-west Indiana
Conference, now in session in this city, and ask most respectfully and earnestly their concurrence in the foregoing preamble and resolutions."

Hon. Henry S. Lane, Mark Jones, and John Brownfield, Esqs., were appointed said Committee. Hon. H.
S. Lane addressed the Conference on behalf of the
Electoral Conference; and at the close of his address, on
motion, the Conference unanimously concurred in the
foregoing preamble and resolutions.

The clerical delegates to the General Conference
were, A. A. Gee, J. C. Reed, N. L. Brakeman, and S.
Godfrey; reserve delegates, A. Wood and L. Taylor.

The reports showed: Members and probationers,
22,010; number of churches, 261; value, $743,268;
number of parsonages, 68; value, $94,118. Contribu-
tions: For Missions, $5,529.52 (being a falling off from
the contributions of the preceding year of $666.76);
Church Extension, $463.60; Bible Society, $1,622.92;
Sunday-school Union, $161.50; Tract Society, $129.62;
superannuated preachers, etc., $1,410.45.

The Conference is earnestly devoted to the good work of fostering our institutions of learning, and directs its patronage to Indiana Asbury University, Fort Wayne College, Stockwell Collegiate Institute, Valparaiso Male and Female College, and Russellville Academy. The Conference expressed its appreciation of Christian education, in connection with Indiana Asbury University, in the following words: "The Church and Conference surely can not complain; for, of the thirty-two who graduated June 22, 1871, seven are already in the ministry, and we believe at least four more will yet enter the regular work. Ten are sons and daughters of ministers; the greater number are members of the Church, and devoted Christians."

NORTH INDIANA CONFERENCE.

THE North Indiana Annual Conference held its twenty-ninth session in Simpson Chapel, Muncie, Ind., commencing March 27, 1872, Bishop Scott presiding. M. H. Mendenhall was elected secretary, and E. F. Hasty, D. P. Hartman, and H. N. Herrick, assistants.

The number of members and probationers reported was 29,856; number of churches, 371½; value, $821,-100; number of parsonages, 91; value, $114,655. The Church contributions were as follows:

For Superannuated Preachers, etc.	$1,469 00
For Missions.	8,719 03
For Church Extension Society	420 38
For the Tract Society	190 95
For the Bible Society	1,910 49
For the Sunday-school Union	217 70
Educational Collection	765 00
For General Conference Expenses	507 97
Extra Missionary Collection	946 56
For Woman's Foreign Missionary Society	421 55

The Electoral Conference of Lay Delegates convened on the second day of the session. Joshua H. Mellett,

Esq., of Newcastle, was chosen as chairman, and C. C. Binkley, Esq., of Richmond, was chosen secretary. J. A. Funk and W. R. West, Esqs., were elected delegates to the ensuing General Conference, to be held in Brooklyn, N. Y., in May, 1872. Congratulations were exchanged between the Electoral Conference of Laymen and the Annual Conference, and addresses were delivered by representatives from each.

The delegates to the General Conference, from the Annual Conference, were, W. H. Goode, Thomas Bowman, Wm. S. Birch, N. H. Phillips, and O. V. Lemon. The reserve delegates were: Ministers, M. H. Mendenhall and L. W. Monson; and for the laymen, G. W. Milburn and A. C. Swayze.

In no part of the state is Methodism advancing more steadily and rapidly than within the bounds of the North Indiana Conference. The General Conference of 1868 having detached that portion of the North Indiana Conference lying in Marion County, and attached the same to the South-eastern Indiana Conference, the Conference adopted a series of strong resolutions against said alteration in their Conference boundary, and instructed their delegates to the General Conference to use their influence to have the former boundary restored. Their memorial was duly considered, both in the Committee on Boundaries and before the General Conference, but the boundaries of Conferences in Indiana were left substantially as they were settled at the General Conference of 1868.

The introduction of lay delegation into the Methodist Episcopal Church, by the General Conference of 1872, marks an epoch in the history of the Church. The freedom from undue excitement, and the harmony and concert of action between the preachers and people,

23

was a very striking proof of the mutual confidence existing between them, and promises well for the future harmony and increased efficiency of the Church. This change in the constitution of the Church received the support of all the delegates from the several Indiana conferences.

Indiana Methodism was well represented in the General Conference of 1872, both by her lay and clerical delegates. And Indiana Methodism was honored in the selection of Rev. Thomas Bowman, D. D., as one of the bishops of the Methodist Episcopal Church.

BISHOP BOWMAN.

BISHOP BOWMAN is a native of Pennsylvania. He was born near Berwick, Columbia County, Pennsylvania, July 15, 1817. His ancestors, for two or three generations, were noted Methodists, distinguished for the fervor of their piety, their fidelity in the discharge of religious duties, and also for their enterprise and frugality in temporal affairs. His parents and grandparents, on his father's side, were Methodists. His grandparents, on his mother's side, were Scotch Presbyterians. His grandfather, Rev. Thomas Bowman, was an efficient local preacher, and introduced Methodism into Columbia and the adjoining counties at an early day. He was an earnest and an indefatigable worker, frequently spending weeks from home carrying on revival meetings. The bishop's father was a steward, class-leader, trustee of the Church, and Sunday-school superintendent during the most of his life. His parents were both noted for their industry and economy. They were remarkably exemplary in the performance of their religious duties, not allowing any thing to interfere with them, either in the family or the Church. The children were uniformly taken to Church. They accompanied their parents not only to public worship, but also to the class-meetings and love-feasts. The bishop was consecrated to God by his parents from his birth, especially by his mother, who earnestly desired that God would call her son to the work of the Christian ministry. He early evinced a fondness for books, and read almost every thing he could find; for books were then less numerous than now, especially books that were likely to interest boys. The bishop's childhood home had much to do in the formation of his character. He was remarkably fond of history and biography, and early stored his mind with a large amount of solid information. At the age of fourteen, through the influence of Rev. George Lane, who was subsequently Book Agent, young Bowman was sent to the Wesleyan Academy, at Wilbraham, Massachusetts. The next year he went to Oneida Conference Seminary, at Cazenovia, New York, it being nearer home. Here, on the first of January, 1833, he was converted to God in one of the most remarkable revivals of religion ever witnessed in our land. Almost every student in the Seminary was converted. Rev. W. C. Larrabee was Principal of the Seminary at.the time. Not a few of the leading men, in Church and State, throughout the land, received an important part of their literary training under the instruction of Professor Larrabee. Immediately on his conversion, young Bowman united with the Church, and determined to do his whole duty as a Christian with whatever ability he had. His piety was of the most earnest, happy, hopeful type, that at once opened before him doors of usefulness, and won for him the society and friendship of the better class of his fellow-students. In the Fall of 1835, he entered the Junior Class in Dickinson College, at Carlisle, Pennsylvania, then under the

Presidency of Rev. John P. Durbin; Drs. Emory, M'Clintock, W. H. Allen, and Mr. Caldwell being Professors. The bishop always expresses himself deeply indebted to these men for his religious growth, and especially to the teaching and preaching of Dr. Durbin.

Having completed the College Course, he graduated in 1837, and studied law one year. His legal studies have, doubtless, been of value to him through life, although Providence designed him for a different sphere of labor. His impressions of duty to preach the Gospel, which had followed him nearly all his life, became so strong that he could not prosecute his legal studies. He accepted license to preach, and, in the Spring of 1839, entered the Baltimore Annual Conference, and was sent to Beaver Meadow Mission, where he had a happy and successful year in a rough field of labor.

In 1840, at the earnest solicitations of the Faculty, he took charge of the Grammar School of Dickinson College, to which he was appointed by the bishop, where he remained three years, most of the time as colleague of Rev. L. Scott, now the venerable Bishop Scott. Mr. Bowman's health being delicate, he then took a supernumerary relation, and for five years did such work as he could. In 1848 he was appointed Principal of Dickinson Seminary, at Williamsport, Pennsylvania. He organized and opened the institution, and presided over it for ten years, leaving a fine property and a school of about four hundred students. During the years that he had charge of the Seminary, he preached as often as any of the stationed preachers, traveling over the country in his own conveyance for nearly a hundred miles in every direction.

In 1858, he was stationed at Lewisburg, Pennsylvania, and at the end of one year was called to the

Presidency of Indiana Asbury University, where he remained until elected by the General Conference of 1872 to the responsible position of Bishop of the Methodist Episcopal Church.

Although most of his life has been given to the work of Christian education, it formed no part of Bishop Bowman's plan of life when he entered the ministry. The pastoral work has always been his delight, and, left to his own choice, that would have been his chosen field of labor; but when he consecrated his life to God and the Church, he determined to do whatever work the Church might call him to do, to do it cheerfully and to the utmost of his ability. Bishop Bowman's willingness to work, and his ability to work well, have caused him to lead a very busy life. While in Dickinson Seminary, he did the work of nearly three men, acting as principal, agent, and steward, averaging from seven to nine hours a day.

His special sermons, lectures, and platform addresses, while they have been models as to matter and style, have been so numerous as to seem to leave but little leisure for the performance of other duties, while they, in fact, have not been taken into the account as any part of his regular work.

More than forty men are now in the active work of the ministry who were under his care and instruction while at Dickinson Seminary, besides those who have gone out from the halls of Asbury University since he assumed the Presidency of that institution. Without his knowledge, in 1864, Bishop Bowman was elected Chaplain to the United States Senate, which place he filled during one session of Congress. The General Conference of 1864 appointed him a co-delegate with Bishop Janes to the Wesleyan Conference, of Great Britain.

In 1859, he received the degree of Doctor of Divinity.

Bishop Bowman's scholarship is thorough, and his career as an educator has been a brilliant one. But, after all, he has been distinguished through life as a preacher. His sermons give proof of having been carefully thought through; but they are never written. The bishop uses no notes in the pulpit. His style is perspicuous, his ideas are never involved, and his hearers are never in doubt about his meaning. His manner is easy and natural, and at the same time earnest and often impassioned. Ripe in Christian experience, and rejoicing in the assurance of faith, he leads his hearers to contemplate, and often to experience, the freeness and fullness of a present salvation. The power of faith and the joy of salvation are exhibited in his own experience, and glow in all his sermons.

While Bishop Bowman's life has been largely devoted to literary pursuits, and much of it spent in literary society, there is no ostentatious display of learning, either in his conversation or his sermons. Few men have as many elements of personal popularity as Bishop Bowman. He is eminently social, and his conversational powers are of the first order. He is so genial and full of sunshine, so hopeful and brave, that his personal presence is felt to be a blessing. His personal popularity, combined with his superior ability as a platform and pulpit orator, cause him to be called on frequently in the dedication of churches, and on occasions where large sums of money are to be raised; and on such occasions the expectations of his friends are never disappointed. Few men, in any part of the connection, were called on as frequently, or invited to go as far, to dedicate churches, as was Dr. Bowman, during the ten years immediately preceding his election to the episcopacy; and few, if any, raised as much money for Church enterprises during that time as he did. Among his first efforts of this kind, after his election to the episcopacy, was in Roberts Park Church, Indianapolis, where he made an appeal to the congregation for a subscription to complete their new church, and the response was a subscription of about thirty-eight thousand dollars. The pastor, Rev. J. H. Bayliss, had prepared the way by a sermon on the preceding Sabbath, and co-operated efficiently in securing the contribution, which, taken all together, was one of unprecedented liberality.

As President of the University, Bishop Bowman was eminently successful. His influence over the young men was almost unbounded. He governed without seeming to do it. There was no display of authority, and yet obedience was promptly secured. The students loved him as a father, and confided in him as a friend. Many a poor young man has been encouraged by him to secure a good education, who, but for his counsel and the inspiration of his hopefulness, would have given up in despair.

The Church has much to hope from Bishop Bowman as one of her chief pastors. And the Methodists of Indiana have only to regret that his residence is removed from among us, and the position that he has so efficiently filled, as President of our chief institution of learning, will have to be filled by another.

Bishop Bowman has hitherto led too active a life to allow him much leisure for the use of his pen. It is to be hoped that, in his present position he will be able to give to the Church, in a permanent form, much that has fallen from his lips in eloquent appeals and in perspicuous and convincing argument. With our present episcopal force, the Church has a right to expect the literary labors, as well as the preaching and executive functions, of her bishops, and that our literature shall be enriched by the contributions of their pens, as well as guided to greater efficiency by the wisdom of their counsels and the inspiration of their zeal.

THE END.

Printed in the United States
103080LV00001B/27/A

9 781425 539788